D1065246

ArkansasTimes Almanac Of Arkansas History

Arkansas Times
Almanac
Of Arkansas History

Arkansas Times / Little Rock
PUBLISHERS

Published by Arkansas Times
201 East Markham, Suite 200
Little Rock, Arkansas 72203
501-375-2985

First Edition 2000

Printed in The United States of America

ISBN 0-87483-598-4

Book Publisher: Ira Hocut
Executive Editor: Bob Lancaster
Cover and Book Designer: Carron Hocut
Project Consultant: Mike Spain

This book is printed on archival-quality paper which
meets the guidelines for performance and durability of the
Committee on Production Guidelines for Book Longevity
of the Council on Library Resources.

ARKANSAS TIMES   PUBLISHERS   LITTLE ROCK

Contents

An *Arkansas Times* Almanac
Short Takes On The Who, Where, What And Why   7

They Made A Difference
100 People, More Or Less, Who Made Arkansas What It Is Today   43

The Top 100
Our Choices For The Blockbuster News Events Of The 20th Century   63

In These *Times*: A Look Back
25 Years Of *Arkansas Times* Reporting   77

Sponsors
Business And History In Arkansas   133

An *Arkansas Times* Almanac

Short Takes On The Arkansas
Who, Where, What And Why

This is a compendium of nearly 200 years' worth of little-known and well-known facts about people, events, critters, pretty places, notorious places, novelties, and products that have made the Natural State famous.

Or infamous, as the case might be.

It is a modest collection of Arkansiana, and makes no claims to being comprehensive. Every one of these items has a longer tale to tell — a tale that often would (and has) filled a volume, or a whole shelf of them.

Together, they give something of the flavor of life in this odd, out-of-the-way, landlocked little province of the midsouth, or midwest, or southwest — a flavor as distinctive as poke sallet or bear stew.

Assorted Distinctions

■ **Tony Bennett** sang his signature song "I Left My Heart in San Francisco" publicly the first time at a concert rehearsal at the Hot Springs nightclub "The Vapors" in 1961. The only audience was a bartender who said, "I'd buy that record." Bennett, in his autobiography published in 1998, credits that remark with inspiring him to record the tune at the next opportunity.

■ **Erskine Caldwell**, author of "Tobacco Road" and "God's Little Acre," said in his autobiography that he and Margaret Bourke-White, the famous photographer whom he later married, consummated their romance at the Albert Pike Hotel in Little Rock on a summer evening in 1936. In *her* autobiography, Bourke-White allowed that it was at Little Rock that Caldwell "fell in love with me," but she discreetly left it at that.

■ **Whitley Strieber**, who as author of "Communion" is perhaps the world's most famous UFO abductee, disclosed in one of his books that he had his first close encounter with alien abductors when they took him from a moving train in Arkansas when he was a boy.

■ At one time in the early 1930s, **Al Capone** and his

Erskine Caldwell and Margaret Bourke-White

entourage occupied an entire wing of the Arlington Hotel while Capone's arch-enemy **"Bugs" Moran** and his gang were ensconced at the Majestic, just a block away. They agreed to peaceably co-exist in compliance with the spa's ancient reputation as a place where even enemies could come together to rest, soak and heal.

■ **Henry Morton Stanley**, the English journalist who became one of the most famous men of the 19th century when he found Dr. Livingstone in darkest Africa, lived for a time as a young man in south Arkansas around 1860, clerking in a general store at a community near present-day Cummins Prison Farm. He was pressured by his neighbors there to sign up with the Confederate Army.

■ **Elvis Presley**, almost as famous at the time for his swirling blue-black hair as for his swiveling hips, got his GI buzz cut at Fort Chaffee on March 25, 1958, shortly after he entered the Army.

■ **Ernest Hemingway** wrote a portion of "A Farewell to Arms" while living in Piggott, the home town of his second wife, Pauline. He dedicated the novel to her uncle, Gus Pfeiffer, a perfume mogul, who had bailed out the Hemingways financially, including paying their passage home from Paris and bankrolling the safari that brought forth "The Green Hills of Africa."

■ **Lucky Luciano**, the mobster, offered **Carl Bailey**, who was Arkansas attorney general at the time, a $50,000 bribe to prevent his extradition in 1936 to New York to face criminal charges; Bailey turned him down.

■ **Hernando DeSoto**, the Spanish explorer who discovered the Mississippi River, is now thought by anthropologists to have died in present-day Arkansas.

■ **James G. Blaine**, the Republican congressman from Maine, lost the 1884 presidential election to Democrat Grover Cleveland largely because of damaging disclosures during the campaign of corruption and influence peddling by Blaine related to his involvement a decade earlier in the financing of the short-lived Little Rock & Fort Smith Railroad. This was the "Ma, Ma Where's My Pa?" vs. "the Continental Liar from the State of Maine" campaign, one of the nastiest in U.S. history.

■ **Billy Sunday** (1862-1935), the evangelist, credited an incident on the Diamond Jo Railroad between Malvern and Hot Springs with first turning him toward a ministerial career. It occurred in the late 1880s, and Sunday was a professional baseball player at the time. The little train

Ernest and Pauline Hemingway

on which he was chuffing toward the Spa rounded a curve and approached a burning trestle: without time to make a safe stop, the engineer blasted the train over the collapsing trestle, barely making it across. A miracle, Billy Sunday believed, that spared him so he could perform his life's work.

■ **Zachary Taylor**, the future president, was military commander at Fort Smith for a time in the 1840s.

■ **Charles "Boss" Schmidt** (1880-1932) of Coal Hill, a burly catcher for the Detroit Tigers from 1906 through the 1911 season, was said to have been the only man ever to give Ty Cobb a sound thrashing in a fistfight.

■ **Clyde Barrow** robbed a corner grocery store at Fayetteville in 1933. He got $20. While he and **Bonnie Parker** were in the area, they also stole the license plate off a local physician's car and put it on their own — the car they were killed in in Louisiana the following year. The bullet-riddled car, with the Arkansas license, is on display at a Las Vegas casino. The store building, now abandoned and owned by a church, has been the subject of a dispute between preservationists who want to save it as a tourist attraction, and the church's pastor and other local authorities who don't think memorializing criminals in that manner is appropriate.

■ **Julia Koch**, then 35, erstwhile Arkansan, was proclaimed queen of New York high society, the "leading fin de siecle society wife" in Gotham City in early 1998. Koch spent her childhood in Conway and was a UCA grad there; then to New York where she was a model for Arkansas-born designer Tracy Mills, later for the haute couture designer Adolpho. She married oil billionaire David Koch in 1996 and they soon after purchased the late Jacqueline Onassis' Fifth Avenue apartment (for $9.5 million) and began remodeling it. Society writers declared her "reign" to be over by mid-1999.

■ One of the oddest literary references to Arkansas was a quotation from **Oscar Wilde**, the 19th century Irish novelist and playwright: "I would like to flee like a wounded hart into Arkansas." He used Arkansas here as a metaphor for a primitive place where nonconformists are better tolerated than in the more "civilized" places. Wilde, who died in 1900, was imprisoned late in life for homosexual activity, and spent his last years bitter and despairing in self-imposed exile in Paris; and it was during this period that he made the wounded-hart-in-Arkansas comment. The quotation gave novelist **David**

Leavitt his title — "Arkansas" — for a 1997 best-selling novel with a homosexual protagonist who has a similar tough time of it.

■ **James John Audubon** discovered, identified, and painted a theretofore unknown bird, a flycatcher which he called the Traill's flycatcher, now called the willow flycatcher, near Arkansas Post in the 1820s.

■ **B.B. King**, the legendary blues singer, named his guitar **Lucille** after an incident in a nightclub in Twist, Ark., in 1949. He was performing there one cold night when a couple of drunk patrons got into a fight over a woman named Lucille, knocked over the kerosene heater, and started a fire that burned the place down. King risked

his life to retrieve the guitar from the burning building. Lucille No. 1 has had 16 successors.

Natural Attractions

■ **Blanchard Caverns**. Not a lot of people know it yet, but this is a more interesting, more spectacular cave complex than Carlsbad Caverns or any other one in the country. Discovered only in the 1950s, not fully explored until the mid-'60s. First tours of it were only 20-odd years ago. Owned and operated by the feds, has two walking trails, either one of which will inspire your awe, but the longer, tougher one isn't for softies.

■ **The Buffalo River.** The prototypical scenic mountain float stream, the country's first National River, runs about 150 miles through the limestone bluffs of the Ozarks to empty into the White River south of Mountain Home. Among the most alluring places on the Buffalo are: (a) Whitaker Point. Familiar to postcard recipients and calendar enthusiasts everywhere, the promontory is surely the most photographed scene in Arkansas. The huge crag in the Upper Buffalo Wilderness juts majestically into thin air, 500 feet above Whitaker Creek. (b) Duck Head. A 7-mile series of Buffalo River bends near Rush look on the map just like a mallard's head. (c) Devil's Tea Table. A small, often unnoticed rock formation high above the river near Rush. It looks like a table, though no one knows how the devil got into the picture. (d) The Nars. A stretch of river above Woolum bordered on one side by a high, narrow rock wall separating Richland Valley from the national river. Climbers who dare tread carefully along the spin of the rock wall, which measures only 2-feet wide at the top. (e) The Elephant Head. Big rock that looks sort of like a pachyderm's noggin, signals boaters that the Buffalo's confluence with the White at Buffalo City is just ahead.

■ **Cossatot River**. Known as the "skull crusher" to the Caddoes who named it, the Cossatot in west Arkansas draws legions of brave and foolish boaters each spring to its dangerous rapids. The gauntlet of rock teeth above Cossatot Falls are particularly attractive and hazardous. Kayakers have given various rapids along the way ominous names, such as "Eye Opener," "The Washing Machine," "Whiplash," and "BMF."

■ **The Diamond Field** at Murfreesboro. You-pick-'em

James John Audubon's Traill's flycatcher

The Buffalo River valley

BOB LANCASTER

diamonds, the real McCoy, free for the taking (if you don't count the small admission charge). You might ought to get on down there and snatch you up a handful before the commercial interests get their mitts on the place and turn it over to the cartel.

Statesmen

■ **James William Fulbright** (1905-95). Fayetteville native; scholarships and foreign-relations whiz. Turned down presidency of Columbia University to go into politics. Harry Truman called him an "overeducated son-of-a-bitch." JFK wanted to make him Secretary of State but balked at his anti-civil rights voting record. As Senate Foreign Relations chairman, he pioneered and embodied establishment political opposition to the Vietnam War. 30 years in the U.S. Senate, rooted out by Dale Bumpers in 1974.

■ **Wilbur Mills** (1909-1992). From Kensett in White County. Congressman 1939-1977. Longtime chairman of House Ways and Means, made "Powerful" the official first name of that committee, according to a New Yorker cartoon. A serious candidate for president in 1972. Father of Medicare; wrote the legislation and saw to its enactment. Came to a rather bad end politically after his alcoholism triggered a couple of spectacular incidents in which he turned up publicly drunk in the company of a rowdy ecdysiast who called herself the Argentine Firecracker. Did twilight penance as an AA speaker.

■ **Augustus Garland** (1832-1899). Grew up in Hempstead County, was a Confederate congressman and senator, a U.S. senator, twice governor, and U.S. attorney general under Grover Cleveland. Might very well have been the first president from Arkansas if he hadn't come along at a time when Southerners weren't even considered for the presidency.

■ **Brooks Hays** (1898-1981). Born at London (Pope County), congressman for 16 years, better known as a

11

literate, homespun storyteller than for his politics. Was head of the Southern Baptist Convention back when it was possible to be a prominent Baptist and have a sense of humor, a sense of honor, and sense. Political career destroyed by his cautious advocacy of doing the right thing during the Little Rock Central High integration crisis.

■ **Martha Beall Mitchell** (1918-1974). Born at Pine Bluff and grew up there; as wife of Nixon administration's Atty. Gen. John Mitchell became one of the key Watergate squealers. "If it hadn't been for Martha, there'd have been no Watergate," Richard Nixon said.

■ **William Jefferson "Bill" Clinton** (1946-   ). Hope native; noted saxophonist and jogger and ladies' man, 42nd governor of Arkansas and 42nd president of the United States. Elected president 1992; re-elected 1996. The first president since Gerald Ford, and perhaps the only other one, to enter office under a name other than the one he was born with. The first Democratic president since Franklin Roosevelt elected to two terms; one of only three Democrats to serve two full terms in the 20th century. The first president since Andrew Johnson to be impeached.

■ **Hillary Clinton** (1947-   ). U.S. First Lady 1993-2000, though Illinois-born, went to the White House via Little Rock. Named one of the nation's top 100 lawyers while with Rose Law Firm in Little Rock, was powerful White House spokesman for health-care and human rights, not so great a newspaper columnist. Her books of nonfiction uplift got mixed reviews. A target of relentless if unproductive investigation by Special Prosecutor Kenneth Starr for 7 years. Likely candidate for U.S. Senate from New York, 2000.

■ **John Roy Steelman** (1900-1999). Farmboy from Thornton (Dallas County) who was a rail-riding hobo during the Depression; struck up a friendship with Harry Truman in Missouri, who, on becoming president, brought him to the White House as a key advisor on industrial relations and postwar reconversion. He became Truman's chief White House trouble-shooter, with Cabinet-level status and the unique title of "Assistant to the President."

■ **Others**: **Joe T. Robinson** (1872-1937) of Lonoke, U.S. senator and Democratic Party vice presidential nominee (with Al Smith of New York) in 1928; **Hattie Caraway** (1878-1951) of Jonesboro, first woman elected to a full term in the U.S. Senate in 1932; **Orval Faubus** (1910-

Augustus Garland

James William Fulbright

Joe T. Robinson

1994) of Huntsville, governor who precipitated the Little Rock Central High School integration crisis in 1957, named one of 10 most admired men in the world in 1958. **James Lee Witt** (b. 1944) of Dardanelle, former Yell County judge, named by President Clinton as head of the Federal Emergency Management Agency, 1993-1999, in which role he won universal, bipartisan praise for turning a moribund agency into one quickly and effectively responsive to national disasters..

Movies

■ **"A Face in the Crowd"** (1957). Directed by Elia Kazan from a Budd Schulberg script, an important anti-McCarthyism fable that came out at the height of the blacklisting movement. (This is ironic since Kazan was one of the notable HUAC Hollywood name-namers.) Andy Griffith had the leading role as a country singer named Lonesome Rhodes who becomes a national sensation as a kind of Cold War Rush Limbaugh. This was Griffith's movie debut (Lee Remick's too) and he became an instant star. Among the other actors here who'd become famous later on: Patricia Neal, Rip Torn, Lois Nettleton. The main character was an Arkie, and much of the movie was filmed in Arkansas — notably in Jonesboro and Piggott.

■ **"Boxcar Bertha"** (1972). Train-robbery movie featuring Barbara Hershey, a major portion of it filmed in and around Camden. Not a very good movie but an important one in that it marked Martin Scorsese's debut as a director.

■ **"A Soldier's Story"** (1983). Shot mostly at Clarendon and at Fort Chaffee near Fort Smith, this is among the best movies ever made in Arkansas. It's a taut suspense story, set in the rural South of 1944, about the murder of a mean, disagreeable sergeant of an all-black Army unit at a training base. Based on a Pulitzer Prize play by Charles Fuller, directed by Norman Jewison, with Howard E. Rollins and Adolph Caesar in the leading roles. Caesar was nominated for an Oscar as the embittered sergeant, and should have won.

■ **"Hallelujah!"** (1929). Legendary director King Vidor's first talkie, filmed on location in east Arkansas and west Tennessee in 1929. With an all-black cast, a melodrama about an Arkansas field hand who goes to the big city and loses all his money in a crap game and endures many subsequent hardships and heartaches. Vidor spent the unheard-of sum of $600,000 of MGM's money on the picture, which white critics called one of the best ever made. They still say that, by the way. Irving Berlin wrote the music for it.

■ **"Rosalie Goes Shopping"** (1989). Big-time German movie made at and about Stuttgart (Ark.), with Marianne Sagebrecht and Brad Davis. A witty, offbeat comedy, a satire on rampant American consumerism; was critically acclaimed but a box-office flop.

■ **"Sling Blade"** (1996). Billy Bob Thornton, who grew up at Malvern, wrote, directed, and starred in this tale of a loveable mental patient released after 25 years in the nuthouse for multiple murders. He made the movie at Benton for a mere $1 million and sold it to Miramax, which made a big national hit out of it. Thornton got best-actor and best-screenplay Oscar nominations — and won in the screenplay category — and became a Hollywood celebrity.

■ **Harry Thomason**, the TV producer, made several Grade B movies — none of them masterpieces — in Little Rock in the early 1970s, including "Encounter with the Unknown," "So Sad About Gloria," "The Great Lester Boggs," and "The Day It Came to Earth," the last of which several critics have ranked among the worst movies ever made. "9-30-55," a movie by **James Bridges**, who grew up in Logan County, was named by the New York Times one of the best movies of the 1970s; it was filmed in the Conway area. "Between Heaven and Hell," with Robert Wagner and Broderick Crawford, was the 1956 Hollywood version of the World War II novel "The Day the Century Ended" by **Francis I. Gwaltney** of Russellville.

Characters

■ **Nellie Forbush**, the Arkansas nurse in Rogers and Hammerstein's "South Pacific" who washed that man right out of her hair nearly 2,000 times on Broadway. Mary Martin was the stage Nellie; Mitzi Gaynor did the movie role.

■ **Rooster Cogburn**, one-eyed federal marshal from Fort Smith in the Charles Portis novel "True Grit," for the portrayal of whom John Wayne won his only movie Oscar.

■ **Lorelei**, the "Little Girl from Little Rock," in the Jule Styne musical "Gentlemen Prefer Blondes." Carol Channing was Lorelei on stage, Marilyn Monroe in the movie version. For many years, "Little Girl from Little Rock" was Channing's signature song.

■ **Karl Childers**, everybody's favorite mass murderer in "Sling Blade." His raspy voice is the purest Arkansas sound ever featured on the silver screen.

■ **The Arkansas Traveler**, folktale character conceived around 1840 by the Little Rock politician and raconteur Sandford K. Faulkner. Others have since assumed the designation, including the novelist Opie Read and the radio comedian Bob Burns.

■ **The Big Bear of Arkansas**. Important American literary symbol is the "creation bear," most notably embodied in William Faulkner's story "The Bear," which drew heavily from the influential story "The Big Bear of Arkansas" written by Thomas Bangs Thorpe (1815-1870) in 1841. The Thorpe story was the centerpiece of what came to be known as the Big Bear school of American fiction. Albert Bigelow Paine, Mark Twain's friend and collaborator, also wrote a story called "The Big Bear of Arkansas."

MAX BRANTLEY

Harry Thomason

Carol Channing

■ **Socks Clinton**, the presidential cat, born in Little Rock.

■ **Betty Boop**, the cartoons' leading lady of the 1940s, was created by a Harrison-born graphic artist named Dan Glass.

■ **Joe Bob Briggs,** self-described as America's foremost and only drive-in movie critic, created by journalist John Bloom, a Little Rock native.

■ **The Royal Nonesuch**, a creature no less fearsome for being non-existent, was created by the King and the Duke in an Arkansas riverside village in the novel "The Adventures of Huckleberry Finn" by Mark Twain.

■ **Precious and Willard.** In Gennifer Flowers' book "Passion and Betrayal," these are the pet names that she says she and the future president, Bill Clinton, gave their respective genitalia.

■ **L.Q. Jones**, the lovable Marine from Cotton Plant, Ark., in "Battle Cry," the 1955 movie version of the Leon Uris World War II novel. The character was so popular that the actor who played the role, Justus McQueen, acted under the name L.Q. Jones in all his subsequent movies.

B.T. Fooks

Food And Drink

■ **Grapette**. Bottled soft drink, flavored with real grape juice, created in Camden in 1926 by a man named B.T. Fooks who had traded his gasoline filling station for a bottling plant. It was so successful that by 1950 there were more than 600 Grapette bottling plants in 38 states. The drink is still marketed outside the United States.

■ **Fried dill pickles**. Invented in Atkins and made famous at the Loner Drive-in Cafe there. Among celebrities who testified to their tastiness: Allen Ginsberg, the Beat poet; and novelist Norman Mailer.

■ **The "cheese dog,"** a frankfurter with cheese hid in the middle of it, invented in Little Rock in 1956 by the Finkbeiner Meat Packing Co. Proved so popular that the company's TV spokesman ran for governor two years later, only to lose in the post-integration crisis landslide for Orval Faubus. A "chili dog," with a minuscule amount of chili inside the weenie, met with less success.

■ **The turnip sandwich**. An anecdotal staple during the Depression, when turnips were often all there was to eat. The turnip sandwich consisted of one slice of turnip served between two other slices of the same turnip.

■ **Mountain Valley Spring Water**. 4,000-year-old mineral water bottled near Hot Springs since 1906, with such devotees as Calvin Coolidge, Anwar Sadat, John Lennon, Muhammad Ali and Secretariat.

■ **The Bradley pink tomato**. Most delicious food of all time, with the possible exception of lemon meringue pie. Several pale-skinned varieties (including the legendary Traveler '76) developed at the University of Arkansas, notably by Dr. Joe McFerran, who directed the UA's tomato-breeding program for 30 years until his retirement in 1987.

■ **Brown-and-serve rolls** were invented at Meyer's Bakery in Little Rock in the 1930s.

■ Recipe for **Alligator Gar a la Chicot**: Dress gar and place on hickory board. Bake in oven at 475 degrees for four hours. Remove from oven, throw away gar, eat board.

Black Studies

■ **Henry Dumas** (1934-68). Born at Sweet Home south of Little Rock, wrote "Ark of Bones" and several books of stories and poems before being shot dead by a New

York City transit authority policeman in what was said to be a case of mistaken identity. Most of his fame was posthumous.

■ **Maya Angelou** (1928-). Author of "I Know Why the Caged Bird Sings" and other autobiographical works, grew up in the Stamps community in south Arkansas. Her poetry includes "A Little Lower than the Angels," written for — and recited at — President Bill Clinton's inauguration in 1993.

■ **Eldridge Cleaver** (1935-1998). Writer, rapist, prison philosopher, Black Panther leader, and unlikely latter-day convert to conservative Republicanism, born in Little Rock, early life in Wabbaseka in Jefferson County. Book that made him famous was "Soul on Ice" (1968); his civil-rights influence was meteoric — brilliant and brief, and was coincident with that of playwright LeRoi Jones. He died in California last year.

■ **Joycelyn Elders** (1933-). U.S. surgeon general 1993-1995, outspoken advocate of sex-education and birth-control information and access for the poor. Fired by President Clinton, who had appointed her to the Cabinet, for advocating masturbation in a question-and-answer session following a speech at the United Nations. Born

Schaal (Howard County), now retired in North Little Rock.

■ **Rodney Slater** (1955-). U.S. Secretary of Transportation 1997 to present. Born in Marianna, he was administrator of the Federal Highway Administration 1993-1997.

■ **E. Lynn Harris**, Little Rock native and UA-Fayetteville grad who, between 1996 and 1999, became the nation's all-time best-selling African American novelist. His works include "Invisible Life," "Just As I Am," "And This Too Shall Pass," and "If This World Were Mine."

Assorted Champions

■ **Scottie Pippin** (b. 1965) of Hamburg. Starting forward for the Chicago Bulls when they won the two "three-peat" National Basketball Association championships, 1991-1993 and 1996-1998. Traded to Houston Rockets when the championship Bulls team broke up; traded again to Portland Trailblazers, 1999. Named by the NBA as one of the 50 greatest basketball players of all time. Member of the "Dream Team" that represented the U.S. and won the Gold Medal in the 1988 Olympics; attended University of

E. Lynn Harris

Maya Angelou

Joycelyn Elders

Scottie Pippin

Central Arkansas at Conway.

■ **Justin Tyler Carroll**, 14, of Wynne won the 68th annual national spelling bee in 1996 at Washington, D.C.

■ **Donna Axum** of El Dorado (1964) and **Elizabeth Ward** of Russellville (1982) were named Miss America in the annual Atlantic City beauty pageant.

■ **Dr. Benjamin Bugg,** Blytheville physician, had the world's longest beard — it was 6 feet, 6 inches long — before being dethroned at a Chicago exhibition in 1893 by a man with a beard an inch longer.

■ **Captain Elmer E. Stubbs** of Jonesboro won the title of World Champion Rifle Shot in 1896 after a contest with the European champion, who was from London. Stubbs liked to show off his marksmanship by shooting plums off the head of his daughter Cora with a .22-caliber rifle at 40 feet.

■ **Louise McPhetridge Thaden** of Bentonville, holder of most of the world's records for women aviators, was named in 1936 winner of the Harmon Trophy as the nation's outstanding woman flier.

■ **George Osborne**, Siloam Springs farmer, got $150, a gold cup, and a plow for winning a national contest to grow the world's tallest cornstalk in 1937. His cornstalk was 19 feet, 2 inches tall.

■ **Judsonia**, in White County, was named "The Most Community-Conscious Small Town in America" by the newspaper Grit in the 1950s.

■ **The Arkansas Razorbacks** men's basketball team won the NCAA championship in 1994.

■ **John (Big John) Tate** of Marion was a 1976 Olympics medalist and WBA heavyweight boxing champion for a brief time in 1979-80. Afterward he became a street bum, mostly in Knoxville, Tenn., and died penniless and forgotten in the spring of 1998.

■ **The world championships of duck-calling** are awarded annually at a festival at Stuttgart.

■ **Sutane Magnolia Belle**, born in 1926 in Columbia County and owned by Magnolia A&M College, was the world's champion Jersey milk cow at producing butterfat in the 1930s. In 1936 Melbourn Walthall of Magnolia milked her every eight hours over 365 days and her butterfat production was 1,043 pounds.

■ **Mark Davis** of Mount Ida won the 1997 Bass Master Classic, the most prestigious of the professional fishing tournaments, and was named Angler of the Year that year by the professional bass fishermen's organization.

■ **Del Hampton** of Fort Smith won the national cackling championship at National Chicken Cluck-Off in Nebraska in 1999.

Products

■ **Bowie knife**. First one thought to have been made in 1832 by blacksmith James Black in Washington, Ark., near present-day Hope. The knife became standard equipment for frontiersmen and came to be called "The Arkansas Toothpick." In the last half of the 20th century, Jimmy Lile Handmade Knives of Russellville produced what was generally considered the world's finest custom-made cutlery.

■ **Climber cars**. A small automobile manufacturing company in Little Rock built about 200 4-cylinder 40-horsepower cars and 100 pickup trucks between 1920 and 1924. The cars enjoyed a reputation for beauty and dependability. At least two of them are known to exist today, one at the Museum of Automobiles at Petit Jean. The Climber plant at Little Rock was on east 17th Street.

■ **Niloak and Camark pottery**. Two famous lines of earthenware produced commercially in Arkansas during the first four decades of this century — the Niloak at Benton, the Camark at Camden. Jugs, crocks, jars, churns, pitchers, and whatnots still highly prized by collectors worldwide.

■ **Klipsch speakers**. In the heyday of stereo — that is, the middle three-fifths of the last half of the 20th century — the speakers designed and built by Paul Klipsch and his associates in a small facility near his hometown of Hope were said to be the best on the market.

■ **Whetstones**. It was discovered before 1890 that the sharpening rocks in the novaculite deposits in and around Magnet Cove and Hot Springs were the best in the country and were comparable with the best in the world,

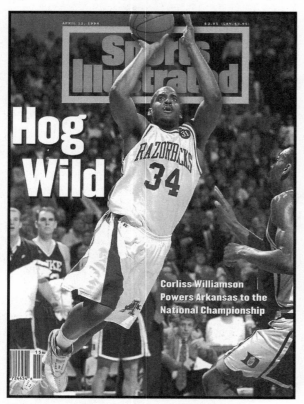

The Arkansas Razorbacks hit the newsstands.

Louise McPhetridge Thaden

which at that time came from Turkey. There's been at least one company mining and marketing them for more than a century.

■ **Glutton Dibbler.** This was the world's greatest topwater fishing lure, designed and patented around 1950 by an Arkadelphia gunsmith named Clyde Key. It was especially deadly on the grinnel, or bowfin. It was awkwardly big, made of cedar wood, and came in six colors—yellow, black, white, frog, perch and pike. Only 24,000 of them were ever made.

Journalists

■ **John H. Johnson**, publisher of Ebony and Jet magazines, born at Arkansas City in Desha County in 1918. His Chicago-based Johnson Publishing Co. was recently said to be the second-largest black-owned business in the country, with 2,600 employees and more than $300 million in annual sales.

■ **Helen Gurley Brown**, editor of Cosmopolitan magazine for 30 years from 1966 to 1996, since booted upstairs, was born at Green Forest in Carroll County in 1922.

■ **William Whitworth**, editor of the Atlantic Monthly magazine 1981-1999, was born at Hot Springs in 1937.

■ **Fred Graham**, Oxford-trained lawyer and longtime CBS News legal correspondent and Supreme Court expert, was born at Little Rock in 1931.

■ **Robert Palmer Jr.**, longtime music critic for the New York Times and preeminent historian of rock music in America, born in Little Rock in 1945. He died in 1997.

Scholars

■ **C. Vann Woodward,** history professor at Johns Hopkins and later at Yale, the leading 20th century Southern historian, born at Vanndale near Wynne in 1908 and grew up at Helena. Author of "The Strange Career of Jim Crow," "The Burden of Southern History," and "Origins of the New South," and other important works about the South.

■ **Vance Randolph** of Fayetteville (1892-1980), Kansas-born folklorist at the University of Arkansas who, starting around 1920, single-handedly preserved much of the folklore of the Ozarks in an encyclopedic bibliog-

THE CLIMBER FOUR

The "CLIMBER" climbs
OVER THEM ALL

You believe in Arkansas.
You live in Arkansas.
The Climber Four is made in Arkansas for Arkansas roads.

BUY A CLIMBER FOUR
AND SAVE THE FREIGHT

Limited Amount of Capital Stock For Sale

THE CLIMBER MOTOR CORPORATION
LITTLE ROCK, ARK.

TEAR OFF AND MAIL — Send me free descriptive matter and catalog CLIMBER MOTOR CORP.,

Advertisement for the Climber automobile

raphy compiled over 50 years, fragments of it published in such popular books as "We Always Lie to Strangers" and "Pissing in the Snow" that continue to sell briskly nearly two decades after Randolph's death.

■ **Dee Brown** of Little Rock, (1908-) authority on American Indian history, the Old West, and the American frontier. Grew up in Ouachita County near Stephens. His book "Bury My Heart at Wounded Knee: An Indian History of the American West" (1970) was a watershed work in American studies; it changed the teaching of American history and it incidentally sold more than a million copies. Brown's 11th novel, "The Way to Bright Star," a critical and popular success, was published in 1998 after he turned 90.

■ **Nannerl Keohane**, (1940-) Blytheville native who is president of Duke University at Durham, N.C. Her father was a Presbyterian minister who moved about frequently, and she grew up in a number of communities in Arkansas, Texas and South Carolina. A 1961 graduate of Wellesley College with a political science doctorate from Yale. Political science prof at Swarthmore College, Penn and Stanford before being named president of Wellesley in 1981. One of her professorial accomplishments was to create the undergraduate feminist studies major. Named Duke president 1993. Vanity Fair magazine named her one of America's top 200 most influential women 1988. Her sister is Geneva Overholser, the former ombudsman and a syndicated columnist for the Washington Post.

■ **Dr. William H. Deaderick** (b. 1876), a physician at Marianna and Hot Springs who wrote the nation's first important medical textbooks of the modern era on malaria, hookworm disease, and other "Southern" illnesses. His major works included "A Practical Study of Malaria," published in 1911, and "The Endemic Diseases of the Southern States," published in 1916. These were the standard medical-school texts for those diseases until the 1930s. As medical director at the Government Free Bath House at Hot Springs in the later part of his career, he became a venereal disease specialist and was editor of the American Journal of Syphilis from 1920 to 1930.

■ **Cyrus Adler** (1863-1940), whom an Arkansas historian described as "the greatest Jewish historian since Josephus," was born at Van Buren during the Civil War. His family left the state soon after the war and it was in Philadelphia and Washington that he completed most of his important literary and theological work, serving as president of the Jewish Theological Seminary of America and resident scholar at the Smithsonian Institution.

■ **Sequoyah** (1760-1843), the lame Cherokee silversmith, developed much of his Cherokee alphabet and syllabary at the Dwight Mission near present-day Russellville during his residence there between 1817 and 1825.

■ **Dr. Moses T. Clegg** (1876-1918). Born in Jefferson County, he was the bacteriologist who first isolated the leprosy bacillus (in the Philippines, around 1910), helping to develop the modern treatment for the ancient disease. He was later superintendent at the Honolulu Leprosarium and at Queen's Hospital there.

C. Vann Woodward

Dee Brown

Cyrus Adler

Sequoyah

■ **Dr. Robert A. Leflar** (1901-1997). Born in Siloam Springs, he was one of the nation's leading constitutional law scholars; wrote the essential textbooks on the subject, and taught at the University of Arkansas Law School at Fayetteville for more than 60 years, and simultaneously at New York University for more than 30 years. He presided over two state constitutional conventions, oversaw the Japanese-American relocation effort in Arkansas in World War II, and orchestrated the desegregation of the UA law school in 1948.

Shady Ladies

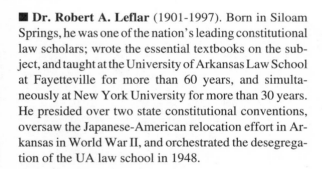

■ **Pearl Starr**, chubbo daughter of Belle the Bandit Queen, operated bodacious bordellos in Van Buren and later Fort Smith from the early 1890s up until around the time of the First World War.

■ **Laura Ziegler**, operated the leading whorehouse on "The Row," Fort Smith's infamous "Street of Sin," around the turn of the century. The house has recently been a visitors center and home to the Fort Smith Convention and Visitors Bureau.

■ **Connie Hamzy** of Little Rock, rock-music's most notoriously lubricious groupie of the 1970s. Known throughout the rock world as Sweet Sweet Connie. Backstage exploits at Barton Coliseum chronicled in Cosmopolitan magazine and memorialized in song by Grand Funk Railroad. Played herself in a 1974 movie titled "Sweet Sweet Connie." Announced 1995 she might run for Congress in 1996 but didn't.

■ **Gennifer Flowers** claimed during the 1992 presidential campaign that she'd had a 12-year love affair with one of the candidates, Gov. Bill Clinton of Arkansas. Her allegations, first reported only in the supermarket tabloid Star, touched off the first great frenzy of what has come to be called "tabloid journalism." She provided amatory details in a 1995 book titled "Passion and Betrayal."

■ **Paula Jones**, a Lonoke native, claimed Bill Clinton propositioned her at the Excelsior Hotel in Little Rock in 1991 when he was governor and she a secretary for the AIDC. Her asking price turned out to be $850,000. That's the amount she finally settled for in a lawsuit charging the president with having violated her civil rights by asking her there in the hotel room to osculate his woody. The suit was dismissed by federal Judge Susan Webber Wright in Little Rock in March 1998, but that decision was appealed and parties settled it in November. Clinton's deposition testimony in this lawsuit became the basis for his impeachment.

Musicians

■ **Scott Joplin** (1869-1917). Self-proclaimed King of Ragtime, born near present-day Texarkana. His "Maple Leaf Rag" made him famous (his first-year royalties amounted to $4) and retains its popularity after a century. Joplin is also said to be the first black composer to have written an opera.

■ **William Grant Still** (1895-1978). Childhood in Little Rock. Became the first important black classical-music composer in the U.S., and the first African American conductor of a major symphony (the Los Angeles Philharmonic). His work, including four symphonies and three ballets, has grown in stature since his death.

■ **Louis Jordan** (1908-75). Father of American rhythm and blues, born at Brinkley. Wrote some of the nation's best-ever popular songs, including "Choo Choo Cha Boogie," "Is You Is Or Is You Ain't My Baby," "Ain't Nobody Here But Us Chickens," and "Saturday Night Fish Fry." Celebrated bandleader (his group was the Tympany Five) and saxophonist.

■ **Emma Dusenbury**, blind folk singer from Mena who became world famous after folk-music historians found her living in dire poverty in the 1930s, came to Arkansas in 1872 as a small child and lived her entire adult life here.

■ **W. Francis McBeth** of Arkadelphia. One of the nation's leading composers of band music and other instrumental and orchestral music. Better known out of state than in, though he has been designated Arkansas's first composer laureate.

■ **Luther Allison** (1939-1997). Born at Widener, near Forrest City, Allison, singer, songwriter, and guitarist, was named top performing blues artist two years in a row in the 1990s.

■ **Albert "Al" Hibbler**, blind jazz singer born Little Rock, 1915. Lead male vocalist for Duke Ellington's orchestra 1943-1952, had five Top 30 popular songs in the 1950s, including the most famous rendition of "Unchained Melody" in 1955. Ten albums between 1952 and 1988.

■ **Thomas Stacy** (1939-   ). Born in Augusta and a longtime player in the New York Philharmonic, he's

Louis Jordan

Emma Dusenbury (standing)

Patsy Montana

Lucinda Williams

Charlie Rich

Jimmie Driftwood

generally considered by music critics to be the world's greatest English horn player.

■ **Sarah Caldwell** (1925-). Founder of the Boston Opera Company and the first woman conductor of the New York Metropolitan Opera, grew up in Fayetteville and attended the University of Arkansas, where she's just returned to teach music.

■ **Mary Lewis** (1897-1941). One of the nation's favorite opera singers in the 1920s and critically acclaimed in Europe, was born in Hot Springs and experienced a storybook childhood as an abused little orphan girl who overcame adversity mainly by the strength of her will and rose to fame and fortune. She's buried in Little Rock.

■ **Others: Rubye Blevins** (1914-1996) who became "Patsy Montana, Queen of Country Music," was born at Jessieville. **Johnny Cash,** the "Man in Black," born near Kingsland in 1932. **William Warfield**, stage singer, born at West Helena in 1920. **Charlie Rich**, "the Silver Fox," born at Colt in 1932. **Elton Britt**, "King of the Yodelers," born at Marshall in 1917. **Jimmie Driftwood** (1907-1998), songwriter and folk-musician, born James Morris, called himself a native of Snowball, Fox, and Mountain View. **Floyd Cramer**, rock-'n'-roll pianist, born at Huttig. **Lucinda Williams**, folk-blues-country-rock singer and songwriter, born in Louisiana in 1953, grew up in Fayetteville. **Iris Dement,** country singer, born in Paragould in 1961. The country music trio **The Browns** — siblings Jim Ed, Maxine, and Bonnie Brown — were from Pine Bluff. Country music singer **Conway Twitty**, born as Harold Jenkins, was a native of Helena. The rock-'n'-roll band **Black Oak Arkansas**, with lead singer **Jim "Dandy" Mangrum**, was from the Black Oak community in Craighead County.

Outlaws

■ **Bill Doolin**, founder of the Wild Bunch, which specialized in robbing banks, trains and stagecoaches in Arkansas, Oklahoma, and Kansas in the 1890s, was born in 1858 on a farm in Johnson County north of Clarksville. Originally a member of the Dalton Gang, he formed his own gang around 1893 and the Wild Bunch became the premier terrorizers of the West until Doolin was captured in a Eureka Springs bathhouse around the turn of the century. Another member of this famous gang was "Ar-

kansas Tom," whose real name was Roy Daughtery. He claimed to have been born into "a family of preachers" somewhere in Arkansas but didn't know the name of the place. He lived long enough to portray himself in a silent movie about the Wild Bunch.

■ **Henry Starr**, horse thief, train robber, and killer, distant kin of Belle by marriage and the last in a long line of Starr family criminals. Twice sentenced by Judge Isaac Parker to hang for murder, he got off on technicalities and got up a gang that robbed banks, trains, stagecoaches, stores, and individuals in northwest Arkansas around the turn of the century. Imprisoned in 1915, he wrote his memoirs and also portrayed himself in a silent movie; was shot and killed while trying to rob a bank in Harrison in 1921.

■ **R. Gene Simmons**, Pope County mass murderer, killed 14 members of his own family and two other people during a rampage in 1987 that was never sensibly explained. Executed by lethal injection 1990.

■ **Cullen Baker**, desperado whose gang killed hundreds of people, many of them freed slaves, in the chaos following the Civil War. Baker's base of operation was the Sulphur River bottoms in extreme southwest Arkansas near Bright Star. Various authorities credited him with killing at least 30 people personally, but the number probably was much higher. Killed by a pursuing posse near the Sulphur River in January 1869.

■ **Frank Nash**, the mobster, was arrested by FBI agents at Hot Springs in 1933 and spirited away to Kansas City, where a trio of mobsters that included "Pretty Boy" Floyd met their train with submachine guns blazing, killing all the lawmen in a Union Station shootout. Their gunfire also accidentally hit Nash and killed him.

■ **Joe Broadway** of Saline County robbed the same bank at Bauxite four different times in the 1960s. During one of the later robberies, he came into the bank and greeted the manager by saying, "Do you remember me?" The manager said, "I sure do," and Broadway said, "Well, you know what I'm here for, then," and gave him a sack and instructed him to fill it with money. Broadway served most of the 1970s in prison for those robberies, was paroled in 1979 and moved out of state.

■ **Jim McDougal,** erstwhile wheeler-dealer and aide to Sen. J. William Fulbright, a native of White County convicted in 1996 of vague Whitewater crimes, sent to

Bill Doolin

"Arkansas Tom"

federal prison in 1997, died in March 1998. He was buried at Arkadelphia.

■ **Mitchell Johnson**, age 13, and **Andrew Golden**, age 11, shot five people to death (four of them little girls) and wounded 10 others in a suburban schoolyard ambush at Jonesboro in March 1998. They were convicted of delinquency in juvenile court; because of their youth, that was the only charge that could be brought against them. The law, since changed, provides that they be released at age 18.

Prophets

■ In 1903, God told a young African American woman named **Ellen Burnett** in an Old Testament-like vision that he would destroy her home town, Pine Bluff, in a great storm at around 5 p.m. on the evening of May 29. Word of her vision got around, and presently got into the city's two competing newspapers and became a bold-headline cause celebre. As the date approached, Pine Bluff was thrown into pandemonium. White authorities arrested Burnett and committed her to a Little Rock asylum, and threatened anyone — black ministers espe-

cially — who publicly repeated her warnings. Nonetheless, by the appointed day, almost half the population of 22,000 had fled the city, effectively shutting down business at the city's hotels, railroads, and factories. Many of these encamped along the highways outside the city, their main concern whether they should watch the destruction and risk turning into pillars of salt. A big electrical storm did in fact hit Pine Bluff that evening, and it might have scared a few people to death. But the toll was small and damage slight. Burnett was asked at the asylum if she wanted to revise the doom date, but she said no, the Lord had only told her about one storm, and had apparently meantime heeded all the prayers, including her own, that he would change his mind and spare the wicked old town.

■ **Tecumseh**, the Shawnee chief who lived in the midwest, visited a Creek settlement in what is now Alabama in 1811 and is said to have predicted there the great New Madrid earthquake that flattened northeast Arkansas and much of the center of the continent later that year.

■ **Dr. Iben Browning**, a New Mexico business consultant without scientific credentials, announced in 1990 that a great earthquake would occur along the New Madrid fault in Arkansas and Missouri on December 3 of that year. As the date approached, a kind of public panic hit Jonesboro, Paragould and other places along the fault. There was a general exodus, and those who stayed stockpiled bottled water, dried food, flashlight batteries and toilet paper. A huge inrush of journalists saw the day itself come and go uneventfully, as has been the case in that region for about 189 years now.

■ **Edgar C. Whisenant**, a retired engineer in Little Rock, reportedly made a quarter million dollars from his best-selling book "88 Reasons Why the Rapture Will Be in 1988." Several times in the late 1980s he named the exact date when the end-of-the-world period called "the rapture" by true believers would commence, having to revise and explain every time one of those dates passed. Attention finally ceased to be paid, and Whisenant faded from the scene.

■ A nameless End of the World watch group spent much of 1976 in a house at **Grannis** near Mena waiting for the Second Coming. There were 24 of them, together for 10 months waiting for the Big Event. The townspeople of Grannis got up a petition calling them a public nuisance, and foreclosers claimed most of their houses, cars, and other worldly goods. Finally, an eviction notice ordered them out of the house. They determined that Jesus would make his triumphal return just before the federal marshals came to enforce the eviction notice, but the marshals showed up on time and the Lord didn't. They afterward dispersed — some moved away, some found jobs in Polk and Howard counties, a few of the younger ones went back to school. All of this attracted enormous press attention, for some reason.

Entertainers

■ **Dale Evans**, Mrs. Roy Rogers, "Queen of the West," grew up in Osceola. She and Roy starred in more than 20 Republic Pictures oaters and hundreds of TV shows. She wrote their theme song "Happy Trails to You" and her horse was named Buttermilk. She and Roy were key investors in the development of the Maumelle community.

■ **Dick Powell** (1904-1963), singer, hoofer and romantic leading man, born in Mountain View. He spent much of his childhood in Berryville, where he got his early musical education.

■ **Alan Ladd**, star of "Shane," born at Hot Springs in 1913.

■ **Gilbert Aronson**, known as Bronco Billy Anderson, the first movie cowboy hero, born at Little Rock in 1882. He made more than 400 "Bronco Billy" cowboy movies, and starred in "The Great Train Robbery," the classic of 1903.

■ **Mary Steenburgen**, Oscar-winning actress, born at Newport, grew up in North Little Rock.

■ **Others**: **Levon Helm** of Marvell, **Lawrence Luckinbill** of Fort Smith, **Melinda Dillon** of Hope, **Tess Harper** of Mammoth Spring, **Billy Bob Thornton** of Malvern.

Literati

■ **John Grisham**, author of best-seller lawyer-novels such as "The Firm" and "The Client," born in Jonesboro in 1955.

■ **Charles Portis**, author of "True Grit," "Norwood," "Masters of Atlantis," "The Dog of the South," "Gringos," born at El Dorado, 1933.

■ **Richard Ford**, author of "The Sportswriter," "Wildlife," and "Independence Day," which won the 1995 Pulitzer Prize for fiction, spent much of his youth in Little Rock living at the Marion Hotel, where his grandfather was manager.

■ **Richard Wright** (1908-1960), author of "Native Son" and "Black Boy," seminal novels about Negro life in the United States, spent much of his youth in Elaine.

■ **Ved Mehta** (1934-), India-born prolific memoirist and nonfiction writer for The New Yorker magazine, spent much of his youth in Little Rock, where he attended Arkansas School for the Blind.

■ **Charles J. Finger** (1869-1950), English-born adventure writer and novelist, a nationally known writer of books for young people, spent his later life in Fayetteville. H.L. Mencken was an enthusiastic fan. Dr. Robert A. Leflar, the legal and constitutional scholar, was his son-in-law.

■ **Others:** Poets **Miller Williams** and **Edsel Ford** of Fayetteville and **John Gould Fletcher** of Little Rock (Pulitzer Prize, 1937); novelists **Ellen Gilchrist, Donald Harington, William Harrison, James Whitehead** and

Dick Powell

Richard Ford

Douglas C. Jones of Fayetteville; novelist **Mary Medearis** of North Little Rock and Washington; novelists **Francis I. Gwaltney** and **B.C. Hall** of Russellville.

Warriors

■ **Stokely P. Morgan** of Camden, a young Navy deck-gunner on Admiral Dewey's flagship Olympia, fired what was said to be the first shot of the Spanish-American War in the fabled Manila Bay engagement on May 1, 1898. He left the service as a lieutenant commander before war's end, and died in 1900.

■ **Douglas MacArthur**, 5-star general born in Little Rock at what is now MacArthur Park in 1880. Said "I shall return" (to the Philippines) and did. Also said, "Old soldiers never die; they just fade away." He did one or the other in 1964.

■ **Herman Davis**. World War I infantry private from Manila. First achieved distinction in the war by killing four German machine gunners, thereby saving an entire American company. Later killed 47 enemy gunners in one encounter, "picking them off as accurately as he had 'barked' squirrels back home in Big Lake," a biographer

wrote. Gen. Pershing listed him fourth among the 100 greatest heroes of the Great War. Returned home from the war to farming until he died at 35 of tuberculosis he had contracted at the front.

■ **Pat Cleburne** (1828-64). Confederate Civil War general from Helena, called the "Stonewall Jackson of the West." Born in Ireland, was a druggist and lawyer at Helena when the war broke out. Commissioned a captain when Arkansas seceded, rose quickly to the rank of Major General in December 1862. Considered one of the best and bravest of the Confederate commanders, his career damaged by his signing of a statement that slaves should be freed and used as Southern soldiers. Killed at the Battle of Franklin in Tennessee in 1864.

■ **Maurice L. "Footsie" Britt** of Carlisle and Lonoke (1919-1995). Football star for the Arkansas Razorbacks and Detroit Lions just before World War II, was the first soldier to win the nation's three highest military honors in a single war — the Congressional medal of honor, the distinguished service cross, and the silver star—for action in Italy in 1944. Also received the top medals for valor awarded to allied soldiers by Great Britain and Italy.

■ **Corydon M. Wassell**, Little Rock physician, became a medical missionary in China, joined the Navy during World War II and was decorated for bravery for saving American servicemen from Japanese on Java. A radio speech by President FDR inspired Cecil B. DeMille to make a movie of the doctor's exploits, starring Gary Cooper. It was titled *The Story of Dr. Wassell* and based on a biographical novel written by James Hilton.

■ **William O. Darby** of Fort Smith, colonel who formed elite Army commando unit that served in North Africa and Sicily in World War II. His story told in a bestseller named "Darby's Rangers," made into a movie in 1957 with James Garner as Darby. Killed in action near the end of the war.

■ **Gen. Wesley Clark**, born Little Rock 1944, was NATO commander in the air war against Yugoslavia 1999. Named Supreme Allied Commander in Europe 1997, and commander-in-chief of U.S. European command. He stepped down at the successful conclusion of the Yugoslav war. A 1966 West Point grad.

■ **Frank Glasgow Tinker** of DeWitt, mercenary American pilot in the Spanish Civil War in January-August 1937, flew combat missions against the Fascists, often duelling with the better-equipped Germans and Italians. Shot down eight enemy planes, and survived an amazing number of close calls with enemy gunners both on the ground and in the air, and with malfunctioning equipment. Disabled by shellshock from the strain of the almost constant combat. Wrote a book about his war experiences, "Some Still Live," published 1938, with the war still unsettled, serialized in the Saturday Evening Post. Hemingway lauded it to Maxwell Perkins, said it provided welcome relief from the "masterpisses" about the war written by "pricks and fakers like Malraux."

Thorncrown Chapel

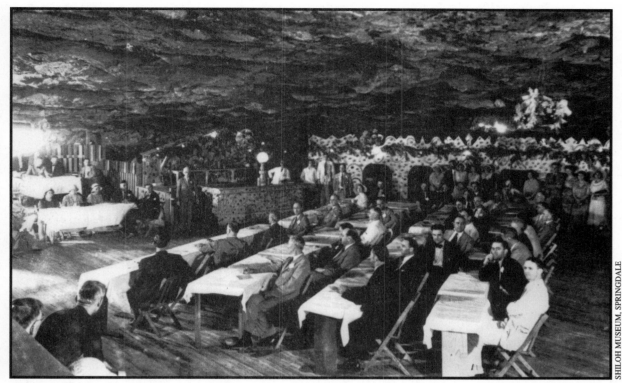

Wonderland Cave and Club

Soon after the book came out, Tinker committed suicide in a Little Rock hotel. Buried in DeWitt with the appropriately enigmatic epitaph "Quien Sabe?" (Who Knows?) on his tombstone. Only 29 when he died.

Structures

■ **Thorncrown Chapel.** Eureka Springs. Designed by Euine Fay Jones of Fayetteville, who was born in Pine Bluff in 1921. The building won for Jones the Gold Medal of the American Institute of Architects. He's the only Arkansas architect ever so honored.

■ **The Old State House**, Markham and Center, Little Rock. Built of handmade brick in 1836, served as state Capitol for 75 years and remains one of our prettiest buildings. Usually described as "one of the best examples of Greek Revival architecture in the South." Recently reopened after a three-year, $4 million refurbishing.

■ **The Old Mill.** On Lakeshore Drive, North Little Rock. Made familiar by way of the opening scene of "Gone With the Wind," the "old" mill was only six years old when the movie came out in 1939.

■ **Wonderland Cave and Club**, near Bella Vista. The "world's largest underground nightclub" opened 130 feet below ground level in a vast limestone cavern in 1930. Has a gymnasium-size dance floor, and some of the nation's leading big-band orchestras played there before the club closed sometime after 1950. Opened again for a time in the 1980s; was purchased in early 1996 by two California businessmen.

■ **Bathhouse Row**, Hot Springs. Still a wonderful eclectic collection of buildings that together tell the story, in stone and metal and wood, of the Gilded Age and its ideals. From north to south, the bath houses are the Superior, the Hale, the Maurice, the Fordyce, the Quapaw, the Ozark, the Buckstaff, and the Lamar. They rose one by one during the 10-year period following the great Hot

Springs fire of 1913, and while a couple have been restored most of them await a rehabilitation that has been promised and delayed several times. If there's ever a revival of hydrotherapy, they might make a dramatic comeback.

■ **Beckham Creek Cave Haven** at Parthenon in Newton County is a 5-bedroom, 6,000-square-foot luxury house built inside a cave near the Buffalo River. The bedrooms rent for $300 a night double occupancy; rough country, so you might want to chopper in: free use of the helipad.

Companies

■ **Wal-Mart**. World's leading discount-retail merchandising chain, headquartered at Bentonville, founded at Rogers in 1962 by Sam Walton, fresh from a flop at storekeeping at Newport. The rest of his story, as the nation's richest man, is, as they say, history. As of early 1999, there were 2,400 Wal-Mart stores, and the company announced late in 1999 that it has more than a million employees worldwide.

■ **Tyson Foods Inc.** Nation's leading chicken grower and processor, headquartered at Springdale. The firm's 1995 sales were $5.5 billion. A recent estimate was that Tyson produces 35 million chickens a week. About a third of its 68,000 employees are in Arkansas.

■ **TCBY Enterprises Inc**. Nation's leading yogurt firm founded by Frank Hickingbotham in a store in the Market Place Shopping Center on Rodney Parham Road in Little Rock in 1981. Three thousand locations in U.S. and 70 nations worldwide.

■ **Aromatique Inc.** Perhaps the nation's leading designer fragrance company — markets special blends of aromatic botanicals gathered from the Arkansas forests and fields — founded at Heber Springs in 1982 by Patti Upton.

■ **Dr. Pilstrom's Tongs.** World's leading supplier of snake-handling tongs, established in Fort Smith in 1970.

■ **Dillard's**. Department-store chain (more than 300 stores in 30 states, with about $10 billion in annual sales as of 1998) founded by William T. Dillard at Nashville, Ark., in 1938, near his home town of Mineral Springs. As of January 1999, the chain had 91,000 employees worldwide.

■ **J.B. Hunt Transport Inc**. Nation's largest publicly held trucking company, headquartered at Lowell, where it was founded by J.B. Hunt in 1969.

■ **Federal Express**. Package-delivery firm started by Fred Smith in Little Rock in 1971, moved to Memphis in 1973 because of greater runway capacity at the airport there. (First night's business for Smith's fleet of jets delivering packages to cities throughout the country: 6 packages.)

Notorious Places

■ **"Little Rock."** The integration crisis at Central High School in 1957 was the first great in-the-field news story covered by the infant medium of television. The broadcast worldwide of pictures of the segregationist mob made "Little Rock" a vivid universal symbol of racial strife. The Central High School Museum is now in a former filling station across the street from the school.

■ **Wolverton Mountain**. Location of a popular song of 1962, written by Merle Kilgore and performed by Claude King. Got as high as No. 6 on the pop music charts. Woolverton Mountain is a real mountain, near Center Ridge in Conway County. Clifton Clowers, the mountaineer who lived there, who had a pretty young daughter, and who was mighty handy with a gun and a knife, died a few years ago.

■ **"Hell on the Border."** This was Fort Smith's nickname between about 1870 and 1910, when it was the prototype frontier shoot-'em-up cowboys-and-Indians town where the Hanging Judge tried to keep the peace. A famous expression of the time: "There's no Sunday west of St. Louis; no God west of Fort Smith."

■ **Trail of Tears**. Cherokees followed several routes during their removal to Oklahoma starting in the 1830s, and at least three of those routes were through portions of Arkansas. One was the water route along the Arkansas River from its mouth all the way into the Indian Territory west of Fort Smith. Another looped south from Missouri into Arkansas near Pocahontas, continued south through Batesville, and then turned west to Oklahoma. A third traversed the northwestern tip of the state, from near Eureka Springs to near Siloam Springs.

■ **Elaine.** Small town in Phillips County near the Mississippi River where in 1919 a week-long racial conflict left a few white people and an undetermined number of

"Hell on the Border."

African Americans, possibly hundreds, dead. "Posses" of armed whites swarmed into the area from surrounding states, and sporadic gun battles flared for several days until Gov. Charles Brough dispatched 500 army troops. In the aftermath, only African Americans were arrested and 11 were condemned but the U.S. Supreme Court, in a famous opinion written by Oliver Wendell Holmes, reversed the convictions and they were eventually freed.

■ **Rose Law Firm**. At 4th and Scott streets in Little Rock, it loosed on the world such courtroom characters as Webb Hubbell, Vince Foster, and Hillary Rodham Clinton. Fundamentalists and conservatives consider it a nest of vipers, one of the most sinister institutions in contemporary America. By romanticizing the genealogy, the firm traces its founding to 1820, when Little Rock was a rude wilderness clearing. Many of the state's best legal minds have been associated with it, including the real founder U.M. Rose, a confidant of Presidents Grover Cleveland and Theodore Roosevelt.

■ **Whitewater Estates**. Abortive land development near Flippin, the focus of congressional and special-prosecutor investigations into financial dealings by Bill and Hillary Clinton in the 1970s.

■ **Mena airport**. A favorite site in some of the more lurid right-wing fantasies about international intrigue during the 1980s. Persistent stories about a connection between Oliver North's gun-running operation to the Nicaraguan Contras and a cocaine-smuggling operation from which George Bush, Bill Clinton and others were supposed to have skimmed profits.

Expressions

■ "You can't get there from here."
■ "It's coming up a cloud." (A storm's on the way.)
■ "It beats a hacking cough." (It could be worse.)
■ "It beats a kick in the butt with a hobnailed boot." (It could be worse still.)
■ "I'm flatter than a one-egg puddin'." (Broke.)
■ "... all dressed up like a lightning-rod salesman."
■ "... cuter than a speckled pup in a red wagon."
■ "... worser abused than a red-haired stepchild."

- "... as clumsy as a cow gigging fish."
- "... as clumsy as a cow on Tom Walkers."
- "... so sick I would've had to of got better to of died."
- "... too poor to paint and too proud to whitewash."
- "... about as graceful as a bird they call the bear."
- "We was so uncivilized we said clemb for clumb."
- "... so hot it'd fry spit."
- "Well, say something or shake a bush." (Speak up.)
- "You ain't just a-woofin'." (Dizzy Dean used to say this. It meant, "You're not kidding" or "You're not just whistling 'Dixie.' ")
- "Well, I'll swan." (Or "I'll swanee.") (This is President Clinton's favorite colloquialism, an expression of surprise or wonderment, and it's probably from the Elizabethan expression, "I'll swoon.")
- "Plague on!" (A non-profane way of saying "Damn!")
- "... shallow as a cow track."
- "... sharp as the edge of town."
- "His biscuits ain't quite done."
- "... finer than frog hair."
- "... grunting." (Ailing, or sick.)
- "Haven't seen you in a coon's age." (A long time.)
- "... a right smart." (Considerable.)

- "... pounced on it like a duck on a Junebug."
- "... hotter than a $2 cookstove." (This is not usually said of the weather, but rather of gamblers on winning streaks.)
- "... playing whaley." (Creating havoc, as in, "This damp weather's playing whaley with my rheumatiz."

Quacks And Charlatans

- **Dr. John R. Brinkley** (1885-1942) was perhaps the nation's alltime most notorious quack, his specialty the wholly fraudulent "goat gland" sex rejuvenation operation in which he or associates removed male patients' defective prostate glands and allegedly implanted healthy billy-goat testicles to restore post-operative potency. Brinkley ran his scam out of Kansas, Mexico, and Del Rio, Texas, before repairing to Little Rock, already rich and famous, in the 1930s. His base here was the Marylake structure at East End on Arch Street Pike that later became a Carmelite monastery. The malpractice lawsuits finally caught up with him in Little Rock, and he went bankrupt after a U.S. appeals court in 1940 declared him "a charlatan and a quack in the ordinary, well-

Dr. Norman Baker

Dr. John R. Brinkley

understood meaning of these words."

■ **Dr. Norman Baker** of Eureka Springs opened a hospital in the Cresent Hotel in that city in the 1930s and treated cancer sufferers with injections said to have consisted of carbolic acid and alcohol and with an orally administered potion made of ground-up watermelon seeds, clover seeds and corn silks. Baker published his own magazine, distributed nationally, and advertised his wares on his own radio station. His fame came almost to rival that of Dr. Brinkley before he was indicted for mail fraud in 1940, convicted and sentenced to four years in prison.

■ In 1908, a Paragould "doctor" named **A.M. Bochner** gave regular blackface comedy shows on the streets of that city at the conclusion of which he invited audience members into a local pharmacy to buy patent medicines of his concoction. He was tried under the state's first medical-practice regulations enacted by the state legislature, and acquitted.

■ Arkansas medical practice was so rife with quackery in the 1880s that the state legislature passed a resolution saying, "... It is the opinion of this House that surgery and medicine are Humbugs, and that all medical colleges should be declared nuisances injurious to the health of the Commonwealth and therefore should be abated."

■ The Journal of the American Medical Association declared in 1939 that the two worst states for quackery were Arkansas and California.

Legends

■ **Saracen** (1735-1832), the Quapaw "chief," was the hero of a tale told as early as 1826 of a mischievous band of Chickasaws who captured a couple of white youngsters near Arkansas Post around 1800 and spirited them away down the Arkansas River, intending to enslave them or eat them or something. Whereupon Saracen, vowing to their distraught parents to bring the children back or not return himself, tracked the culprits down and effected an amazing single-handed rescue.

■ **The James Gang**, including Jesse and Frank and two of the Younger brothers, supposedly robbed a stagecoach at present-day Malvern in 1874 and stole all the passengers' valuables — but returned an old man's money and pocketwatch when he told them he had been

Wild Bill Hickock

a Confederate soldier.

■ **Sam Houston, Stephen F. Austin** and **Jim Bowie** supposedly met in Washington, Ark., in 1832 and plotted the revolution that would lead to Texas independence. In some accounts, **Davy Crockett** was in on the plotting. It's true that all of those men made their way through Washington at various times, but the lamplight plot at the Washington inn is just a good story.

■ The community of **Gilbert** always records the lowest temperature of any of the reporting weather stations in Arkansas, and native Gilbertians claim it's because of the **Blowing Cave** on the Buffalo River. A current of frigid air rose from the cave year round, and after several people froze to death some years ago, the community got together and walled it off, the wall including a heavy door to be opened only when someone had an exceptional amount of meat or produce that required refrigeration. The cold current circulating underground continues to keep the Gilbert surface colder than the surrounding countryside.

■ **Wild Bill Hickock** supposedly was captured in Pine Bluff by Confederate authorities in 1863 while he was on a spying mission for the Union Army. He was disguised as an old hillbilly farmer with a mule and a hounddog. He escaped with great derring-do on the night before his scheduled execution, and made his way back to safety behind the Union lines in north Arkansas. The story is oft-repeated and even made its way in part into Shelby Foote's monumental Civil War history. The historian Dee Brown remembers Camden as the site of the capture in the version he heard. Contemporary historians discount the tale as romantic fiction.

Sports Heroes

■ **Dizzy Dean** (1911-1974). Real name Jerome Herman Dean, born in the now vanished hamlet of Lucas in Logan County. Won 133 games for the St. Louis Cardinals between 1932 and 1938 on the strength of a fastball that was said to be flat-out dizzying. Great year was 1934 when his record was 30-7. Record in 1935 was 28-12. His little brother Paul Dee Dean, also born at Lucas, also pitched for the Cardinals in that period. No slouch either. During each of those two banner years of Dizzy's, Paul won 19 games, one of them a no-hitter against the Dodgers in 1934.

■ **Lou Brock** (1939-), born at El Dorado, had 3,023 hits and 938 stolen bases in 18 major-league seasons, mostly with the St. Louis Cardinals. Generally regarded as one of three or four of baseball's all-time best base runners.

■ **George Kell** (1922-), third baseman for the Athletics, Tigers, Red Sox, White Sox, and Orioles between 1943 and 1957, born at Swifton. Best years with Detroit between 1946 and 1951 when he hit over .300 each season six years in a row, including .343 in 1949. During a 10-year stretch with the Tigers, he missed hitting .300 only twice — and those two years he hit .299 and .296. Lifetime major-league average was .306 in 1,795 games.

■ **Travis Jackson** (1903-), born at Waldo, shortstop for the New York Giants, 1922-1936. Hit .290 lifetime in 15 major-league seasons, including .339 in 1930.

■ **Brooks Robinson** (1937-), Hall of Fame third baseman for the Orioles (he followed George Kell in the position), born in Little Rock. He might have been the best ever hot-corner glove man, with a record 16 Gold Glove awards.

■ **Lon Warneke** (1909-1976), the Arkansas Humming-

Brooks Robinson

Johnny Sain

Lon Warneke *Dizzy Dean*

bird, born at Mount Ida. Won 192 games pitching for the Cubs and Cardinals in the National League between 1930 and 1945. Won 80 of them for the Cubs in the same span when Dizzy Dean was starring for the Cardinals. Pitched a no-hitter for Cards against Cincinnati in 1941.

■ **Elwin "Preacher" Roe** (1915-   ). His name was Elwin Charles Roe, born at Ash Flat. Won 127 games pitching for the Pirates and Dodgers between 1944 and 1954. Best year was with the Dodgers in 1951 when his record was 22-3.

■ **Johnny Sain** (1917-   ). Born Havana (Yell County). Won 20 games for the Boston Braves four times in five years between 1946 and 1950. Was the second half of the Braves' famous winning prescription of "Spahn and Sain and pray for rain."

■ **Arky Vaughan** (1912-1952). Born at Clifty. Shortstop for Pirates and Dodgers between 1932 and 1948, hit over .300 10 years in a row and 12 years out of 13. Lifetime average of .318 in 1,817 games.

■ **Linwood "Schoolboy" Rowe** (1912-1961). The same year (1934) Dizzy Dean won his 30 for the Cardinals, Rowe was 24-8 for the Detroit Tigers in the American League. So Arkansas pitchers dominated both leagues.

Rowe was born in Waco, but spent his youth in El Dorado, where he was a famous schoolboy athlete. In 16 major league seasons, all but one with the Tigers and Phillies, he was 158-101. That great '34 season was his second, and he never again won 20 games.

■ **Charles "Sonny" Liston** (1932-1971). Heavyweight boxing world champ most famous for having lost the title in 1963 to young mouthy Cassius Clay, who went on to be Muhammad Ali. Clay TKO'ed him with a phantom punch to the arm. Liston apparently born in Forrest City, though at times he said Pine Bluff or Little Rock. He was one of a family of 25 children.

■ **John Daly** of Dardanelle won the PGA Tournament in 1991 at age 25. Became an overnight sensation, the nation's most popular golfer, because of his ability to consistently hit the golf ball much farther off the tee than anyone else. Booze and emotional problems dimmed his prospects for several years but he made a dramatic comeback in 1995 when he won the British Open. He has struggled since.

■ **Don Hutson** (1913-1997). Leading NFL pass receiver, born at Pine Bluff. He was wide receiver for the Green Bay Packers 1935-45 and twice was NFL Player of the Year. He led the league in receptions eight times, and in scoring five years in a row. Oldtimers who saw him play said Lance Alworth, who came along 30 years later as a Hall of Fame receiver for the Arkansas Razorbacks and the San Diego Chargers, reminded them a lot of Hutson. Frank Deford, the sportswriter, called Hutson "the greatest receiver in pro football before Jerry Rice." (Alworth, incidentally, was the first American Football League player inducted into the NFL Hall of Fame, 1978.)

■ **Others: Paul "Bear" Bryant**, legendary football coach, born at Moro Bottoms in Dallas County in 1913. **Hazel Walker**, basketball player, played for Ashdown High School and had her own professional team in Little Rock from 1949 to 1965. **Sidney Moncrief** of Little Rock, basketball player for the Arkansas Razorbacks and Milwaukee Bucks, now head basketball coach at UALR, born 1957. **Steve Little** (1956-1999), kicker for the Arkansas Razorbacks, set an NCAA record that still stands (he shares it with Texas kicker Russell Erxleben) by kicking a 67-yard field goal in 1977. **Dan Hampton** of Jacksonville, a Razorback All-American in the late 1970s, was recently named all-time greatest Chicago Bears defensive lineman (1979-1990) by a Chicago newspaper.

Place Names

■ **Apt.** (Craighead County) An early resident remarked, during a town meeting to choose a name for the place, that it was pointless to do so because the railroad coming through town soon was apt to want to name the place for one of its officials.

■ **Armorel.** (Mississippi County). Plantation boss Robert E. Lee Wilson named this community near the Arkansas-Missouri border with the first two letters of the two states and his own first three initials.

■ **Ink.** (Polk County). Named inadvertently by local postal officials while filling out a Post Office form for naming the town. Near the box in which they were to write the proposed name, the form instructed them to "Write in ink," so they did.

■ **Tomato.** (Mississippi County). Said to have been named by a child who, when elders gathered at the general store couldn't agree on a name for the place, pointed to a tomato soup can on the shelf and said, "Why

Arky Vaughan

Elwin "Preacher" Roe

not name it Tomato?"

■ **Hector.** (Pope County). Said to be named for President Grover Cleveland's bulldog.

■ **Standard Umpstead.** (Ouachita County). Named for Sid Umpstead, a landowner on whose property the Standard Oil Company made a big oil strike in 1921.

■ **Toad Suck.** (Faulkner County). Origin unknown. Probably all the theories about what it means are wrong and it derives from something nasty and wicked that the pioneers did.

■ There are communities in Arkansas named **Ralph, Waldo,** and **Emerson.**

Novelties

■ **The Arkansas Do-Nothing.** Toy or make-work device with a handle which, when cranked rapidly and with considerable exertion, moved parts of the device about with ferocious pointlessness.

■ **The Arkansas Go-Getter.** Said of a man who lives off his wife's paycheck. "I take her to work in the morning, and when she gets off in the afternoon I go getter."

■ **The Tucker Telephone.** Torture device once used on

Linwood "Schoolboy" Rowe

ARKANSAS SPORTS HALL OF FAME PHOTO

prisoners' genitals by a sadistic warden at the Tucker Unit of the state penitentiary, now on display (the telephone, not the warden, and not the genitals) at the prison museum at Tucker.

■ **The rural mailbox mounted on a plow.** Georgia claims to have originated this landscape prettiment (near Valdosta in 1933) but the claim is dubious; of undoubted historical authenticity, though, is the one in background of the photographs of hooligans harassing Norman Thomas, the Socialist Party leader, near Birdsong in Mississippi County, in 1934.

■ **The pooch kick.** Named by Frank Broyles, head football coach of the Arkansas Razorbacks, when he tried to introduce it in the 1966 Baylor game. Hogs had the ball on the Baylor 29, fourth down, late in the game, rain falling. Broyles sent in the punter, Martine Bercher, with instructions to pooch kick, pinning the Bears back against their own end zone. Center snap sailed over Bercher's head, Baylor recovered near midfield, went on to score and win the game — the first regular-season loss for the Hogs in two and a half years. The pooch kick lives in infamy, even though the first one didn't even get kicked.

■ **The Concatenated Order of Hoo Hoo.** A group of timber barons got stranded at Gurdon in 1892 and, with nothing better to do, passed the time by creating a fraternal order of lumbermen, with a lot of silly titles, rituals, and nomenclature. Improbably, the organization survived and evolved into a genuine industrial fraternity, one of North America's largest. It still exists, its international headquarters now in Canada. There's a Hoo Hoo museum in Gurdon.

■ **The Tinkle Pot.** A musical toilet invented by Frank Headlee of Searcy, it became a national fad in 1957, at about the same time as the hula hoop and the coonskin cap.

■ **The Hog Call.** The triple woo-pig is said to have erupted spontaneously at an Arkansas football game at Fayetteville sometime around the First World War, not long after the Razorback had supplanted the Cardinal as the UA sports mascot.

■ **The Hog Hat.** A drawing made for the Smithsonian Institution in 1880 of pottery and other art objects found in Indian burial mounds in east Arkansas includes a mysterious container or decorative piece that looks amazingly like one of the red plastic hog hats that became popular in the 1960s. Archeologists haven't deduced from this that prehistoric Native Americans hereabouts used the razorback as the mascot for their sports teams, but perhaps they should have.

Weird And Colossal Stuff

■ **Christ of the Ozarks** at Eureka Springs. Largest concrete Jesus statue in North America at 70 feet, and maybe the sternest-visaged one on earth. Commissioned by Gerald L.K. Smith, the anti-Semite. Nearby is a 10-foot-square section of the Berlin Wall with a verse from the 23d Psalm scrawled on it in German.

■ **The Osborne Christmas lights** at Little Rock, Hot Springs, and other Arkansas cities. Grew in the early 1990s into one of the world's most garish seasonal spectacles but scaled back in 1994 by order of the state Supreme Court. Part of the 3-million-light display was moved to Walt Disney World in Florida; bits and pieces of it have since been seasonally displayed at Warren, Hot Springs, Little Rock, and elsewhere.

■ **The Coin Harvey Pyramid** at Monte Ne. Meant to be a monumental tribute to the contemporary civilization, built of concrete and native fieldstone and rising 130 feet from atop a Boston Mountain peak, with the mechanical

An 1880 drawing of objects found in Indian burial mounds in east Arkansas. Can you find the Hog Hat?

The Osborne Christmas lights

and electronic marvels of the age stored inside, for the edification and instruction of the successor civilization 10,000 years hence. As with the Tower of Babel, construction on it (started around 1925) was never finished; and the exhibits and memorabilia were never amassed. Ruins now covered by an arm of Beaver Lake. William H. "Coin" Harvey (1851-1936) was perhaps the nation's best known economist in the first decade of the 20th Century — a Chicago retiree to the Ozarks in the 1920s; his theories went the way of his pyramid. He formed his own political party, had its convention in Monte Ne, and won its presidential nomination in 1928 — but proved no threat to Hoover or Al Smith.

■ **King Crowley**, stone statue of the head of a proto-Indian purportedly unearthed by a Jonesboro jeweler and amateur archeologist named Dentler "Deefy" Rowland near his home town in 1924. The stone head had inset copper eyes with silver pupils, gold earrings, and a copper "heart" embedded at the top of its "chest." It was regarded by some authorities as evidence of occupation of the site by an ancient race of giants, possibly related to the Aztecs. Smithsonian archeologists proclaimed it a fake, and Rowland subsequently admitted having created it, but some Arkansas scholars continued to champion its authenticity up to the time it disappeared in 1950.

■ The paintings of **Donald Roller Wilson** of Fayetteville. Avant-garde extravagantly-priced photo-realistic renderings of sartorial apes and cigarette-smoking cats. The titles of the paintings sometimes run to several thousand words.

■ **The Bob Burns Bazooka.** Comical musical instrument, a horn made out of some sections of gas pipe and a funnel. Burns, the radio humorist from Van Buren, built the thing and used it as a prop in his monologues and movie-comedy bits in the 1930s. It was such a famous item that the World War II anti-tank weapon, which bore a certain awkward resemblance to it, was named for it.

■ **The New Holy Land** complex at Eureka Springs features what it calls "the only complete lifesize reproduction of Moses' Tabernacle in the world."

■ **Albert Pike's** books on ancient philosophy, meditations on Hebrew, Hindu, and Zoroastrian themes, thousands of pages long, considered essential texts by Freemasonry, and utterly impenetrable to the uninitiated. Pike (1809-1891) born in Boston but came to Arkansas in 1832 and spent nearly 40 years here as a kind of oddball frontier renaissance man.

■ **The Big Shootout.** Texas 15, Arkansas 14 in what is still called the college football Game of the Century at Fayetteville, 1969.

■ The **largest single nugget of zinc** ever mined, weighing 70 tons, was quarried in Marion County in 1893.

■ **J. Oscar Humphrey**, who was state auditor in the World War II era and who had no arms, was said to have been unsurpassed in two unlikely areas of endeavor: penmanship, and his ability to drive an automobile.

■ **The Petrified Farmer.** A rash of state and local Sunday "blue" laws in the 1880s banned practically all non-church Sunday activity in Arkansas, even such leisure pursuits as hunting and fishing. In rural Pike County, a farmer who sneaked off on a Sunday afternoon fishing trip was said to have been turned to stone by an angry Almighty. He subsequently crumbled, and rocky pieces of him were scattered along the Caddo River. The site where this miracle supposedly occurred became a shrine visited by thousands of teetotaler true-believers over the next 20 years.

Monsters

■ **The Fouke Monster**. Although there'd been reports since 1946 of a weird creature in the Sulphur River bottoms south of Texarkana, the sightings that made a sensation in the supermarket tabloid newspapers occurred in 1971. They led to three movies about the creature — "The Legend of Boggy Creek," "Return to Boggy Creek," and "The Barbaric Beast of Boggy Creek, Part II" (there was no Part 1) — on whose authenticity the jury is still out. Depicted as a sort of redneck Sasquatch.

■ **The White River Monster**. First reported in the 1930s near Newport, speculated to be a strayed sea serpent or reliquary riverine dinosaur; pretty much dismissed now even by the congenitally credulous as having been just a silly hoax.

■ **The Heber Springs Water Panther**. A furry underwater creature — a "horrid, man-like form covered with fur" — given to "hellish screams and agonizing moans," according to W.C. Jameson, the chief folklorist of the

J. Oscar Humphrey

Albert Pike

Detail from a Donald Roller Wilson painting

region, that is said to haunt the deep woods along the Little Red River and to live beneath the waters of Greers Ferry Lake.

■ **The Gowrow**. A 20-foot tusked dinosaur-like monster, one of which supposedly was killed in Searcy County in 1897, according to Vance Randolph. Randolph also said another lizard-like monster, called a **jimplicute**, was reported near what is now North Little Rock in the 1880s, but he speculated that this creature was an invention of disfranchised ex-Confederates during Reconstruction intended to frighten ex-slaves who had been elected to public office — so they'd not come to Little Rock to attend to their official duties. Other names given by Ozarkers to various monsters once said to haunt the hills: the **snawfus**; the **willipus** or **wallipus**; the **galliwampus**, an overlarge panther or mountain lion; and a bird-like creature called the **giasticutus**, possibly

The Gowrow

a specimen of the creature called Mothman who created a sensation in the 1960s after several sightings in the midwest and on the East Coast.

■ **Others**: Pine Bluff and Springdale have reported Bigfoot-type monsters. The Gurdon Light is said to represent a railroadman's ghost. Hamburg once had similar ghostly light, said to have resembled a railroader's lantern.

They Made A Difference

100 People, More Or Less,
Who Made Arkansas What It Is Today

This is a roster of people who have had a hand, one way or another, for better or worse, in making Arkansas what it is today.

Influential people; people who wrought important changes in the state's psychology, its landscape, its reputation, the way it goes about its business.

It's a list that goes back nearly 500 years, and that will continue to expand in the 21st century. It's not meant to be exhaustive, and it's by necessity arbitrary, even capricious, and a little quirky. To answer just one question about some obvious omissions: being rich is its own reward.

The roster might be as notable for the famous people who didn't make the list as for the obscure people who did; and it might be a little bit of a scandal that some of people on the list never laid eyes on Arkansas, or set foot in it. One of the names is not even a person; it's a fruit.

We started out to pick 100 influential people, and if the final list doesn't have quite 100, it has might near it. And anyhow you'll probably want to round it out with your own nominees — those many deserving who, through oversight or plain foolishness — we left out.

ROBERT E. LEE WILSON (1865-1933)

As recently as the first decade of the 20th century, a vast portion of east Arkansas — up to 200,000 acres of the Mississippi Valley flatlands lying east of Crowley's Ridge — was still up for grabs. Much of this area was a swampy waste, the so-called "sunk lands," and a fierce struggle for the property developed. Did the state or the federal government own it? And how should it be disposed of? On one side were the bigtime cotton farmers who wanted to drain the area with a great network of ditches and canals and then buy and farm it; and they were resolutely opposed by the timber interests, the sportsmen, and a big commercial fishing industry that wanted those wetlands to stay that way. Most small farmers also opposed reclaiming the land, fearing the drainage-district fees would amount to a new and ruinous form of taxation. The seesaw struggle often erupted into violence, and leaders on both sides — and the judges who had to decide the issue — had to face down lynch mobs. Wilson was the most prominent of the drainage advocates, and once wrote proudly of himself that he was "the first man to start the drainage of rivers and lakes in Arkansas." Born in Mississippi County, he was or-

phaned at age 13 and soon after began farming on a small plot with a mule that was his only inheritance. He began trading small pieces of cleared land for larger tracts of undrained swamp, and had accumulated more than 2,000 acres by 1894 when he founded the town of Wilson. By 1920, the entire population of that town of nearly 3,000 worked for him—everybody except the postmaster and the railroad agent—and his circumscribing plantation, drained by the system he had brought into being, was said to be the biggest cotton farm in the world.

ISAAC C. PARKER (1838-1896)

For practically the entire 19th century, Arkansas had a well-deserved reputation as the most murderous province in America. The killings here were so scandalously common in the territorial period that the Arkansas Gazette campaigned frequently for public lynchings to "send a message" to the criminals. Then the statehood period was launched by the flat-out bowie-knife murder of a state legislator on the floor of the House of Representatives by the House speaker. Desperadoes ran riot over the state in the chaos following the Civil War, and west Arkansas was particularly bloody, with the Indian Terri-

Robert E. Lee Wilson

Isaac C. Parker

tory, where there was effectively no civil authority whatever, offering quick and easy criminal refuge. Judge Parker, the "Hanging Judge," was the first official to have much of a law-and-order impact on this desperate situation. He was a Missouri Republican sent to Fort Smith in 1875 to preside over the federal District Court and during the next 21 years he sentenced 151 men to hang, 83 of whom were executed on the famous gallows. For the first 14 years of his tenure, his sentences were not appealable. His famous force of 200 hard-riding federal marshals broke the back of the criminal empire that had terrorized Arkansas for a generation, and Judge Parker's success in bringing justice into this woolly region went a long way toward redeeming the state's reputation.

SAM WALTON (1919-1992)

Not merely because he was the nation's richest man did Sam Walton become one of the most influential of Arkansans. It was more a matter of his having changed the way that most people in Arkansas, and in much of the country, shop for necessary household goods. In rural and small-town Arkansas — and to some degree in big-town Arkansas — "going to Wal-Mart" has become in the 1990s the chief form of public entertainment. It's a daily pilgrimmage, whether you buy anything or not — and inevitably you do. And that change in the public shopping habit has resulted in shutting down thousands of small-town mom-and-pop businesses that simply couldn't stand the heat of Walton's brand of discount-merchandising competition. The loss of this element of the Arkansas business community has changed what our small towns are — their look and character — and surely there will be long-term consequences concerning what manner of people this new variety of small town will turn out. Food for thought.

DR. JOHN C. BRANNER

In 1887, Dr. Branner, the state geologist, began the first comprehensive survey of the mineral wealth of Arkansas. He didn't find much of the fabled gold and silver that had inspired explorers for 400 years, but he did find (in a pile of dirt and rock being used to surface the new Little Rock-Pine Bluff road) an even greater treasure: bauxite. The ore was part of the largest deposit in North America, centered in Saline County. Commercial mining began in 1899, peaked in World War II, and was a 20th century

Sam Walton

economic mainstay. Among the other mineral treasures Dr. Branner found and identified was a small deposit of kimberlite in Pike County that he correctly predicted would contain diamonds. His geological reports filled 20 volumes, and among his other scholarly works was a compilation of places and geological features in the state with French names.

JOHN TYSON (D. 1967)

The Arkansas poultry industry is now the nation's largest, producing more than a billion chickens a year. It's the state's biggest agricultural industry now, producing nearly $2 1/2 billion a year. The industry can be traced to the spring of 1936 when John Tyson of Springdale put 500 chickens into wooden crates on the back of his flatbed truck and drove them to Chicago, where he sold them for a $235 profit. He kept out $15 of the money to buy gas for the trip back home, and wired the rest to Springdale with instructions to buy another 500 chickens and have them crated up and ready to go when he arrived. "Within a year," according to a corporate history written by Marvin Schwartz, "Tyson was hauling loads of Arkansas chickens to new markets in Cincinnati, Detroit, Cleveland,

Memphis and Houston." As soon as he was able, he bought a hatchery and began selling baby chicks to growers from whom he then bought them back and marketed them. The Tyson firm incorporated in 1947 and by 1952 output was 12,000 chickens a week and annual sales topped $1 million for the first time. More people in Arkansas now make a living in the poultry business than in the timber business, and the industry has impacted the environment, the landscape, almost as much as it has the economy.

JIM JOHNSON (B.1924)

"Justice Jim" Johnson was the state's best-known segregationist hothead in the 1950s and 1960s. A Crossett lawyer and state senator, he was already a founder of the Citizens Council of Arkansas and only 30 years old when he ran for attorney general and lost in 1954 — only 32 when he ran for governor as a segregationist firebrand in 1956, losing to Orval Faubus, the racial "moderate" in the race. Johnson's strong showing in that race — and his success in promoting a nullification amendment to the state constitution — is said to have provoked Faubus into following the segregationist course he took in the 1957 integration crisis at Little Rock Central High School. Johnson has been credited (by Faubus, Winthrop Rockefeller, and himself, among others) with having pressured Faubus, through intimations of incipient violence, among other means) into his defiant stand. Johnson influenced Arkansas history in at least a couple of other ways, too. He headed George Wallace's third-party presidential campaign in Arkansas in 1968, and Wallace would never have carried the Arkansas vote in that election without him. Johnson also turns out to have been a main conduit for much of the damaging information and misinformation that led to many of the Whitewater and sex-and-murder allegations against President Bill Clinton.

THOMAS HART BENTON (1782-1858)

The abolitionist movement was gaining momentum in the 1830s when Arkansas began pressing for admission to the Union. The path to statehood for a slaveholding area was suddenly chancy and treacherous, and Arkansas's territorial delegate in Congress, Ambrose Sevier, had neither the clout nor the skill to negotiate it. So the task

John Tyson (right)

Jim Johnson

Thomas Hart Benton

Daisy Bates

fell to Benton, the leonine Missouri Democrat who was called Old Bullion because of his artful oratory on behalf of Andy Jackson's monetary policies. Benton successfully linked Arkansas's admission as a slave state with that of Michigan as a free state in 1836, and piloted the legislation through Congress. He was the grand-uncle of Thomas Hart Benton, the 20th century Missouri painter. Benton County in northwest Arkansas and its county seat Bentonville were named for the senator, as was the city of Benton in Saline County.

DAISY BATES (1914-1999) AND THE LITTLE ROCK NINE: THELMA MOTHERSHED, ELIZABETH ECKFORD, JEFFERSON THOMAS, ERNEST GREEN, MINNIJEAN BROWN, CARLOTTA WALLS, TERRENCE ROBERTS. GLORIA RAY, AND MELBA PATTILLO

For those caught up in the storm of the 1957 Little Rock

Central High School crisis, Daisy Bates was a symbol, but for those in the eye of that storm — the nine students who desegregated the school — she was much more than that. She was their spokesman, their protector, and their counselor, and the source of much of the courage they needed each day. During the crisis, she acted as a buffer between the students and the outside world, as a kind of lightning rod to draw political, media and racist attention from them onto herself. For her efforts, she became perhaps the most vilified Arkansan of the century, and there were serious efforts to bomb her home. Mrs. Bates and her husband, L.C. Bates, had published a black-oriented newspaper, the Arkansas State Press, here since 1941. A boycott by white advertisers forced the paper to shut down in 1959, but Mrs. Bates revived it again 25 years later.

ANONYMOUS CHEROKEE FARMERS

The Cherokees owned a big parallelogram of northwest Arkansas for about a decade until their removal in 1828, and during that time they planted Arkansas's first peach orchards. They were excellent farmers and their beautiful farmsteads and well-kept orchards in the Arkansas River valley hastened their expulsion by covetous settlers. Without them to tend it, the Arkansas peach crop evolved slowly, and became commercially important only in this century. It faded to one of the state's lesser crops after the Second World War, now valued at about $4 million a year

BRUCE HUNT, J.J. VICTOR, DR. SAMUEL BUSEY

Hunt was a Tulsa oil speculator and Victor a consulting geologist in Oklahoma in the early 1900s. Victor was sure south Arkansas sat on a big oil pool, and he persuaded Hunt to go to Union County in 1919 to buy up oil leases. Hunt was broke but rustled up $250 with which he leased 12,000 acres in a tract west of El Dorado. Victor surveyed the tract and he and Hunt together got a Tulsa oil company to come drill a test well. In April, 1920, these drillers hit a monster pocket of natural gas that almost blew up Union County but produced no oil. Their success did encourage other drillers, however, including a company that put down two dry holes near El Dorado before going broke that summer. Enter Dr. Busey, a colorful doctor-turned-geologist who had just returned to the U.S. via Bolivia and Mexico and was looking for oil wells to buy. He bought 51 per cent of the company that had drilled those dry holes — and lured two other well-heeled local investors. They put down a third well, the Busey No. 1, that fall, and on Jan. 10, 1921, it erupted in a gusher so powerful it drenched El Doradoans two miles away. The strike started the oil boom that, by 1924, had transformed Arkansas into the fourth leading petroleum producer among the states. Oil is still an important element in the south Arkansas economy. Only about half the oil reserves there have been retrieved.

JOHN H. WALKER

Walker is said to be responsible for the Missouri bootheel becoming a part of Missouri rather than Arkansas. The northern border of Arkansas was originally proposed to be a straight line to the Mississippi River, taking in the bootheel counties of Dunklin and Pemiscot and part of New Madrid county. Walker had a bigtime cattle farm at Caruthersville (just north of Blytheville) and the story is that when Arkansas Territory was organized in 1819,

Walker knew that Missouri soon would be admitted to the Union and his holdings would be much more valuable in the U.S. than out. He lobbied the necessary officials, including Congress, rather lavishly, and got the bootheel border "jogged" around him, for about 50 miles down the St. Francis River.

F.W. TUCKER, SID B. REDDING, ALICE FRENCH, THEODORE ROOSEVELT

At the dawn of the 20th century, Tucker was co-owner of the plantation at Clover Bend in Lawrence County where novelist Alice French (her pen name was Octave Thanet) lived part-time and which she used as a kind of Arkansas Tara in her books. President Theodore Roosevelt was an admirer of French's writing, and when she visited the White House at his invitation in 1906, she recommended Tucker as a back-home Republican he could rely on. With TR's backing, Tucker soon became GOP chairman in Arkansas and a presidential advisor. Roosevelt consulted with him and with Redding, a Little Rock GOP stalwart, about including large blocks of public-domain lands in western Arkansas in the Arkansas National Forest (later called the Ouachita National Forest) in 1907. Tucker and Redding were key inputters at the White House Conference on Conseration in early 1908, which led to the creation of the Ozark National Forest in northwest Arkansas in 1908 and to its expansion the following year. Partly because of pressure by loggers, partly because the national forests were a Republican creation, the state legislature petitioned Congress in 1909 to remove the state from participation in the national-forests program, and in 1910 President William Howard Taft did withdraw some of the Ouachita lands, but eventually the state wound up with more than 1.5 million acres of national forest.

HERNANDO DE SOTO (1500-1542)

De Soto and his bedraggled band were the first Europeans in what is now Arkansas. They crossed the Mississippi near present-day Helena in 1541 and spent a couple of years tromping around future Arkansas looking for gold and abusing the hospitality of the native people. DeSoto

Hernando de Soto

Robert Crittenden

himself is now thought to have died in east Arkansas. His trek here was of little historical importance, but the disease germs he and his men brought along — measles and smallpox chief among them — probably decimated the native population, thus altering the future course of Arkansas's development. "There is a striking contrast between the areas of dense population encountered by the Spanish and the few small towns near the Arkansas River found by the French 130 years later," the archeologists Dan and Phyllis Morse have written. "The thousands of warriors, towns of 400-500 houses, paramount chiefs, and highly developed societies were gone. Epidemic disease spread by the Spanish has long been suggested as the ultimate cause... ."

ROBERT CRITTENDEN (1797-1834)

He was only 22 when he came from Kentucky to Arkansas Post in 1819 to serve as secretary of the new Arkansas Territory. Because the first territorial governor was delayed five months getting here, the opportunistic Crittenden assumed the power to make key political appointments and called a hurry-up election to get his man elected as

territorial delegate to Congress. This gave him a formidable base on which he built the first important Arkansas political machine, which set a standard for grasping, crony-ridden politics that more often than not has been the standard ever since. One advantage Crittenden had over his political-machine successors was that, all else failing, he could just flat-out bump off the competition—evidence his dispatching Henry W. Conway, the congressional delegate, in an 1827 duel. Crittenden was also a key figure in Arkansas getting rid of its Indian tribes. He was fluently deceitful and mendacious in negotiating the various Arkansas tribes, particularly the Quapaws, into want, homelessness, and despair. His contributions in that regard were a major factor in establishing Arkansas's permanent borders. He died at 37 after suffering a seizure while trying a case in a Vicksburg courtroom.

JULIAN HOGAN, FRANK STORY

Hogan was budget director in the state comptroller's office and Story was a state Board of Fiscal Control official during the 1945-1949 administration of Gov. Ben T. Laney. Together they forged the Revenue

Stabilization Act of 1945 (amended in 1947), which brought modern, efficient fiscal management to the state government and gave the state agencies a measure of financial stability from one biennium to the next. A model provision of the act prohibits deficit spending by the state, a provision that has kept the state solvent through good times and bad for more than 50 years now.

BENJAMIN CLARK, JESSE JAMES, WILLIAM STEVENSON, JOHN P. CARNAHAN

Carnahan, a Cumberland Presbyterian minister, preached the first Protestant sermon in Arkansas at Arkansas Post in 1811. Clark and James were the elders who in 1818 founded what is thought to be the first Baptist church in Arkansas — a log hut not far from present-day Pocahontas. The church had 12 members. Today, Baptist churches claim more members by far — nearly a million — than any other denomination in the state, though some of those churched resent being lumped into a generic Baptist category. (This Jesse James, incidentally, was apparently no kin to the desperado.) Methodism is the second most popular affiliation in Arkansas — with about 250,000 adherents. Stevenson was one of its first torchbearers in the state, coming from South Carolina in 1814 to establish the first Methodist "circuit" of rural chruches and brush arbors in the Arkadelphia area. By 1818, there were four circuits in what is now Arkansas, and Stevenson was presiding elder. Frontier churchgoing was more civilized by this time though it was considered a rather routine Sunday service at Batesville in 1818 when the circuit-rider and the menfolk of the congregation had to beg pardon during the hymn-singing to go out and kill a bear that was trying to tear the churchhouse down. The first Catholic clergymen in present-day Arkansas, incidentally, weren't French, as you might expect; they were eight Spanish priests who were part of the De Soto expedition of 1541-42. At least three of them died here. Their presence didn't have much of a mitigating influence on the Spaniards' cruel treatment of the native people.

DAVID O. DODD (1847-1864)

At age 17, he was hanged as a Confederate spy by federal authorities in Little Rock in 1864. Arkansas had pro-

David O. Dodd

Sanford K. Faulkner

duced no war heroes to speak of — our greatest officer, Pat Cleburne, the Irish apothecary from Helena, didn't fire the public imagination somehow — and this child filled the void, serving as a symbol of Southern defiance and as a personification of the war's tragic naivete. He was born in Texas but his storekeeper parents were Arkies who returned here soon after his birth to open a store at Benton. About 6,000 people watched his execution on the grounds of what is now MacArthur Park. He is buried in Mount Holly Cemetery.

SANFORD K. FAULKNER (1803-1874), THOMAS W. JACKSON (1865-1934)

Faulkner is thought to have first written down words and music in the 1840s to the famous fiddle tune, "The Arkansas Traveler." He was born in Kentucky, settled as a cotton farmer in Chicot County in 1829, moved to a plantation below Little Rock about 1840. He fought for the Confederacy, lost his fortune in the war, held several minor government posts subsequently. While he drifted into obscurity, however, his folktale-tune became an international favorite, and by the end of the century was said to be one of the world's best known and best loved. Arkansans were ambivalent about it, though, the boosters already concerned about its effect on the state's "image." If the Arkansas Traveler spawned the stereotype of the Arkie as backwoods yokel, Thomas Jackson immortalized that stereotype in 1903 with his paperback jokebook, "On a Slow Train Through Arkansaw." A whole genre of "slow train" books and pamphlets, published to amuse train riders in the midwest during the great railroad era, preceded Jackson's book, and he simply made Arkansas the butt of the stale jokes and anecdotes that he amassed and strung together, drawing loosely on his experience as a Springfield, Mo.-based railroad brakeman. His book sold 9 million copies, stayed in print for 50 years, inspired countless imitations, and made careers for Bob Burns, Lum and Abner, the Clampett family, and others of the hillbilly persuasion.

GERALD L.K.SMITH (1898-1976)

Smith, who started his public career as a Louisiana

Gerald L.K.Smith

preacher stumping the hustings for Huey Long, brought a new vitality to the Arkansas tourism industry in the 1960s by transforming the small town of Eureka Springs into a lurid mecca for fundamentalist Christians. He staged the Passion Play of Oberammegau in a vast amphitheater, raised a giant Christ of the Ozarks in imitation of the Christ of the Andes, and bankrolled a number of other "religious" ventures, including a museum filled with Bibles. None of this was accomplished without controversy, Smith having established a solid, hard-earned reputation as the nation's leading anti-Semite, and the "sacred projects" are still anathema to a large segment of the American community. Smith never disavowed his anti-Semitic views; in fact he used the opportunity of the publicity surrounding the new tourist attractions to sedulously affirm those views, with the result that Arkansas tourism, now one of the state's principal industries, acquired an enduring taint. After nearly 40 years, that stain has faded only a little.

DR. THOMAS SMITH

Dr. Smith was a St. Louis physician who discovered Arkansas while treating wounded Union troops here in the Civil War. He moved to Helena at war's end and was delegated to the state constitutional convention of 1868, at which he authored and got adopted a provision setting up the state's first public school system. To implement the system, Dr. Smith, who was 60, was named the state's first superintendent of public instruction. The prospects for educating Arkansas weren't good. Two-thirds of the state's adults were illiterate, and most considered book learning an extravagance and public education a vaguely shameful kind of "charity." Practically all black youngsters were unschooled, and it was thought that schooling "ruined" them for field work. There were no facilities or standards for teacher education; public buildings suitable for conversion to schools were scarce because of the recent war's ravages; and there was little capital for new construction. But Smith was undaunted, and agitated up a great deal of public and political support for the public school system he was able to put together over the next few years—a system ensconced into the 1874 state constitution under which we still operate. Dr. Smith also organized and was the first president of the first professional association of teachers in Arkansas, and has been called the father of the University of Arkansas since

he was ex-officio chairman of the board that directed that the university be established.

RENE ROBERT CAVELIER (SIEUR DE LA SALLE) (1643-1687), HENRY DE TONTI (1660-1704)

The Spaniard DeSoto and the Frenchmen Marquette and Joliet visited what is now Arkansas before La Salle ventured down the Mississippi River with his flotilla of river rats and priests in 1686. But La Salle became the first really influential person in the region because he had the audacity to step ashore near the mouth of the Arkansas River and lay claim to the entire Mississippi River valley. He claimed the land for France and its king, but also claimed big chunks of it for himself. He gave these away as generously as he claimed them, including one in the Arkansas River bottoms to his faithful subordinate De Tonti. De Tonti designated six of his men to establish a fort at the place, and planned to settle down there himself and take up wilderness farming, but never got around to it. The fort became Arkansas Post, the midcontinent hub of European commerce and the jump-

Rene Robert Cavelier (Sieur de La Salle)   *Henry de Tonti*

52

John M. Morris

Mr. and Mrs. William Fuller

ing-off place for modern Arkansas. Because it was his idea, De Tonti became known to historians as the Father of Arkansas.

MR. AND MRS. WILLIAM FULLER, MR. AND MRS. JOHN M. MORRIS

These folks were pioneers in the development of the Arkansas rice industry. They were in-laws — the Fullers from Ohio, the Morrises from Nebraska — who moved to the Carlisle area of Lonoke County to farm in the 1890s. They experimented with a rice crop on the Grand Prairie there as early as 1897, but it was 1904 before they harvested a successful crop. Meantime, their congressman, Joe T. Robinson of Lonoke, had landed a federal grant to fund rice research at an agricultural experiment substation at Lonoke, and studies there proved the feasibility of profitable rice production. In 1906, the first rice mill was built at Suttgart, and by 1910 Arkansas farmers were producing a million bushels of rice a year. In the 1970s Arkansas became the top rice-producing state in the nation.

C.A. LINEBARGER, F.W. LINEBARGER, AND C.C. LINEBARGER

In the Roaring Twenties, when the automobile was making its first impact on the Ozarks, the Linebarger brothers, real estate dealers from Dallas, moved to Benton County in northwest Arkansas to develop a rural resort-retirement community at Bella Vista. Theirs was the first notable effort to promote Arkansas as a retirement haven, and it was a big success. Their first year in business, 1919, the Linebargers built 45 resort cottages and two lodges with a total of 80 guest rooms. By 1928, there were 700 cottages, all occupied, and more than 5,000 registered guests, and the brothers had brought in a full range of utility services, a post office, physicians, and shops and stores to provide all the essential goods and services. They even built a big-band nightclub in a large cave on the property. They sold Bella Vista in 1947 and it was sold again in 1963 to John A. Cooper Sr., who enlarged and redeveloped it along the lines of the Cherokee Village retirement community he'd built in Sharp County. By 1990, Arkansas was second to Florida in the percentage of its population who were retirees.

SAMUEL FORDYCE
(1840-1919)

He was born in Ohio, moved to Hot Springs in 1876 for the waters to treat the pain he continued to suffer from Civil War wounds. He helped develop Hot Springs as a federal reservation but his main influence in Arkansas was as a railroad man. An old war buddy of his became president in 1880 of the Texas & St. Louis Railway Co., and he enlisted Fordyce to take over mapping the route through Arkansas of a narrow-gauge line the company wanted to run from St. Louis into central Texas. This was the "Cotton Belt Route" of what eventualy became the St. Louis Southwestern Railway. It cut a diagonal through Arkansas — from Piggott to Texarkana, opening to agriculture the hardwood swamps and virgin prairies of northeast Arkansas, and creating the modern timber industry of south Arkansas by opening the vast pine forests. Fordyce covered every foot of the route many times (usually alone, riding a mule), securing right-of-way grants from often recalcitrant backwoodsmen, sometimes changing the route to accommodate aspiring hamlets that he liked: Jonesboro, pop. 250, for example. Completion of the Cotton Belt line in 1883 changed the map of Arkansas permanently, making major railroad towns out of cities like Pine Bluff and Texarkana, and creating a slew of new communities, including Fordyce, which was named for him.

THOMAS JEFFERSON
(1743-1826)

His opportunistic and perhaps illegal purchase of the Louisiana Territory in 1803 confirmed the destiny of the future state of Arkansas as American rather than French or Spanish or allegiant to some other colonial or homegrown power. What would have happened if he hadn't bought this big old piece of woods sight unseen? The fledgling United States would have been penned east of the Mississippi, its further development permanently blocked off. A vast Canada-like province might have coalesced west of the river, and another in what is now the American southwest, from Texas through California. A tumultuous tripartite American history comparable to the mess in Europe might have evolved, and people different from us would be here to contemplate it. Certainly there would have been no Arkansas except for the river, the post, and a small Indian tribe too friendly for its own good.

Samuel Fordyce

Thomas Jefferson

DR. T.W. FLY,
DR. T.B. BRADFORD,
DR. E.A. CAMPBELL, AND
DR. J.F. WILSON OF DALARK,
DR. W.P. JACOCKS
OF CONWAY,
DR. ALBERT G. MCGILL
OF CHIDISTER,
DR. MORGAN SMITH
OF LITTLE ROCK,
DR. C.W. GARRISON
OF LITTLE ROCK,
DR. S.J. MCGRAW
OF EL DORADO, ETC.

These doctors were among the unsung heroes who, starting in 1910, were sent forth by the Rockefeller Sanitary Commission for the Eradication of Hookworm Disease to test rural Arkansans for the parasitic disease that had blighted two generations. In the next six years, they and their assistants tested more than 50,000 people in 58 counties, determining for the first time just how extensive the disease was and developing a systematic strategy for fighting it. It was thankless, nasty, and often heartbreaking work, but by bringing a new medical treatment to the sufferers, and educating them in the sanitary procedures that would help them avoid the disease, the doctors took a giant step toward eliminating this historic horror. The Rockefeller Sanitary Commission subsequently turned its attention to the more frustrating task of trying to conquer malaria, and many of these doctors were influential in that work, also.

ADOLPHINE TERRY
(1882-1976)

For more than 40 years, Adolphine Terry was the leading proponent of women's rights and women's influence in Arkansas public affairs. She was prominent in the suffrage movement early in the 20th century, and it was she who organized the Women's Emergency Committee to "straighten out the mess the men had made" of the Little Rock school system during the desegregation crisis in 1957-1958. She was a 1902 honors graduate of Vassar College, organized the state's first PTA, and helped create public libraries in many Arkansas communities. She was the poet John Gould Fletcher's sister, and wife and widow of Con-

Adolphine Terry

gressman D.D. Terry. Before she died in 1976, she provided that her home — the historic Pike-Fletcher-Terry Mansion in Little Rock — would become the Decorative Arts Museum of the Arkansas Arts Center.

CALVIN COOLIDGE
(1872-1933)

On March 24, 1929, in the very last act of his presidency, Calvin Coolidge vetoed a bill approved by the Congress to create a 163,000-acre Ouachita National Park in west Arkansas. Why he vetoed the bill, no one knows. The park would have been 35 miles long, 12 miles wide—about three times as big as the entire state parks system of today. It would have taken in much of Polk County, a big chunk of Montgomery, and smaller pieces of Howard and Pike. The National Parks Service had vigorously opposed including it in the National Parks system—an opposition that might have derived from a visit to inspect the parksite by Arno B. Cammerer, assistant parks service director, who got chiggers on him during a walk over some of the property. Coolidge's veto might also have been a parting partisan shot at Sen. Joe T. Robinson, who had been a champion of the park and had also been the opposition Democratic party's vice presidential nominee in the bitter 1928 election of just a few months before.

H.S. MUNDELL, "BENNY DAVIS"

A Cherokee woman who ran a farm in Benton County is said to have planted the first sizeable apple orchard in northwest Arkansas before 1840, and she continued to manage the orchard with slave labor until the Civil War. Mundell bought the farm in 1866, expanded the orchard, and soon was selling all the apples he could grow for 50 cents a bushel to freighters hauling them by wagon to Kansas City. His success, with the coming of the railroad in the 1880s, prompted the development of a vast apple industry in that region — and of a supplemental canning industry that these days concentrates on chicken soup and vegetables. The peak year for Arkansas apple production was 1919, when the state led the nation with 7 million bushels of 300 apple varieties. The most popular variety: the Benny Davis, a striped apple that sold especially well in the southern markets. Its namesake is

forgotten but an old story around Springdale was of a Louisiana fruit-stand operator who told an Arkansas tourist: "That man Benny Davis up there sho' do grow the apples." Only a tiny remnant of that great apple industry (less than $2 million a year) survives today.

C. HAMILTON MOSES, HARVEY COUCH, WINTHROP ROCKEFELLER

Moses, a Hampton native, was a prominent lawyer and behind-the-scenes politician and from 1919 to 1956 an Arkansas Power & Light Co. executive, first as general counsel and then as president and board chairman. He and his predecessor as AP&L's c.e.o., Harvey Couch, a Columbia County native, devoted a lot of time in the years between the world wars to recruiting outside industry for Arkansas. They created an in-house industrial development department at AP&L to court new industry, and during one period brought trainloads of New York capitalists on excursions to Arkansas in the hope of luring new businesses here. But the state had few incentives to offer these potential developers, and Moses and Couch turned their efforts toward creating some. With other business

Harvey Couch

Winthrop Rockefeller

leaders they organized in 1943 the Arkansas Economic Council. This group, which later merged with the state Chamber of Commerce, developed a broad-based plan for industrial development that included creative and novel economic approaches. The group's efforts culminated in 1955 in establishment of the Arkansas Industrial Development ment Commission which, under the chairmanship of Winthrop Rockefeller, developed the industrial program that exists in the state today. Rockefeller, a New York City native, a John D. grandson and governor from 1966-1970, turned the state's developmental emphasis in the direction of tourism and the service industries, away from manufacturing.

JOHN BARNHILL (1903-1973), FRANK BROYLES

Barnhill taught Arkansas how to stop worrying and love the Hogs. He took an old negative image, the razorback pig, and transformed it into one that's been a source of great vitality, controversy, and coffee-counter conversation in the state for 50 years. He came to Arkansas in 1946

Frank Broyles

John Barnhill (second from left)

after a meteoric wartime coaching stint at the University of Tennessee in his native state, lured here by what he saw as the unique opportunity to unite a whole state behind a single football team. When the Razorback team of that first Barnhill season made it to the Cotton Bowl, he seized on the enthusiasm to get Razorback Stadium in Fayetteville enlarged and War Memorial Stadium in Little Rock built. Multiple sclerosis sidelined him in 1950, but as UA athletic director he continued to build the Razorbacks into a powerful state symbol. In 1958, he hired Frank Broyles, who would succeed him as athletic director, as head football coach, and Broyles built the university football team — and eventually the entire Razorback sports program — into one of the nation's elite.

SCOTT BOND (B.1852), PICKENS W. BLACK (B.1861)

Born a slave in Mississippi, Bond became perhaps Arkansas's all-time most successful black farmer — with 4,000 acres near Madison in St. Francis County in east Arkansas, with more than 400 families working the timber milling operation, the cotton fields, the gravel mining operation, the cattle operation, and one of the state's largest peach orchards. Bond turned down a $2 million offer for the property before the First World War — back when $2 million was a considerable amount of money. His success as an east Arkansas planter was all the more unlikely in that it occurred in the most repressive period of the Jim Crow era, and in the heart of the most vigorously racist part of the state. By showing that it could be done, against all odds, he became the state's most important African American role model. A remarkably similar life story is that of Pickens W. Black, also born into slavery (in Alabama), who came to Arkansas as a penniless, half-starved runaway at age 14. He wound up in rural Jackson County working at odd jobs and saving practically every penny till he had enough to purchase a 40-acre farm, which he eventually built into a spread of several thousand acres, supporting 360 families, centered around the Blackville community (near Newport), which was named for him. His son told a newspaper interviewer in 1971: "My father did something unheard of for a black man, and most white men, of that time.... He actually created something from nothing with no education or help from nobody. He was one in a million."

Scott Bond

George. W. Donaghey

GEORGE. W. DONAGHEY (1856-1937)

With no money to spend on a state prison system during the Reconstruction era, the state of Arkansas made its penitentiary a paying proposition by turning it into a slave-labor-for-hire operation. Prison inmates were leased out to labor contractors who in turn rented them out in work gangs to railroads, coal mines, cotton plantations and other businesses. Their working conditions were unregulated, and prisoners routinely died from overwork and neglect, the horror stories emerging in a series of spectacular press accounts starting around 1880. From the time he became governor in 1909 Donaghey determined to end the convict-lease system but he was stymied at every turn by a corrupt state legislature and a majority of the state Penitentiary Board. He finally forced the issue in 1912 by virtually emptying the prison — issuing pardons to 360 convicts and soon after to 45 more. He promised to keep releasing prisoners until the lease system starved for want of chattel. The dramatic move focused such attention on the system that the authorities had little choice but to abolish it. This was the first great prison-reform measure in Arkansas, and there wouldn't be another for more than 50 years. Winthrop Rockefeller, in his final act as governor in 1970, commuted the sentences of the 15 convicts on Arkansas's Death Row, and he cited Donaghey's earlier bold move as a precedent and inspiration.

ANTHONY DAVIES, ABNER THORNTON, WILLIAM M. BALL, ET.AL.

These were the crooked or inept bankers who ruined early Arkansas's financial reputation. Ringgold, a Batesville state senator, and Davies, a Chicot County legislator, were, in the first General Assembly in 1836, the principal advocates of creating two Arkansas banks— the Real Estate Bank, which opened in 1839, and the State Bank of Arkansas, in 1837. Each of these had a main office in Little Rock and branches around the state. It's typical of the ethics of the era that, having drawn up the charters of those banks, Davies became president of the Real Estate Bank and Ringgold cashier of the Batesville branch of the State Bank, and each became his own biggest customer. Both banks had failed by 1844, leaving thousands of investors ruined. Two accountants who surveyed the wreckage in 1857 attributed the failure to "mismanagement, gross incompetency, rascality, and thievery" by the officers and directors of the banks. Ringgold and Davies weren't alone in this great scam: legislative colleagues and political cronies galore availed themselves of the ridiculously easy credit and big unsecured loans extended by the banks they had created. Thornton, an obscure figure, might have been the only bank official criminally charged. One of the lesser accusations was that he had absconded to Mexico with $10,000 of State Bank funds. Ball, president of the Fayetteville branch of the State Bank, made off to Texas with $50,000. The banks were capitalized by bond issues backed by the state, and the state defaulted on the bonds. The state formally repudiated the debt by a vote of the people in 1884. The longterm effects of all this were summarized in 1906 by W.L. Worthen in his book, "Early Banking in Arkansas": "No enemy could have so seriously injured the state of Arkansas, even by the most studied and assiduous efforts, as did the men who were entrusted with the management of these banks. ...The slow development of this state, due to disinclination of outside capital to invest here, is in great measure chargeable to the gross mismanagement of these two banking corporations."

W.B. WORTHEN (1852-1911)

Worthen almost single-handedly obliged the state of Arkansas finally to come to terms with that old banking disaster, to face up to it politically and historically, and to start taking steps to repair some of the damage from it that continued into the 20th century to hamper the state's growth and development. He did so with an unflinching investigation of the matter, commissioned by the Arkansas Bankers Association, and a lucid, stunning report on that investigation, published in 1906 as that book "Early Banking in Arkansas." It's one of the few absolutely essential texts in the study of Arkansas history, but good luck trying to find a copy. Even archival copies are extremely rare anymore.

CLYDE ELLIS (1909-1980)

He set in motion actions that changed the face of Arkansas forever, most notably seeing to it that the rural areas of the state got electric power. He never broke the hold of the utility monopolies, but he deftly maneuvered around them. As a state legislator in 1933 he developed model legislation that brought rural electric co-ops into being. He was elected to Congress in 1938 on a platform of cheap electricity in every home, and was largely responsible for getting hydropower generation included in the plans for the dams that were in the works for the White River. He became a leading spokesman for hydroelectric power, and the great dam complex in northwest Arkansas was long recognized as chiefly his legacy.

JOHN RUST (1892-1954)

He invented the mechanical cotton picker that brought to a merciful conclusion one of history's worst occupations. There were other earlier cotton pickers but the one that Rust built with his brother, after having worked on it practically all his life, was the first one efficient enough to persuade farmers to buy it to use in place of stoop labor. The first version of the Rust machine was marketed in 1927, but Rust spent 20 years (most of that time in Memphis) making improvements and refinements. He

moved to Pine Bluff in 1949 and lived there the rest of his life. He devoted much of his later life to bringing the cost of his machines down a level that virtually all cotton farmers could afford one, and he funneled much of the money he made from the invention into a trust fund used to help displaced field hands learn other work.

HENRY SHREVE (D. 1851), JOHN L. MCCLELLAN (1896-1977), ROBERT KERR

Early Arkansas had no roads to speak of, and no railroads at all, so most settlers came by water. It was a tough way to travel before the steamboat simplified matters in the 1830s, and it was Captain Shreve (d. 1851), a Pennsylvania Quaker and lifelong riverboat man, who altered paddlewheeler's design so that craft could ply the Western waters. Shreve also built the "snagboat" used to clear the waterways of the timber snags that the French boatmen called chicots, or teeth, and this greatly facilitated steamboat traffic first on the Ohio, then on the Mississippi and Arkansas rivers. Shreve's greatest challenge was removing the so-called Great Raft on the Red River,

John Rust

ARKANSAS HISTORICAL QUARTERLY

Clyde Ellis

John L. McClellan

UNIVERSITY OF ILLINOIS PRESS

Vance Randolph

a mass of logs, trees, and mud flats that clogged the river for 100 miles north of present-day Shreveport, La. (named for him). The raft was a major deterrent to the settlement of southwest Arkansas, and Shreve attacked it for seven years, finally claiming victory though the raft did too, hanging on until the invention of nitroglycerine exposives around 1850. Without Shreve's contributions, the settlement of Arkansas would surely have proceeded much differently. With the abandonment and dismantling of the railroads in Arkansas in the last half of the 20th century, it appeared that river traffic might return to commercial prominence —notably traffic on the $1.2 billion Arkansas River Navigation Project created in the 1970s by legislation piloted through Congress by Sen. McClellan of Arkansas and Sen. Kerr of Oklahoma. McClellan also had a big hand in the Ouachita River development project that made that river navigable upstream to Camden in the 1980s.

VANCE RANDOLPH (1892-1980), BLANCHE ELLIOTT

Much of the folklore of the Ozarks, and many of the arts

and crafts, would be lost now without these two people. Randolph, a native Kansan, started collecting and writing the folklore of the region around 1920. He searched out tales and stories from Arkansas and Missouri mountaineers for 25 years with virtually no academic encouragement. During that time, he lived hand to mouth and pretty much invented the methodology of modern folklorists. Even as late as 1958 not a single publisher had shown the slighest interest in his definitive collection of more than 2,500 scrupulously annotated folktales, "Ozark Folklore: A Bibliography," which afterward was hailed as a landmark in the field, and he finally sold it to the University of Arkansas for $500. Eventually more than 20 volumes of his work saw print. Elliott, a Washington County native, became a Benton County home demonstration agent after graduating from the UA in 1924, and revived the Benton County Rug Weavers Assn., which served as an umbrella organization for a number of handicraft preservation programs during the Depression. In 1953, the Northwest Arkansas Handweavers Guild sponsored a weeklong weaving study course at Elliott's 1832 farmstead home at War Eagle; the public was invited to view their handiwork when the course concluded, and a great throng showed up. This inspired the guild to sponsor an arts and crafts fair the following year, and the War Eagle Fair quickly grew into one of the nation's leading annual crafts shows.

JOHN LAW (1671-1729)

Law was a mad genius, a Scottish economist who, in the interregnum in Paris after the death of Louis XIV in 1715, gained control of the French economy, and tied it to the fortunes of a New World colonization scheme of his called the "Company of the Mississippi and the Occident." He converted France's monetary system from gold to paper, which gave the country a giddy, 2-year illusion of sudden wealth and made Law the most popular man in Europe. But the only backing for this blizzard of paper money was a harvest of jewels, furs, precious metals, Indian slaves, and agricultural riches that Law planned to reap in the new Louisiana territory, which he envisioned as a sort of reclaimed Eden where he would establish a colony of 6,000 riches-gatherers attended by African slaves. He sold billions of shares of stock in this phantom colony, but found precious few colonial volunteers. He reserved for himself a "duchy" of Arkansas River bottomland near Arkansas Post, and persuaded a few hundred would-be settlers to emigrate there in 1719, shortly before the great "Mississippi Bubble" burst, throwing all of Europe into a financial panic. These settlers, whom Law had supplied with a boatload of slaves from Guinea, hacked at the wilderness for a couple of years before melting away. Thus the only legacy to Arkansas of John Law and his grand scheme was to introduce black slavery here — a blight that would continue in the region for 140 years, with consequences that are still being felt.

ORVAL FAUBUS (1910-1994)

He was born on a farm near Combs in Madison County, and had something of a directionless career as a strawberry picker, postal worker, rural schoolteacher, and small-time politico before Gov. Sid McMath made him a satrap in the state Highway Department in 1948. When McMath left office in 1953 Faubus returned to Madison

John Law

County apparently doomed to obscurity, but he reappeared in 1954 to run for governor. He managed to force the incumbent, Francis Cherry, into a runoff, wherein Cherry panicked and launched a smear campaign against him, portraying him as a communist, thereby assuring Faubus's election. Faubus established a vaguely liberal record in his first term, but then in his second he transformed the attempted integration of Little Rock Central High School into the nation's greatest constitutional crisis since the Civil War. He rode the notoriety of the crisis to six two-year terms as governor — a record tenure at the time, matched only once since. His influence on Arkansas's reputation as a nexus of Southern racism has begun to fade after 40 years, and his most enduring influence probably will turn out to be his statement in 1967 opposing the damming of the Buffalo River — the single most decisive step in the saving of the Buffalo in its wild, free-flowing state as the country's first National River.

The Top 100

Our Picks For The Blockbuster News Events Of The 20th Century

What are the top Arkansas news events of the 20th century? Our nominations are listed here.

Some of them came quickly to mind — the '27 flood, Central High School then and after — and some took more digging and overtime with the microfilm.

These aren't the most important news events now — or anyhow that's not the basis of their selection. Some of these 100 had no lasting importance whatsoever.

But these events did make some noise, stir some stink, generate some headlines — and perhaps they had a little bit of influence on shaping us into whatever we are as a state here in the morning light of the 21st century.

Bill Clinton elected president, twice

1▩ Integration crisis at Little Rock Central High School, 1957. Gov. Orval Faubus calls National Guard to bar entrance to nine African-American students; President Dwight Eisenhower sends 101st Airborne Army troops to see that the nine students are safely enrolled. The state-federal confrontation is called the most serious U.S. constitutional crisis since the Civil War.

2▩ Bill Clinton, Hope native and Little Rock resident, elected U.S. president, 1992.

3▩ Bill Clinton re-elected U.S. president, 1996.

4▩ Elaine Race Riot, 1919. A few white people and an undetermined number of African Americans, possibly hundreds, are killed in a week of violence. White mobs calling themselves "posses" caravan into the area from surrounding states, and sporadic gun battles flare for several days until Gov. Charles Brough sends in 500 army troops. In the aftermath, only African Americans are arrested — 87 of them sent to prison, 11 condemned — but the U.S. Supreme Court reverses the convictions of these last and they are eventually freed.

5▩ Flooding on Arkansas and Mississippi rivers devastates one-fifth of Arkansas, 1927.

6▩ Jonesboro school shootings, 1998. Five killed,10 wounded, by two murderers ages 11 and 13.

7▩ England Food Riot focuses national attention on the Depression's economic devastation of rural Arkansas, 1931. (The Red Cross reported late that year that more than 500,000 Arkansas people were receiving food allowances amounting to no more than 60 cents per person per week. At one point 21,912 people in Chicot County, out of a total population of 22,646, were subsisting on Red Cross aid.)

8▩ Bill Clinton survives presidential impeachment, 1999.

9▩ Gov. George Donaghey cleans out state penitentiary, pardoning about 360 convicts as a way of pressing for reform of the prisoner-lease system that allowed min-

The crisis at Central High

ing companies, plantation owners, and other private contractors to hire out prison work gangs, 1912.

10 Little Rock public high schools closed under scheme devised by Gov. Orval Faubus to avoid integration, 1958. Faubus elected to a third term that year, winning the vote in all 75 counties.

11 Whitewater, 1992-98. Failed north Arkansas land development of the 1970s becomes the focus of a $50 million special prosecutor investigation and national news media obsession, the object of which is the destruction of the Clinton presidency.

12 Federal court testimony concerning strap beatings and crank-telephone torture leads to state prison system being declared unconstitutional, 1966-70. Scandal is sensationalized in 1969 with unearthing of skeletons at Cummins Unit.

Elizabeth Eckford taunted at Central High, 1957.

13■ Buffalo River saved from damming, 1965; made first National River, 1972.

14■ Arkansas River Navigation Project, which Life magazine had called the greatest pork-barrel boondoggle in history, is completed and dedicated, 1969-71.

15■ Influenza brought to U.S. by returning World War I soldiers kills 7,000 people in Arkansas, more than three times the number of Arkansas people killed and wounded in the war, 1918.

16■ A lynch mob goes on a two-day rampage in Little Rock, 1927. When the mob can't force authorities to hand over a teen African-American suspect in the murder of a white girl, it takes the suspect in another case and lynches him — hanging him, shooting him 200 times, burning him, and dragging him around town behind a car. Gov. John Martineau is finally persuaded to send in the National Guard, which discovers a member of the mob directing traffic at 10th and Broadway with the lynching victim's charred arm.

17■ Postwar agricultural vagaries effect profound and fundamental changes in the Arkansas lifestyle, 1945-50. These include farm consolidation and particularly mechanization, perhaps most importantly the mechanical cotton picker developed by John Rust, a Pine Bluff resident in his last years, in consequence of which the number of Arkansas farms is reduced by two-thirds, sharecropping and tenant farming are virtually eliminated, and farm labor is almost totally dispersed, giving a powerful boost to the urbanization and industrialization of the state.

18■ A riot and pitched battle between union and non-union coal miners at Hartford near Fort Smith leaves

Arkansas City in the 1927 flood

Sharecropper families evicted at Parkin, 1936, for having talked with union organizers

two dead and a number of coal mines destroyed, 1914. Strikers drive out U.S. marshals attempting to enforce court order, and President Woodrow Wilson sends four units of U.S. cavalry into the area to restore order.

19 A strike by Missouri-North Arkansas Railroad workers triggers two bitter years of labor violence in and around Harrison, resulting in lynchings, floggings, and the dynamiting of bridges and tracks, 1921-23.

20 Southern Tenant Farmers Union formed by east Arkansas sharecroppers, born in turmoil and violence with a multiracial governing board during white supremacy's heyday, 1934. Claims 31,000 members by 1938 but declines quickly after that as many of its destitute members leave farming.

21 "Relocation centers" for West Coast Americans of Japanese ancestry established at Rohwer and Jerome in southeast Arkansas, 1942. At peak population, each of the concentration camps has about 8,500 people in-

Japanese-American children interned at Jerome perform a patriotic pageant, 1943

terned. Later in the war, German and Italian prisoners-of-war, including a big contingent of Rommel's Afrika Corps, are stationed in these camps.

22 The University of Arkansas becomes the first integrated public institution of higher learning in the South when a black student named Silas Hunt is admitted to the Law School in the spring semester, 1948. Hunt, of Texarkana, is a vet who'd been wounded in the Battle of the Bulge. He dies of TB the following summer.

23 Worst tornado day in Arkansas history, with 111 killed, 772 injured, across the state, March 21, 1952.

24 Arkansas becomes home to 18 Titan intercontinental ballistic missiles with nuclear warheads, 1961.

25 Sen. J. William Fulbright of Arkansas becomes leading congressional critic of Vietnam War, 1966.

26 Vast illegal gambling operations that had flourished for 50 years at Hot Springs are closed for good by State Police, 1967.

27 Wilbur Mills of Kensett, chairman of the House Ways and Means Committee, is arrested while cavorting drunk in the Tidal Basin near Washington with an exotic dancer named Fanne Foxe. Thus begins a scandal that ruins Mills' distinguished political career, 1974.

28 "Balanced Treatment Act" passed by state legislature and signed by Gov. Frank White requires that "creation science" be taught in public schools as alternative to evolutionary theory, 1981. The law is declared unconstitutional, 1982, after federal court trial in Little Rock in which many scientific luminaries testify.

29 Women win voting rights, 1918. 40,000 women vote that year in the Democratic primary. The 19th Amendment extends voting privileges to women in national elections, 1920.

30 Ronald Eugene Simmons murders 16 people in Pope County over Christmas holidays, 1987. He's executed, 1990.

31 Arkansas Gazette publishes last issue, 1991.

32 Flood of Mississippi River hits northeast Arkansas as hard as the great flood of a decade earlier had hit southern half of state, 1937.

33 Jonesboro Church War, 1930-33. A firebrand itinerant preacher manages to polarize Jonesboro Baptists and trigger riots, assassinations, arsons, bomb-throwings, murders, assaults on public officials, and other felonies by warring factions of the faithful. At one point it takes the National Guard with machine guns to restore order.

The 1937 flood, photographed near Forrest City by Walker Evans.

Reforestation in newly created Ozark National Forest, about 1910

34 Vast portions of west Arkansas are included in Ouachita and Ozark national forest preserves, 1907-08.

35 Little Rock Air Force Base begins to take shape on the site of a largely abandoned WWII fuse and detonation ordnance factory at Jacksonville, 1953. Base activated, 1955.

36 First hydroelectric dam (Remmel, on the Ouachita River near Hot Springs) begins general electrification of Arkansas, 1924.

37 Arkansas voters approve an initiated act making it a crime to teach evolution in Arkansas public schools, 1928. It is ruled unconstitutional by the U.S. Supreme Court in 1968.

38 Sen. Huey Long of Louisiana campaigns in Arkansas for the election of Hattie W. Caraway of Jonesboro

Joe T. Robinson conferring with President Franklin D. Roosevelt

to the U.S. Senate, 1932. She wins, becomes the first woman elected to a full term in the Senate.

39 Arkansas Power & Light Co. uses its influence with Sen. Joe T. Robinson to persuade federal government to scrub plans for a federal hydroelectric project on the Arkansas River — a project that is ultimately implemented on the Tennessee River as the Tennessee Valley Authority, 1930s.

40 Little Rock School District voters oust segregationist school board members and see high schools reopened despite demonstrations and threats by segregationist mob, 1959.

41 U.S. Sen. Joe T. Robinson of Lonoke is chosen by Gov. Al Smith of New York as his running mate and Democratic nominee for vice president, 1928.

One of the Ozark National Forest's first fire lookout towers

42 Creation of Bella Vista resort-retirement community in Benton County presages development of retirement industry in Arkansas, 1918.

43 Jeff Davis of Russellville, with Populist rhetoric and a Progressive program, bolstered by ruralist, racist stump bombast, becomes the first Arkansas governor elected to a third term, 1906. Only two other governors, Orval Faubus and Bill Clinton, would serve more than two terms in the 20th century.

44 Statewide prohibition begins, 1915. Ends, 1933.

45 Gov. Jim Guy Tucker, caught up in Special Prosecutor Kenneth Starr's widely cast Whitewater net, is convicted on felony charges and forced to resign, 1997.

46 Long inactive Ku Klux Klan revives in 1922 and becomes a dominant force in Arkansas public affairs, 1924. It begins to wane again in1925, and has all but disappeared by 1928.

47 Armed draft resisters in the so-called Cleburne County Draft War thwart effort by National Guard to round them up for military service in World War I, but are eventually starved into submission, 1918. Arkansas draft evaders and deserters in World War I number more than 8,700.

48 Thugs storm a meeting of Jehovah's Witnesses on Asher Ave. in Little Rock, shooting seven people and beating others with metal pipes, in the most serious Arkansas incident of violence against the sect for its resistance to the draft and military service in World War II, 1942. In the aftermath, police arrest only Jehovah's Witnesses, including those most seriously injured, and charge them with disturbing the peace.

49 State of Arkansas refuses in 1935 to shoulder any of the relief burden of the state's impoverished people, in response to which Harry Hopkins, federal welfare czar, threatens to cut off all federal relief to the state. Gov. J. M. Futrell then recalls legislature, saying "unless hungry mouths are fed, angry mobs will be running loose in this state," and the state approves some revenue-raising measures including a tax on liquor, a dog- and horse-racing tax, and a 2-cent sales tax.

50 Attouney General Carl Bailey turns down a $50,000 bribe offer to prevent extradition of mobster Lucky Luciano to New York from Hot Springs, where he had been arrested, 1936.

51 The establishment of 16 planned resettlement communities in Arkansas promises to put more than 40,000 of Arkansas's most economically distressed into new homes on government-owned farm complexes at Plum Bayou, Lakeview, Dyess and other sites, but the program becomes politically embroiled and only 1,400 people have been resettled when the program dies after the start of World War II.

52 The Civilian Conservation Corps is one of several public works agencies that change Arkansas's physical environment by building schools, courthouses, roads and bridges in difficult terrain, parks and other public facilities, 1930s.

53 A state constitutional amendment eliminates the poll tax, the last impediment to full African-American participation in Arkansas elections, 1964.

54 Epidemics of yellow fever and smallpox occasion quarantines, including rail service cancellation, in a dozen Arkansas cities, among them Texarkana, Pine Bluff, Helena, and Newport, 1905.

55 Sam Walton of Bentonville is named America's richest man, worth more than $3 billion, by Forbes magazine, signifying the explosive growth of his discount-merchandising company, Wal-Mart, into one of the nation's biggest corporations,1985.

56 Freshman U.S. Rep. Asa Hutchinson of Fort Smith is one of 13 House Republicans who lead the impeachment of Bill Clinton.

57 "On a Slow Train Through Arkansaw," by Thomas Jackson, is published as a paperback in 1903 and sells at least 9,000,000 copies thereafter, its author claim-

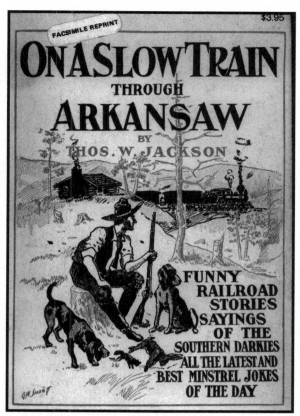

Thomas W. Jackson's infamous book

ing it to be history's greatest bestseller after the Bible. It has a profound and lasting influence on Arkansas's "image."

58 Lily Peter of Marvell, millionaire farmer, brings Eugene Ormandy and the Philadelphia Orchestra to Little Rock for two evening concerts, including the world premiere of a work by composer Norman Dello Joio, 1969.

59 Dr. Joycelyn Elders, erstwhile state Health Department director, is named U.S. Surgeon General, 1993; is fired by President Bill Clinton, 1994, for remarks that were interpreted as condoning masturbation.

60 Total deaths from lynchings in Arkansas between 1889 and 1919: 214. Eighty percent of the victims are African Americans.

61 Soybeans supplant cotton as state's No. 1 cash crop, 1965; peak production for Arkansas soybeans is 1979 when they bring in just under $1 billion.

62 Faubus-Rockefeller gubernatorial race, 1964. Sets the tone for Arkansas politics for the remainder of the century.

63 Paula Jones of Lonoke sues President Clinton for sexual harassment, 1994. She claims he propositioned her in a Little Rock hotel room in 1991 when he was governor and she a lowly state employee. Testimony in her lawsuit provides most of the material for the Clinton impeachment.

64 Arkansas poultry industry surpasses $1 billion in sales for the first time, 1984; produces more than a billion broiler chickens for the first time, 1992; both sta-

Orval Faubus in his most famous campaign photo

UNIVERSITY OF ARKANSAS LIBRARIES/SPECIAL COLLECTIONS

tistics reflect the emergence of Tyson Foods of Springdale as the nation's leading food-processing firm.

65 South Arkansas oil boom, 1921. The state is pumping 77 million barrels of crude oil annually by 1925, after which production declines.

66 The state's greatest fire destroys 50 square blocks at Hot Springs, 1913.

67 Funded by John D. Rockefeller's Sanitary Commission, state doctors and health workers begin the tedious field work promoting sanitation and nutrition reforms that culminate in the elimination of malaria, pellagra, hookworm disease, and other ancient scourges of rural Arkansas, 1916.

68 Weyerhaeuser, the timber and paper giant, inaugurates clear-cutting in southwest Arkansas, denuding many scenic vistas covering thousands of acres at a whack, and replanting them as pine plantations, 1969. Other corporate forestry companies, notably International Paper, were clear-cutting smaller tracts in the mid-60s, and the U.S. Forest Service was experimenting with the practice, under the euphemistic name of even-age timber management, as early as 1962.

69 Henry Starr, legendary frontier bank robber and nephew-in-law of Belle Starr, is shot and killed while attempting to rob a bank in Harrison, 1921. Starr had been shot at least twice in earlier bank robberies, had beaten two death sentences by Judge Isaac C. Parker, and, during a rare period of parole, had starred as himself in a silent movie about his criminal career.

70 U.S. Sen. William F. Kirby of Texarkana becomes one of the nation's leading proponents of keeping the United States out of World War I, 1917.

71 In one of Arkansas's few serious flirtations with McCarthyism, incumbent Gov. Francis Cherry paints his Democratic primary opponent Orval Faubus as a radical alumnus of "hammer and sickle" Commonwealth College at Mena who had retained his "Communist leanings," 1954. The tactic backfires — Arkansas never developed a taste for hardline anti-communism — and the consequent sympathy vote helps Faubus win the election.

72 Term-limiting legislation passes and within six years has wrought fundamental changes in Arkansas politics, the most revolutionary of which is that seniority is no longer much of a factor — much less the pre-eminent factor — in political power formulations, 1992.

73 Three 8-year-old West Memphis boys murdered and dumped in a drainage ditch, 1993. Three teenage West Memphis boys convicted in the case, 1994.

74 After President Harry Truman proposes sweeping civil rights reforms in 1947, Gov. Ben T. Laney of Arkansas and other Southern political leaders organize the offshoot white supremacist States Rights Democratic Party — nicknamed the Dixiecrats — which considers Laney but finally nominates Strom Thurmond of South Carolina (yep, the same one) for president,1948. Sid McMath, elected Arkansas governor in 1948, and Sen. J. William Fulbright help keep the state loyal to Truman in the 1948 presidential election.

75 Interstate highway system makes Arkansas major east-west national transportation corridor, spawns major trucking industry centered in Fort Smith, and eliminates passenger rail service in Arkansas, 1956-72.

76 Gun battle in Lawrence County between law-enforcement authorities and Posse Comitatus militia elements leaves sheriff and prominent militiaman Gordon Kaul dead, 1983.

77 Arkansas utility customers learn that they'll have to pay up to $3 billion as their share of construction costs for the Middle South Utilities' Grand Gulf nuclear power plants on the Gulf coast, even though Arkansas is slated to receive none of the electric power generated by the plants, 1984.

78 The Fort Smith Fourteen, radical militia militants charged with "seditious conspiracy" to overthrow the government, assassinate government officials and

Mississippi County child with rickets, 1937

blow up government buildings (including the one in Oklahoma City that was indeed blown up seven years later) are acquitted by an all-white federal court jury in Fort Smith, 1988.

79 Carry A. Nation makes Arkansas the hub of her hatchet-wielding terrorism campaign against saloons, chopping up bars in Fort Smith, Hot Springs, and elsewhere in the state after moving first to a farm at Alpena and then into Eureka Springs, where she dies after suffering a stroke while making a temperance speech from a buggy in Basin Circle, 1909.

80 A B-47 bomber from Little Rock Air Force base explodes over Little Rock, killing three crewmen — two civilians on the ground die as debris falls over the Hillcrest area, destroying ten homes and an apartment complex and damaging 124 other residences, 1960.

81 Clinton public-education reform package includes pioneering teacher-testing requirements and biggest-ever jump in teacher salaries, 1983.

82 As House Ways and Means chairman, U.S. Rep. Wilbur D. Mills of Kensett develops the legislation creating Medicare and pilots it through Congress, 1965.

83 The Senate Permanent Subcommittee on Investigations, in hearings chaired by U.S. Sen. John L. McClellan of Camden, permanently vitiates big labor's political influence by charges of corruption and racketeering particularly against the Teamsters' union, whose top leaders are eventually jailed, 1957.

84 Drought ushers in Great Depression by almost obliterating Arkansas agriculture, with cotton production dropping by a half and corn production by 70 per cent in a single year, 1930. It is estimated that by the end of that year a third of the Arkansas population is subsisting on wild game, mainly rabbits and squirrels.

Wilbur Mills in his Medicare heyday

85 A flash fire in one of the Titan II missile silos near Searcy kills 53 workers, 1965.

86 After a 26-year hiatus, capital punishment resumes in Arkansas with the execution of murderer John Edward Swindler, 1990.

87 In the drive for prohibition, the Mississippi County sheriff and a posse of militia raid a bootleggers' enclave on Island No. 37 in the Mississippi River; in a bloody shootout, the sheriff and several militiamen are killed, the bootlegger who shot them dies from a beating he takes when he's arrested, and another of the bootleggers is lynched in his Crittenden County jail cell, 1915.

88 Former U.S. Sen. Dale Bumpers summarizes Clinton impeachment defense case in heralded oration to the Senate, 1999.

89 Old West-style shootout on the courthouse square at El Dorado leaves three dead, three wounded, and sets off a violent feud that precipitates other ambush murders and requires National Guard intervention two different times, 1902.

90 Arkansas Razorback men's basketball team wins NCAA championship at Charlotte, N.C., by a score of 76-72, over Duke, 1994.

91 Elvis Presley loses his much-shrieked-over greasy ducktail when, after joining the Army, he gets his first G.I. buzzcut at Fort Chaffee near Fort Smith, 1958.

92 Biological and chemical warfare facilities at Pine Bluff Arsenal ordered shut down by President Richard Nixon and converted to health and toxological research, 1969-71.

93 Joe Broadway of Saline County becomes modern romantic outlaw by robbing the same bank at Bauxite four different times in the 1960s. During one of the later robberies, he comes into the bank and greets the manager by saying, "Do you remember me?" The manager says, "I sure do," and Broadway says, "Well, you know what I'm here for, then," and hands him a sack and instructs him to fill it with money. Broadway serves most of the 1970s in prison for those robberies, is paroled in 1979 and moves out of state.

94 11 die and nearly 100 injured as an American Airlines plane from Dallas crash-lands at the Little Rock National Airport during a violent thunderstorm, 1999.

95 Townspeople foil a Eureka Springs bank robbery there by an infamous Oklahoma gang, killing three of the robbers and capturing the other two after heavy gunfire disables the getaway car, 1922.

96 Arkansas loses "Big Shootout" football game to Texas, 15-14, with President Nixon in attendance, 1969.

97 Half an hour before he leaves office, President Calvin Coolidge vetoes legislation to create a 165,000-acre Ouachita National Park in west Arkansas centered on the Little Missouri River, 1929. It would have been roughly three times as big as today's entire state parks system.

98 Heat wave produces a record 20 straight days of 100-plus temperatures, June 30-July 19, 1980.

99 Arkansas becomes No. 1 rice-producing state, 1962.

100 The Institute of Science and Technology at the University of Arkansas at Fayetteville is dismantled under heavy political pressure — including U.S. Rep. Boyd Tackett's rhetorical drumfire against "subversive foreign intellectuals" said to be associated with the postwar research going on there, 1951. One historian, Michael B. Dougan of Jonesboro, has compared the short-lived Fayetteville institute to one in North Carolina that keyed that state's development of its redefining Research Triangle. "Arkansas had its opportunity but chose another road," Dougan wrote.

In These *Times*: A Look Back

25 Years Of *Arkansas Times* Reporting

These are articles that appeared in the *Arkansas Times* in the first 25 years of that publication (1974-1999). They seem to us fairly representative of the scope and range of the reporting and writing that have characterized the *Times* in its first quarter-century.

We tried to make it more of a representative collection than one of those "best of" deals — a sampler that modestly betokens the changes that have occurred in Arkansas over that estimable span and that also shows that the more things have changed (the faces, the issues) the more they remained the same going into the new century and new millennium.

Given the choice, we opted for the whimsical piece over the thumbsucker, the light one over the message-weighted, the short one over the colossus. Veteran *Arkansas Times* readers will be familiar with the names of many of the contributors in this section, and we hope these keepsake articles rekindle memories of some of the other great work with which those contributors have filled the *Times* over the years.

The Smell Of Possum

In The Beginning, There Was The *Union Station Times*

BY BILL TERRY

The beginnings in 1974 of the *Arkansas Times*, nee the *Union Station Times*, were not sonorous — unless you define them in terms of the windy clatter of the ramshackle office at 1215 West Second St. (near the Union Station), of the gurgle of the chain-pull toilet that broke the stillness of concentration—when there was concentration—and of the arguments between people with more purpose than proficiency.

There were other problems. Like money. You might expect a magazine project such as the Times to have begun with a stake, a modest bankroll to turn on the heat and lights, pay the printer and a few salaries, and buy a little equipment, like a lock for the door. The bankroll totaled $400, gleaned from a few friends who risked $50 to $100 and never expected to see the money again. The printer took it all for the first issue, which appeared Sept. 5; with 32 pages, twice monthly then, on black-and-white pulp, but with a sanguine red stripe across the upper-right corner that read "Maiden Voyage."

A few more investors were discovered, so the door remained open — but without a lock, since there was nothing to steal except an ancient typewriter and a couple of chairs. The one desk consisted of four concrete blocks and a board. A thief would have made us proud. The heat didn't work either, and nobody did anything about it; why bother when one of the windows was jammed open because of building warp? One morning we found that an overnight snow had covered the typewriter as neatly as a bush.

There were other shortages. No regular salaries were paid for almost three years, and to provide the intermittent wage for writer Arlin Fields, publisher Alan Leveritt drove a taxicab, presenting Fields with the exciting sum

of $50 on Friday — some Fridays — his pay for the week. Writers, editors, and artists, as is generally the case when you don't pay them, were scarce. The same for advertisers; the magazine had none the first issue and only a sprinkle for a year or so after. Looking back on that first issue, and on the vicissitudes of the time, brings to mind Dr. Samuel Johnson's observation about a dog walking on its hind legs. "It's not done well," he said, "but you're

FEBRUARY 1977: The first "slick" cover; inside pages were still newsprint.

THE SMELL OF POSSUM

An all-Arkansas magazine needed the appropriate tang

The beginnings in 1974 of the *Arkansas Times*, née the *Union Station Times*, were not sonorous —unless you define them in terms of the windy clatter of the ramshackle office at 1215 West Second Street (near the Union Station), of the gurgle of the chain-pull toilet that broke the stillness of concentration—when there *was* concentration—and of the arguments between people with more purpose than proficiency.

There were other problems. Like money. You might expect a magazine project such as the *Times* to have begun with a stake, a modest bankroll to turn on the heat and lights, pay the printer and a few salaries, and buy a little equipment, like a lock for the door. The bankroll totaled $400, gleaned from a few friends who risked $50 to $100 and never expected to see the money again. The printer took it all for the first issue, which appeared September 5: thirty-two pages, twice monthly then, on black-and-white pulp, but with a sanguine red stripe across the

upper-right corner that read "Maiden Voyage."

A few more investors were discovered, so the door remained open—but without a lock, since there was nothing to steal except an ancient typewriter and a couple of chairs. The one desk consisted of four concrete blocks and a board. A thief would have made us proud. The heat didn't work either, and nobody did anything about it; why bother when one of the windows was jammed open because of building warp? One morning we found that an overnight snow had covered the typewriter as neatly as a bush.

There were other shortages. No regular salaries were paid for almost three years, and to provide the intermittent wage for writer Arlin Fields, publisher Alan Leveritt drove a taxicab, presenting Fields with the exciting sum of $50 on Friday— some Fridays—his pay for the week. Writers, editors, and artists, as is generally the case when you don't pay them, were scarce. The same for advertisers; the magazine had none the first issue and only a sprinkle for a year or so after. Looking back on that first issue and on the vicissitudes of the time, brings to mind Dr. Samuel Johnson's observation about a dog walking on its hind legs. "It's not done well," he said, "but you're surprised to see that it is done at all."

So, how to account for the *Times*'s good fortune? Of course, the miracle of luck had something to do with it. Also, if you survive long enough and things begin to work out, you start to develop a pattern, or formula, for success. In our case, it all had to do with the smell of possum.

But first, about luck. There was a bit of it. The big break, though, came with the Writer's Conference of 1976, to which the *Times*, as sponsor, charged admission and from which the magazine earned a clear profit of just over $1,400. It was the first real money we'd ever had. It was fast and easy, since we didn't pay anything to the invited writers who held seminars, nor rent to the old Seafarer Restaurant, where the event continued for three days. But we gained something more valuable than money: the allegiance of well-known writers. They made a notable list: the late Francis Irby Gwaltney, B. C. Hall, James Whitehead, Miller Williams. We also made the acquaintance then of Dee Brown, who would later write stories for the magazine. In the years that followed, these people wrote and campaigned for us as contributing editors. They brought us prestige and quality, and the first thing

you knew, the *Times* had a following and soon a verifiable circulation. I don't remember what it was exactly; it was around ten thousand, but we were on our way. Other writers were sending material now, and the magazine expanded to seventy-two, eighty, and even one hundred pages.

Now, about this possum business. I'm not sure exactly what the smell of possum is, and I'm not sure I want to know. The phrase comes from Miller Williams, who back in the Seventies told us that no matter how slick and fancy the *Times* got, it ought to have a little of this possum scent; i.e., it ought not to get too sophisticated ("We don't need another *New Yorker* down here," Williams said), and ought to maintain a kind of earthy touch.

So, we had a little sex in the magazine, including a nude on the cover once. A little tic, it does more or less describe the format, one eschewing the commonplace and unshackled by conformity and sometimes decency. We won some awards, made some enemies, and drew a swarm of critics—one woman in particular who, when this possum idea was first discussed in the *Times*, wrote in to say, "I don't know how you have the smell of possum about you when you've got a skunk for an editor." A reference at the time to myself.
— *Bill Terry*

JULY 1978: The magazine cut its teeth on Little Rock cops-and-robbers intrigue.

ARKANSAS **Times**

The Hastings Tapes

surprised to see that it is done at all."

So, how to account for the *Times's* good fortune? Of course, the miracle of luck had something to do with it. Also, if you survive long enough and things begin to work out, you start to develop a pattern, or formula, for success. In our case, it all had to do with the smell of a possum.

But first, about luck. There was a lot of it. The big break, though, came with the Writers Conference of 1976 to which the *Times*, as sponsor, charged admission and from which the magazine earned a clear profit of just over $1,400. It was the first real money we'd ever had. It was fast and easy, since we didn't pay anything to the invited writers who held seminars, nor rent to the Old Seafarer Restaurant, where the event continued for three days. But we gained something more valuable than money: the allegiance of well-known writers. They made a notable list: the late Francis Irby Gwaltney, B.C. Hall, James Whitehead, Miller Williams. We also made the acquaintance then of Dee Brown, who would later write stories for the magazine. In the years that followed, these people wrote and campaigned for us as contributing editors. They brought us prestige and quality, and the first thing you knew, the *Times* had a following and soon a verifiable circulation. I don't remember what it was exactly; it was around 10,000 but we were on our way. Other writers were sending material now, and the magazine expanded to 72, 80, even 100 pages.

Now, about this possum business. I'm not sure exactly what the smell of possum is, and I'm not sure I want to know. The phrase comes from Miller William, who back in the 1970s told us that no matter how slick and fancy the *Times* got, it ought to have a little of this possum scent; i.e., it ought not to get too sophisticated ("We don't need another *New Yorker* down here," Williams said) and ought to maintain a kind of earthy touch.

So we had a little sex in the magazine, including a nude on the cover once. A little sex and a little of this and that; one issue, for example, bashing doctors and exploring the value of whores, a cover story on the stupidest and the smartest Arkansas legislators, and some cops-and-robbers stuff.

As much as I hate to use the word eclectic, it does more or less describe the format, one eschewing the commonplace and unshackled by conformity and sometimes decency. We won some awards, made some enemies, and drew a swarm of critics — one woman in particular who, when this possum idea was first discussed in the *Times*, wrote in to say, "I don't know how you have the smell of possum about you when you've got a skunk for an editor." A reference at the time to myself.

—Arkansas Times, *September 1989.*
The author is a former Times *editor.*

Bud Richards And The Scottish Play

BY MIKE TRIMBLE

It was one of those conversations that friends of long standing have, the kind in which we recall how silly we were in our college days in the vain hope of proving to ourselves that we are not nearly so silly today.

"Can you believe," she said, "that we once sat down and seriously discussed whether or not Ray Charles was a genius?"I immediately cast doubt on my own intellectual progress by responding that there didn't seem to me to be any doubt, then or now, that Ray Charles was indeed a genius, but that I was still willing to discuss it seriously — up to and including the use of dueling pistols — with any tin-eared, gourd-headed sucker who wished to argue in the negative.

She gave me a look. It was the same sad, affectionate look she had given me many years before when, as a college freshman, I had proposed marriage to her five minutes into our first date. (It never came to anything. She immersed herself in the world of art. I dropped out of school to become a Grub Street hack, trying to buff a literary sheen onto newspaper accounts of car wrecks and quorum-court meetings. We keep in touch, though.)

"Have you ever seen a genius?" she asked in that way of hers that says she already knows the answer, and it doesn't help my argument any.

"I cannot say definitely that I have seen a genius," I said huffily, not willing to concede the point entirely. "But I have seen genius. Without the 'a'."

The look softened. I had regained some ground by splitting a semantic hair.

"Tell me about it," she said.

So I told her about Bud Richards and *Macbeth*.

IT WAS 1961, AND THE SENIOR class of Bauxite High School — all 31 of us — were suffering senior English under the watchful eye of a teacher referred to as Miz Trimble in my hearing and Old Lady Trimble when I was out of earshot. She was my mother. Still is.

The psychological dynamics of having one's mother for a high school teacher — or, for that matter, having one's son for a pupil — seem to me a neglected area of scientific research. The whole thing was a familial and social minefield, to be navigated by intuition alone. For instance, I knew instinctively that no matter what else I let slide, I would get my English homework in on time, and in good order. For her part, my mother understood and accepted that I would occasionally attempt to disrupt class decorum as a way of proving that, while I might be the teacher's son, I was not the teacher's pet. I, once again in my turn, expected — actually counted on — the disciplinary hammer to fall as hard on me as on my classmates. Maybe harder.

And so the ball bounced back and forth: a compromise here, a nonnegotiable position there; a liberty taken here, the consequence of that liberty there. It was as complicated as any Mid-East ceasefire ever negotiated, and it was made even more remarkable by the fact that never a word passed between us about it. I still count it as a miracle that it never broke down completely.

It came close once, but that was nobody's fault. It was on one of those sultry early-September afternoons at the first of the school year, when my mother had given us some time at the end of the period to get ahead on our homework, work on extra-credit book reports, or stare slackjawed out the window, as we saw fit. All of a sudden, my mother interrupted the reverie to make an announcement.

"Look class," she said. "Isn't this strange? I've got this cramp in my hand from holding a pencil too long. It doesn't hurt, but I can't move any of my fingers. I can't figure out why they cramped in that position."

She showed us the offended right hand. It was indeed

cramped, all the fingers curled tightly into a fist.

All but one.

"Isn't that something?" she said.

It was something, all right. It was something that my mother — raised in polite New Orleans society, schooled in the classics at LSU, and married to a man so gentle that the word "damn" never passed his lips in my presence, let alone hers — did not even know existed.

"Would you just look at that!" my mother said. And everyone did —everyone except me. I simply lowered my face into my hands as pandemonium took over. Pleased and surprised at the uproarious reaction — she was never opposed to laughter in the classroom, only anarchy — my mother continued to gesture toward the farthest corners of the room, unknowingly fulfilling the secret yearning of God knows how many longsuffering teachers and causing me to try to disappear beneath my desk, certain that our fragile alliance had been shattered to smithereens.

Somehow, it had not. I survived the mortification of the day (yes, to my shame, I was mortified more *by* my mother than *for* her, something I felt guilty about for years until I became a parent myself and learned that mortifying one's children is more than inevitable, it's practically one's duty), and I did not mention the incident to her that evening. I have never mentioned it to her, as a matter of fact, and when she reads of it (she checks this stuff out carefully for errors in grammar and syntax), somebody is going to have to explain it to her. It is not going to be me.

Well, where were we. Oh, yes, it was 1961, we were seniors in a tiny Arkansas high school, and we were about to wrestle with William Shakespeare. It was not our first encounter. We had tackled Julius Caesar two years earlier, and it had not been a pretty sight. The 11th grade had been given over to American literature, thus we had been given a year to rest up.

This year's assault was to be on *Macbeth*, and my mother created a small stir in class when she announced that we would give a readers' theater presentation of the play — no sets, costumes, or stage action, just the "actors" reading their roles from their desks. Shakespeare can seem dull and impenetrable just squatting there on the page, she said, but the words would come alive when spoken aloud, even without sets or props. An advantage

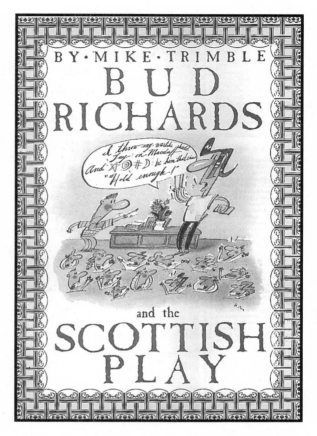

of the readers' theater format would be that we could pause anywhere we wished to discuss the action, examine the characters' motives, or look up "bodkin" in the dictionary.

We were skeptical but curious. Roles were assigned, and the reader-actors were advised to read ahead as much as possible to avoid complete bumfuzzlement upon encountering such words as "benison" or "thither." I was cast as Duncan. It was, it seems to me now, another of those silent compromises between my mother and me. It was an important role in the play, but not a dominant one; I would be killed early in the second act. Those of my classmates for whom being chosen for such a thing was anathema would not be able to say that I had got out of it by virtue of being the teacher's son; those for whom being chosen was a big deal wouldn't be able to say I got a fat part for the same reason.

The role of Macbeth went to Bud Richards.

Bud's real first name was Ralph, but everyone save a few teachers — my mother among them — called him Bud. My mother was no stuffed shirt in the classroom, but she believed in a certain amount of formality between teacher and student. She would no more call Harvey Hamilton "Goober" than she would allow him to call her "Frannie." (The only exception I can recall her making was for Jiggs Bono. I don't know what Jiggs' first name was, and maybe my mother didn't either. I wouldn't be surprised if Jiggs' parents didn't know what his first name was. He had been called Jiggs since the day he was born.)

Bud lived in West Bauxite, also known as Swamp Poodle, or sometimes just Poodle. Bauxite proper was a company town. All the houses, the general store, the picture show, the hospital — everything — was owned by Alcoa, which maintained the town in order to staff its bauxite mines and refining plants. I guess you could call it corporate communism. West Bauxite was, by comparison, a tiny spot of free enterprise on this socialistic landscape. People there owned their own houses, or rented from someone who did, and there were privately owned businesses: Putty Hendrix's grocery, Charlie's Cafe, Earl Lindsey's Esso station, and Elmer Sheaf's Thrifty Store. There was an informal subdivision within Swamp Poodle that we called Stuckeyville, because many members of that family had begun houses there, though none had ever finished one.

Some town people tended to look down their noses at Swamp Poodle, but I don't think any of us kids did. If anything, we probably considered it the best part of town, or at least the most interesting. You could win real money on the pinball machines down at Earl Lindsey's Esso, and it was said that a grown-up could even place a bet on a horse race there during the Oaklawn season. Charlie Gibbs cooked up fine cheeseburgers in his cafe, and he would let us young bloods hang around and curse, as long as there were no ladies present. We thought Swamp Poodle was a fine place, and Bud Richards was proud to live there.

It might not be accurate to say that Bud Richards was the most "popular" kid in school, because even back then and even in so small a place, the word "popular" toted a lot of phony baggage around with it — things like looks, social standing, the ability to throw or catch a football.

It is more accurate to say that Bud was probably the best-liked kid in school. Honest, open, and possessed of a perpetually sunny disposition, Bud was universally liked, even by those teachers who sometimes became frustrated with his casual outlook on life and secondary education.

This is not to say that Bud Richards was not intelligent; he was. But he channeled his intelligence into the pursuits he considered most important: fixing up old cars, making beautiful and substantial furniture in the school shop, and deciphering the dirty parts of "Be-Bop-a-Lula."

Bud was never a rebellious or impertinent student. He realized that his teachers had a job to do, and, being a naturally helpful kid, he was anxious to help them do it.

I remember one day in civics class, when Coach Bass was drilling us on one of those long lists of dull facts that everybody has to learn in civics but nobody remembers. Coach was going down the roll asking questions. "What is the compensation for work?" he would ask. (The correct answer was "wages.")

It was Bud's turn.

"Bud, what is the compensation for shelter?" Coach asked.

(The answer was "rent.")

Bud scrootched up his face. He wanted to help Coach by answering the question. He liked Coach Bass. Coach Bass liked Bud; Bud was a good halfback. Bud thought some more.

"You mean shelter like a tent, Coach?"

"No, Bud, like where you stay."

"You mean like where I live?"

"Right, Bud! Where you live! Now where do you live, Bud?"

"Swamp Poodle, Coach."

"Your house, Bud! Your house! What does your daddy give for that house y'all live in?"

That cleared it up. You could almost see the light bulb click on over Bud's head. He broke into a big grin, obviously pleased that he was going to be able to help Coach Bass do his job.

"Forty-five dollars a month, Coach!"

I DO NOT KEEP UP WITH the world of classical literature, but it is my dimly held impression that *Macbeth* has only lately been rehabilitated by scholars to its former status as one of Shakespeare's finest plays, maybe even the finest. For a while there, if memory serves, *Macbeth* was given the sort of second-string status that serious critics sometimes reserve for works of art so glorious that their appeal extends beyond the insular confines of academia and into the world at large. As I said, I am not sure about that, but I do know that there is a longstanding superstition in the theatrical world that the play is unlucky, and that many actors refuse to speak the play's name in a theater. They call it "the Scottish Play." I once asked an actor acquaintance of mine about the origins of the superstition, and he didn't know much more about it than I did. There were stories of actors dying violent, untimely deaths while involved in productions of *Macbeth*, he said, and he had also heard that in Shakespeare's time, many people thought that the verses uttered by Hecate and the three witches were authentic incantations, therefore tainting the whole play with evil.

One thing for sure, he said: the superstition was still alive, and a lot of people were dead serious about it.

"I was out of town doing a play," he recalled, "and we were sitting in the theater just talking when I happened to refer to *Macbeth*. The director jumped all over me. I thought she was joking at first, but she was serious. And this wasn't some far-out person; this was a woman whose work I really respect."

AND SO BUD RICHARDS was to be our Macbeth. The happiest, most contented, and most guileless of us all was to portray the tortured, ambitious nobleman in a play so shrouded in moody lore that those most closely associated with it dared not speak its name.

IT TOOK US ABOUT THREE days to complete our reading of *Macbeth*, what with all the pauses for recapitulating the action, interpreting obscure passages, and quelling the general hilarity when Lady Macbeth uttered the word "nipple." At first, Bud seemed to consider the whole thing a lark, and my mother had to reprimand him a couple of times for acting silly as he read his lines.

But it was not long before something about the play seemed to seep into Bud's consciousness, and all of us could tell that it began to matter to him. He had jokingly adlibbed a few lines early on, stringing hithers and thithers into amusing nonsense phrases only to be brought up short by my mother. Later on, he was to depart from the script again, but these were not the improvisations of a young man playing the fool; they were the missteps of an actor so deeply immersed in his role that he momentarily forgets what is real and what is theater.

After being exhorted by Lady Macbeth to screw his courage to the sticking place and do the murder that will make him king, Bud responded, "Good grief, woman!" The rest of us immediately looked toward my mother, waiting for her to pounce on Bud again, but she did nothing. I guess she was the only one — except for Bud — who realized what was going on, that "Good grief, woman!", while it might not be what Shakespeare wrote, was certainly what he had in mind.

Later on, when Banquo's ghost appeared to reproach Macbeth for his latest murderous episode, Bud rose unbidden from his desk, pointed a trembling finger at Banquo across the room, and shouted: "Oh, Lordy! You can't say I done it! Don't wave those gory locks at me!"

As *Macbeth* had come alive earlier for Bud Richards, it came alive at that moment for me. All the evil, all the false courage summoned to commit a cowardly deed in the name of ambition, all the guilt and fear coming home to roost, suddenly became clear to me, and compelling. And it wasn't Shakespeare's "gory locks" that did it; it was Bud Richards's "Oh Lordy!" I have since seen actors who got money for it do that scene as written; they did not move me half so much.

On the last day of our reading, Bud was subdued as we filed into the room at English period. He had obviously read ahead; he knew he was a goner. Malcolm and Donalbain had finally got their act together, and under the able generalship of Macduff, Macbeth's former buddy, were coming to claim their birthright. The witches had screwed up Macbeth with trick prophesies: the insurgents had carried bushes in front of them and Macduff's mama had given birth in the Hollywood Way. The jig was up, and Bud knew it. As Macduff, played by a skinny, timorous young man named Turkey Ridling, issued the final demand for surrender — "Yield thee, coward!" — Bud slowly rose from his seat, his book in one hand and his pencil in the other, gripped as though it were a sword. This time, he read his lines just as the man wrote them.

"I will not kiss the ground before young Malcolm's

feet," Bud roared.

"And to be baited with the rabble's curse.

"Though Birnam Wood be come to Dunsinane,

"And thou opposed, being of no woman born,

"Yet I will try the last. Before my body

"I throw my warlike shield: Lay on, Macduff,

"And damn'd be him that first cries 'Hold, enough!'"

The room was dead silent. Bud dropped his book on the floor and glared across the room at Turkey Ridling, who appeared terrified. Bud sneered, and his lips silently formed the words, "C'mon, sumbitch."

Turkey blanched and shook his head. You couldn't have got him out of that chair with a hand grenade.

I looked quickly toward my mother, to see if she had caught Bud's unauthorized profanity. She could not have missed it; she was looking right at him, but she said nothing.

So Macbeth was slain, the scene changed, and within a minute's time, the surviving players had figuratively exeunted to catch the coronation over at Scone. The Scottish Play was over.

AND THAT, I TOLD HER, was the time I had seen genius. Not "a" genius, unless you want to count Shakespeare himself, but the quality of genius. It was all over the place in that classroom for three days. First of all, there was the genius — quite possibly accidental — of some forgotten, faceless bureaucrat in the state Education Department who had seen fit to put *Macbeth* in the hands of teenage savages. While it is a play whose murky depths are still being explored by heavy hitters in English Departments everywhere, it is also a thumping good story, as replete with action, intrigue, and gore as any modern-day splatter flick. I can't imagine any red-blooded American youth not taking to *Macbeth* if he or she gives it half a chance. To while away the time until the magic takes hold, young scholars can keep their eyes open for the crude jokes about booze, urine, and impo-

tence, in the same way they look (or used to look) for bare-breasted natives in the National Geographic.

And what of Bud Richards's performance as Macbeth? Dare I say it was a work of genius? I will go this far: I will say that it was *touched* by genius; Bud's, Shakespeare's, Earl Lindsey's (Earl wrote poetry, did I tell you that?), somebody's. I was mesmerized by his reading: we all were, even my mother. Genius at work? Maybe not, but something, something good.

(Here's something else good to think about. Bud still lives in the Bauxite school district: he has a grandbaby now. One of these days — you can count on it — some beehived-hairdoed mama is going to raise unshirted hell at a school board meeting about teaching that filthy Shakespeare to her innocent young 'uns. Bud Richards is going to be there, and he's going to listen quietly for a while, and then he's going to stand up and say, "Wait a dadblamed minute lady..." Then he is going to tell them about *Macbeth*. It is a comforting scenario.)

Finally, I must make bold to put in a word for my mother, a teacher of English and literature. I would guess that most teachers, when adding up their accomplishments tend to remember best those students who went on to do great things. I do not know if Bud Richards has done great things, but I consider him a triumph of the art and science of teaching, and I hope my mother does, too. She lured Bud into the world of great literature, if only for three days, and gave him his creative head once he got there. Even more important, she somehow knew the role that he should play. When we looked at Bud, we saw a kid who put pinstripes and a flame job on his football helmet and did a startlingly accurate imitation of a chicken. My mother looked and saw the Thane of Cawdor.

"Like Michelangelo," my friend interrupted. "He looked into the stone and saw an angel."

Exactly, I said. Exactly.

—Arkansas Times, *September 1988*

Good Night, Mrs. Crawford, Wherever You Are

BY DON HARRELL

One small, dark corner in the oft-reexamined Maud Crawford story deserves illumination. Shortly after her highly publicized 1957 disappearance in Camden, her husband Clyde saw that he could no longer keep her car properly serviced, so he made an offer to my father, who bought it for me to take to college.

Dad was a friend of Maud's — they had clerked in a Camden law office at about the same time — and I think he took the car both to help Clyde and maybe to have something of Maud's as a token of their friendship. I was a sophomore at Hendrix and was excited about having my own car for runs to Johnny's restaurant and Palarm. My friends and I named it Maud.

It was a dark-blue, two-door Mercury, 1956 model, shaped like a smooth black-eyed pea with an uninterrupted arc extending from the top of the front windshield back to the tailpipe. Washed and shined, it looked like a Butch-waxed pompadour.

One night that spring — it was April 1957 — I was double-dating to the show, and when we parked across the street from the Conway Theater I pulled the front seat forward to let the other couple crawl out from the back. Just then my friend Nelson snapped up a small piece of paper that had been wedged under the front seat and had fallen free. It was a grocery store receipt with a cash-register printout of several items that totaled around twenty dollars. The stamped date was the same day Maud had disappeared — March 2, 1957 — and on the back was scrawled a Camden telephone number in pencil.

Like one of the Hardy boys, I sent it to Chief B.G. Cole in Camden with an explanation of how it had come to light. In a few days he wrote back that he appreciated my help and would file the receipt with other clues. He added that he would let me know more as things developed, and I began preparing my testimony for the grand jury.

Two years later I graduated from Hendrix without hearing anything more from Chief Cole or my clue. Maud was traded in on something more streamlined — a black '59 Chevy with fins — and I went about the business of living my life.

As years passed, people in Camden came to regard its most celebrated personage with curiosity and wonder. Everyone had memories of Maud, and whenever the subject of her disappearance came up we trotted them out for comparison. I had known Maud chiefly as a friend of my parents' and by reputation as a practicing lawyer. She stood apart in a town where most working women were either schoolteachers or nurses. That's changed now, but 30 years ago it was remarkable that Maud had made it in a man's world.

A couple of specific memories linger. She used to walk her fierce Dalmatian with the leash wrapped around her waist, so that he pulled her along the sidewalk in a slow glide. Once I saw her stopped in her car at the red light in front of Cleveland Avenue School, singing what sounded like a hymn and pulling pins from her hair. They were those big hairpins women wore in the 1940s. My mother used them when she wrapped her hair around what they called a rat. Maud didn't know I saw her because I was lying in the tall grass in front of Frances Benson's house, eating a Popsicle.

Dad always said that, being a brilliant lawyer and strategist, Maud could easily have planned her own disappearance and brought it off without a hitch. If she had wanted to, that is. He could lay out a plan to the last detail, from the way she might have pulled her money out of the bank over several years to the Greyhound bus that whisked her from Camden to some exotic spot in Alaska. A variation of the script put her in the South Seas.

Subscribers to this theory were given a jolt early in 1958 when the Associated Press wire ran a picture of a sixtyish woman sticking an envelope in an outdoor mailbox in Milwaukee. It looked for the world like Maud, and as I recall a Camden policeman flew up there to check her out. But it was only a loyal Braves fan making sure she ordered her tickets for the first day of the World Series. Other clues from around the country were equally unproductive.

Being from Camden has always meant holding to one version or another of Maud's disappearance. Everybody has one. I've always favored Dad's, and over the years it's the scheme I return to when others get shot down or seem stretched. I like it because there's no tawdry violence in it. There are no bitter feuds or unsolved questions about where a body is buried. It's simple and clean. It just has Maud flying off to Central America or Hong Kong, her feet up in a Pan Am jet, putting Camden behind her along with Clyde and all those documents she had to fiddle with down at the courthouse.

This wasn't Dad's only theory about what happened to Maud. It was one of them. Each person was allowed to hold several at the same time. In fact, that's one of the frustrations of being from Camden: we keep close track of all these plots, and still we've never found out for sure which one is right. If there's a single wish on the lips of a dying Camden native, it's that somebody will say for sure what happened to Maud — before the end comes.

I guess I want to know right along with everyone else. But at the same time something in me doesn't want to find out at all. This may be Camden heresy, but deep down I hope they never establish what happened to Maud. I'd just as soon they left her alone.

If you ask me, it's something like diving for the Titanic. I wish Dr. Ballard and his Woods Hole team only the best, and I'll continue to read every word about their search. It's a fascinating story. But when I think of it I don't really want to see that rusted chandelier, or the grand staircase, or those tragic little ratchets that held the lifeboats. I pray they'll never show us whatever it is they discover when they finally get down to steerage. As long as the facts are in question, it's better to make up your own version of what might have happened.

Same thing with Maud. For me, she entered long ago my own private mythology of Camden. It's a wide pantheon that includes gods and heroes, villains and creeps, and Maud enjoys a right high spot in that firmament. I want to keep her there, but how can I if they start digging around in all that tattered reality?

Which reminds me. Several years ago my wife and I took a trip to Mexico City to see the burial mounds and visit a cousin who was living there at the time. Late one afternoon we came out of some museum or other, our heads filled with native images and colors, and I looked up to see Maud's blue Mercury coming straight at me — or at least her identical twin. Anyone who's been to Mexico City knows the shock of seeing all those cars we drove in the 40s and 50s — Henry Js, Kaiser-Fraziers, Nash Rambler convertibles.

Well, here comes Maud, careening at 80 miles an hour down a boulevard, heading straight for the curb I'm about to step off of. Dents and bumps cover her body. The blue is sun-bleached to an almost-white, and a web of cracks covers the windshield so that I can't quite see the driver. It's a cruel and shabby reminder of my lost youth. And for a second, as it rounds the corner, I could swear I see Maud behind the wheel, her mouth fixed in a wide, singing O and hair pins flying in the hot wind.

By the time I race to the corner for a better look, the old thing has disappeared in a thick cloud of purple exhaust. My wife asks what on earth I'm doing, and I laugh and say it looked like somebody I used to know a long time ago. But I must be wrong. And anyway, it doesn't matter, since whoever it was has managed to get away.

Wherever you are, Maud, I hope they never find you.
— Arkansas Times, *October 1986.*

The Country Correspondent

BY DEE BROWN

One of the onerous jobs assigned to me [as a teenage printer at the Harrison Times in the mid-1920s] was setting the country correspondence into type, weekly letters that came in from the mountain communities of Boone and adjacent counties around Harrison. Most of the writers were women, and their letters chronicled the comings and goings of people in their neighborhoods — births, deaths, weddings, etc. These were printed in the big weekly edition of the Times, which went mostly to these rural communities.

It was slow work setting the country correspondence in type, because much of it was written in pencil on cheap gray tablet paper supplied by the Harrison Times. The first batch of these letters that I saw was brought to me by John [Newman, the paper's editor and co-owner], who explained how I was to handle them. First, I was to watch for any item that might be newsworthy enough to excerpt and use in the daily Times. If I saw anything interesting I was to call it to John's attention. Second, whenever the spelling or grammar was very bad, I was to correct it ...

My favorite correspondent was a Mrs. Livingston of the Compton community. She loved outrageous metaphors and similes. Instead of simply reporting that hog-killing time had brought fresh meat to the Thurman farm she would write: "The Thurmans have greasy chins this week." In reporting weddings, she would write a long paragraph describing the groom's appearance — his suit, shirt, necktie, socks, shoes and haircut, and then would add offhandedly that the bride wore the traditional white.

One week in Mrs. Livingston's letter I noticed a possible news item for the daily and showed it to John: "Mr. Cole, who is staying at our house, has discovered a cave near Compton. He says it is the largest cave in the Ozarks."

John was not impressed. "The Ozarks are full of caves," he said. "People are always discovering new caves. Set it without a head and we'll stick it in the daily news bits."

The next week Mrs. Livingston had another report on Mr. Cole and his cave. About halfway down the page, sandwiched between a wedding and a burned barn, was this: "Mr. Cole has been gone for three days. It is feared he may be lost in the cave he discovered."

John was busily setting slugs for a difficult full-page ad, and he was annoyed when I interrupted him. But his eyebrows and cigarette holder shot up when he read the two brief sentences. "That could be news," he said. Back in those days the story of Floyd Collins trapped in Sand Cave in Kentucky was still fresh in everybody's memory. John frowned a minute, and then said: "Call up Mrs. Livingston and see what's going on out there."

The Compton community had only two or three telephones, however, and Mrs. Livingston was not one of the subscribers, but eventually a neighbor summoned her to a phone. Mrs. Livingston said she did not know any more than what she had written in her weekly correspondence. Mr. Cole was still missing. She promised to call collect if anything new developed.

When I informed John that nothing was going on out at Compton, he was still struggling to finish the ad by press time. "I think we should notify the Associated Press anyway," he said. "How about you calling the AP? Their number is pasted on the phone. Just read off what Mrs. Livingston wrote and tell the man that's all we know."

I found it extremely exhilarating to be talking to a representative of the Associated Press, and next morning when the Arkansas Gazette ran a brief item on its front page about a man believed to be lost in a cave, I felt a sense of real power. I had helped make news that everybody in the state was reading. And I also noticed either the AP man or a copy editor at the Gazette had provided the mysterious Mr. Cole with initials. He had become

A.B. Cole. Somehow I felt that I had helped create him.

About midmorning a call came from the Gazette, wanting to know whether a search had begun yet for A.B. Cole. John insisted that I get on the phone. "It's your story," he said. "You handle it." All I could say was that we had no further information from Compton. The Gazette man was disappointed and refused to hang up until I promised to call him the minute we heard anything.

That afternoon one of the editors of a Memphis newspaper telephoned; he said they were running the brief item about A.B. Cole. And he asked: "Shall we send a reporter to cover the search?" He wouldn't believe me when I told him that as far as we knew no search had yet begun.

The next morning the Gazette carried a small follow-up item over its back pages, stating that nothing further had been learned of the whereabouts of A.B. Cole. That afternoon a St. Louis paper called and said they wanted a full account of the A.B. Cole story, with photographs. I replied that there was nothing new, but that we would keep them informed.

By this time I had become obsessed with A.B. Cole, and I knew I would have to go out to Compton and find out more about him and his cave. I talked with Bill Farley [another young printer] about it and he immediately became enthusiastic. Neither of us had a car, but Bill assured me that we could hitch-hike out there Sunday morning.

And so early Sunday morning we were standing at the road fork outside Harrison which led to Compton. After we'd waited an hour, I insisted that we start walking. "But it's twenty miles to Compton," Farley protested. "Up and down the mountains."

"We can walk there before sundown," I said. "If A.B. Cole is lost in that cave, the world ought to know about it."

Farley thought I was crazy, but he was game. We had walked about a hundred yards when a car pulled up beside us. The occupants were a man and wife whom Farley knew, and they were going out near Compton to tend their ginseng plants. Ginseng-growing on shady Ozark slopes was a fairly profitable undertaking then; the dried roots were collected in Harrison for shipment to China, where high prices were paid for them in the belief that gensing would restore virility and cure all ailments afflicting man.

The ginseng growers let us off in front of the Livingstons' white frame house, and we went up and knocked on the door. A rather pleasant-faced plumpish woman opened it. She was wearing what in that place and time would be described as a Sunday dress. I told her I was a reporter for the Harrison Times. She was impressed and immediately invited us in. "Are both you boys from the Times?" she asked. I told her we were.

"Are you the Newman boys?"

"No, ma'am," I said and introduced Farley, explaining that we worked for the Newmans. "I called you on the phone the other day," I said. "About Mr. Cole." I told her we had come out to Compton to find out more about Mr. Cole and his cave.

"Mercy," she said, "it's dreadful thinking of that poor man lost in that cave forever."

"Well, isn't anybody doing anything about it?" I asked.

She replied that since what had happened to poor Floyd Collins nobody around Compton wanted to set foot in a cave.

I asked: "Doesn't Mr. Cole have any friends or relatives here?"

She said no, that he was from somewhere way up in Missouri. He'd come to Compton to buy oak timber for a stave company and had been boarding with the Livingstons. After he'd found the cave, he'd been more interested in exploring it than in buying timber.

About this time Mrs. Livingston's husband came in, and they took us across a hallway to show us Mr. Cole's room. There wasn't much to see — a table top covered with crystal rocks, a couple of lanterns on the floor. A blue suit and some muddy work clothing hung in a closet.

When I asked Mr. Livingston whether he didn't think a search party should be looking for Mr. Cole, he replied that no one knew for sure he was in the cave. "Maybe he found another cave," he said, "and got lost in *it*. Lots of caves around in these hills." But he did agree to take Bill Farley and me to see the entrance to the cave. We carried along one of Mr. Cole's lanterns.

We had to walk for some distance across the hills, and along the way Mr. Livingston entertained us with horror tales about men lost in caves until their skeletons were found years afterward.

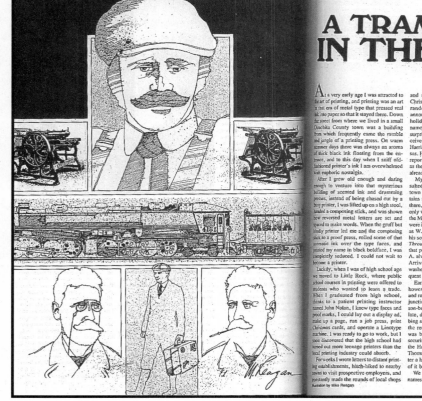

A TRAMP PRINTER IN THE OZARKS

By Dee Brown

At a very early age I was attracted to the art of printing, and printing was an art in that era of metal type that pressed real ink into paper so that it stayed there. Down the street from where we lived in a small Ouachita County town was a building from which frequently came the rumble and jangle of a printing press. On warm summer days there was always an aroma of thick black ink floating from the entrance, and to this day when I sniff old-fashioned printer's ink I am overwhelmed with euphoric nostalgia.

After I grew old enough and daring enough to venture into that mysterious building of scented ink and drumming presses, instead of being chased out by a busy printer, I was lifted up on a high stool, handed a composing stick, and was shown how reversed metal letters are set and spaced to make words. When the gruff but kindly printer led me and the composing stick to a proof press, rolled some of that aromatic ink over the type faces, and printed my name in black boldface, I was completely seduced. I could not wait to become a printer.

Luckily, when I was of high school age we moved to Little Rock, where public school courses in printing were offered to students who wanted to learn a trade. When I graduated from high school, thanks to a patient printing instructor named John Nolan, I knew type faces and proof marks, I could lay out a display ad, make up a page, run a job press, print Christmas cards, and operate a Linotype machine. I was ready to go to work, but I soon discovered that the high school had turned out more teenage printers than the local printing industry could absorb.

For weeks I wrote letters to distant printing establishments, hitch-hiked to nearby towns to visit prospective employers, and constantly made the rounds of local shops and newspapers. Several weeks before Christmas I sent out a batch of letters at random to towns around the state, announcing my availability during the pre-holiday season as an expert printer of names upon Christmas cards. To my great surprise, just before Thanksgiving I received a reply from the publisher of the Harrison *Times* in Boone County, Arkansas. He could use me for a month. I should report at the earliest possible date, he said, as the Christmas card printing season was already beginning.

My family was aghast when they consulted a map and found that Harrison was a town buried so deep in the Ozark Mountains that no one we knew had ever been there, or had ever heard of the place. The only way to get to Harrison was by way of the Missouri & North Arkansas, which we were informed was the railroad that Thomas W. Jackson had used as the model for his scurrilous joke book, *On a Slow Train Through Arkansaw*. A neighbor told us that people who lived along the M. & N. A. always referred to it as the May Never Arrive, and that it was notorious for washed-out bridges, loose rails, and frequent accidents. I was warned not to go.

Early one chilly November morning, however, I boarded the Missouri-Pacific and rode up to Kensett, where there was a junction with the M. & N. A. The Harrison-bound train finally arrived two hours late, drawn by a clanking, hissing, throbbing steam locomotive. I got aboard, and the realization suddenly struck me that I was bound into the unknown, my only security being a letter from the publisher of the Harrison *Times*, who signed himself Thomas Newman, Esq. I had read his letter a hundred times and knew every word of it by heart.

We were passing through towns whose names I had never heard before — Mount Pisgah, Letona, Pangburn, Snell, Higden, Edgemont — each being impressed upon my memory because I have forever been fascinated by place names. As we began to move up into the hill country, a train butch in a shiny blue-serge suit and hard-visored cap came through the car. I asked if he had any books, and he brought a basket of them for me to make a selection. I chose *Jesse James and the Great Train Robbery* and became so involved in it that I forgot we were traveling through the very country in which Jesse had operated in the flesh. I remember once or twice lifting my eyes to glance out the window. The train was climbing alongside a crooking stream which was alive with rapids and sparkling little waterfalls. Sometimes I could see the locomotive up ahead swinging in and out as it rounded curves, and sometimes the engine would be reflected in the creek below, creating an illusion of stream and train racing happily toward some pleasant destination.

When we reached Harrison, darkness had fallen. I felt lost and lonely there on the cinder platform in the chill November night, listening to the panting of the weary locomotive. All the other passengers who got off hurried away to familiar havens, but I had to search out a place to stay. I managed to find my way to the courthouse square, which the last time I saw it was almost exactly the same as it was in the late Nineteen Twenties. I found a hotel of sorts, above a drugstore, and the desk man eyed me suspiciously after I inscribed my name and Little Rock address. "Little Rock? What you doing so far from home, boy?"

"I'm here to work for the Harrison *Times*," I said.

"Oh? The Newman brothers."

"Mr. Tom Newman," I explained.

"Yeah. And John. Tom hires and John

FEBRUARY 1984 ARKANSAS TIMES 63

Illustration by Mike Reagan

At the edge of a clump of blackjack oaks and almost concealed by an overhang of brown sedge grass, he showed us a crevice about six feet long. It resembled a half-open mouth. We got down on our knees and peered into the blackness. There was just enough space for a man to crawl inside.

After several minutes of nervous joking, we lighted the lantern and took a look inside. The smooth walls were curved and wet. We could see a narrow ledge just below the entrance, and gathering our courage we crawled inside and dropped down on the ledge. That was as far as we went. We called out Mr. Cole's name as loudly as we could, and listened, but all we could hear were echoes. When we climbed back outside, Mr. Livingston did not appear to be surprised at our quick return. We went back to his house, had Sunday dinner with him and his wife and listened to some more of his cave horror stories until the ginseng growers came by and took us back to Harrison.

That night I wrote the story of Mr. Cole and his cave. I brooded over it, dragged in every lurid adjective I'd ever heard of, and borrowed from the horror tales Mr. Livingston had told us as well as what I could remember of the tales of Edgar Allan Poe. Next morning I was down at the Times office early so that I could use the typewriter. I typed up one piece for the St. Louis paper that had asked for a feature story, and a similar one for the Arkansas Gazette, and got them off in the mail by special delivery before starting to work at the Linotype.

For the first time since becoming a printer, I didn't enjoy setting type that day. It struck me as being a rather mundane occupation in comparison with the heavenly experience of putting words together *before* they were set into type. Also I was restless. I could hardly wait to see my creative journalism printed in the two newspapers that had been granted the privilege of receiving my compositions.

I fully expected Wednesday's edition of the Gazette to have my cave story headlined on the front page, but it wasn't there. Far over in the back of the paper was a one-paragraph item stating that A.B. Cole, the missing man of Compton, still had not been found. When the St. Louis paper arrived, I searched it carefully, but there was nothing, not even a line. I was crushed.

Next day the usual weekly Compton letter arrived from Mrs. Livingston. Evidently the visit Bill Farley and I had made to her house on Sunday was the event of the week. "Two young newspaper reporters from the Harrison Times ..." was her opening line. Farther down was another item dropped in as casually as a mention of the weather. I couldn't believe what I was reading. I looked around for John to tell him about it, but he had gone out somewhere. Not long afterward, he returned in company with a well-dressed stranger carrying a briefcase.

Waving his cigarette holder in my direction, John said to the stranger: "Here's your young correspondent." He then explained to me: "This is Mr. Williams from St. Louis. His paper sent him here to do a piece on that man in the cave. I told him you know more about it than anybody else."

The St. Louis reporter said: "Young man, that was quite a story you sent us. Not our style exactly, but it inspired my editor to send me down here to do some digging into the missing Mr. Cole."

I pushed my chair back from the Linotype and stood up to shake hands. My face was burning with embarrassment and I couldn't say a word.

"I've hired a car to drive out to Compton," the St. Louis reporter went on. "I wonder if you could give me the names of some people I might talk with out there."

"Well, sir," I stammered, "I don't think there's much use of your going out to Compton now."

"Why not?" he asked in a somewhat startled voice.

I reached down and picked Mrs. Livingston's letter off the top of my file of country correspondence and pointed to a paragraph far down on the page. The reporter put on his glasses and began reading. "Good God," he cried.

"Let me see it," John said, reaching for the sheet of paper. He read the paragraph aloud: "Mr. Cole who was feared lost in a cave has returned from Kansas City where he went for a visit."

The reporter from St. Louis was peering at me through his glasses. "Boy," he said, "you sure brought me on a wild goose chase." He started laughing and then John joined in, but at that time I couldn't see anything funny about any part of it. I was convinced that my brief career as a writer of words was ended forever, and that I was destined to spend the rest of my life setting other people's words into type.

—Arkansas Times, *February 1984*

A Thousand Ways To Die

BY MICHAEL HADDIGAN

VARNER — From a thousand ways to die, each condemned man finds his own.

Earl Van Denton was a nervous prisoner in his last days. Paul Ruiz was impassive, and Kirt Wainwright was jumpy, expressive and cheerful.

Denton refused to eat for three days before his execution, saying he wanted to fast. Ruiz refused some meals, but drank gallons of coffee, snacked on junk food and smoked cigarette after cigarette. Wainwright talked politics and football with his guards, paced his cell and listened to the radio. He ate every meal as if it were his last.

The three convicted murderers died by lethal injection on Jan. 8 at the Cummins Unit near Varner. Logs kept by Death Watch guards accounts of execution witnesses and interviews with prison officials offer an outline of their final days.

On Jan. 5, a cloudy Sunday morning, the three took their last breaths of Free World air as they traveled under heavy guard from Death Row at the Tucker maximum security unit to Cummins prison.

Tucker Max was something like home to Denton and Ruiz. The two, convicted and sentenced to death for the murders of two men, had been on Death Row a good portion of their adult lives. But after 18 years of court fights, stays and delays, the pair finally had an execution date that would stick.

Wainwright was a relative newcomer. He was convicted and sentenced to death in 1989 for the murder of a Prescott convenience store clerk.

After their arrival at Cummins on Sunday, the three were searched and placed in separate cells where guards would watch them every minute of their remaining days.

For men whose lives were slowly leaking away, they remained remarkably faithful to the habits of a lifetime. Ruiz carefully brushed and combed his hair several times

a day, and each man faithfully brushed his teeth and showered. The three watched daytime television talk shows, napped, read newspapers and generally turned in early at night.

For Denton, the wait seems to have been the hardest. A guard noted how Denton spent the better part of an hour his first day.

"11:02 a.m. — Inmate lying on bunk looking up at ceiling.

11:15 a.m. — Inmate lying on bunk looking at ceiling.

11:30 a.m. — Inmate lying on bunk looking at ceiling.

11:45 a.m. — Inmate lying on bunk looking at ceiling."

At noon Sunday, he asked guards to pass a small bag of coffee from his personal effects to Wainwright. Then he listened to his radio until the batteries went dead.

Wainwright ate a stout lunch of chicken and rice, egg salad, bread, cake and coffee. He paced quietly in his cell and later met for three hours in a conference room with relatives, spiritual adviser Linda Taylor and her daughter Tisha Edwards. He'd developed an affection for her over the course of her visits.

Late in the afternoon, Wainwright polished off a dinner of salmon, sweet potatoes, greens, green beans and two cups of tea,

Ruiz also met with his spiritual adviser that day.

That night Wainwright spoke with his father by phone for the last time. He talked with his mother in a separate 20-minute call before going to sleep at 9:30 p.m.

Denton watched television until 10:20 p.m., then went to sleep. Ruiz smoked, watched television and went to sleep 20 minutes later, snoozing so soundly that a guard noted his snoring at midnight.

On Monday, the prisoners were taken out of their cells for official photographs and to be weighed. Denton visited with his spiritual advisor during the day and listened to his radio for hours that night before falling asleep.

Denton was still not eating.

Ruiz refused regular prison meals, but ate chocolate and nachos during an afternoon visit with his spiritual adviser. Complaining of congestion, Ruiz was given cough medicine and a decongestant. He worked a crossword puzzle, watched "The Simpsons," read legal documents and snacked on cinnamon rolls.

After visiting again with Taylor and Edwards, Wainwright was given a tranquilizer and muscle relaxant, Valium. Again, he ate a full meal.

Prison officials visited the inmates to outline the execution procedures. The reactions of Denton and Ruiz went unnoted. But a guard wrote, "Inmate Wainwright [responded] with a little laugh ... attitude appears upbeat."

But soon the strain on all three began to show.

Tuesday night, Denton began vomiting.

He told a guard that taking over-the-counter pain medication on an empty stomach had made him sick. The guard asked if he needed medical help.

"No," Denton said. "I'll be okay."

Ruiz, after a day of visiting and gulping down coffee, nachos and snack cakes, had stomach problems of his own. A nurse gave him a muscle relaxant, some Pepto-Bismol, Tylenol and a decongestant.

At 3:53 a.m., Wednesday, the day of his execution, Ruiz awoke.

"What time is it?" he asked the guard.

Around the same time, Denton woke up vomiting. A prison nurse examined him and found his life was in no danger. The inmate slept fitfully until almost 10 a.m. but the vomiting continued. An injection meant to stop the vomiting offered some relief.

Wainwright started off his last day with a big breakfast of apple juice, eggs, chicken sausage, oats, biscuits and gravy, jelly and butter. He ate it all.

Wainwright watched television, read the paper and looked over some letters. About noon, he asked a guard to pass some cakes from his personal property to Ruiz and Denton. From Denton, he received some coffee in return.

Ruiz spent much of the morning talking quietly with his spiritual adviser, holding her hand through the cell's

mail slot as they spoke. Ruiz refused lunch, watched the Maury Povich talk show and worked a crossword puzzle.

By early afternoon, Denton was felling better. He napped, met with his attorney and his spiritual adviser. He drank a little Seven-Up to settle his stomach.

At 3:05 p.m., Ruiz began his last meal of seedless grapes, salad, breadsticks, crackers and three cups of coffee. He saved some leftover grapes. After his last shower, Ruiz had a smoke, combed his hair and slapped on some after-shave lotion.

"Damn these grapes are good," he said as he finished them off.

At 6:51 p.m., the "tie-down team" stood outside Denton's cell. With the arrival of the seven guards who would take him to the Death House and secure him to the gurney, the guards' log on Denton closed.

From then on, his execution went by the book.

Inside the chamber, the guards secured Denton to the gurney with straps across his chest and arms. A strap and a plastic band held his head in place. Catheters that would carry the lethal chemicals into Denton's body were inserted into his arms. A white sheet covered Denton up to his chin.

At 7:05 p.m., officials opened a curtain, allowing 11 citizen witnesses to see into the chamber through a one-way mirror. Two reporters, from the Associated Press and the Southwest Times Record of Fort Smith, were with the witnesses.

Asked if he had any last words, Denton simply said, "No."

Volunteer executioners, blocked from the witnesses' view by a barrier, then began the flow of three lethal chemicals — Pavulon to paralyze Denton's muscles, sodium pentothal to stop his breathing and potassium chloride to stop his heart.

The witnesses watched in dead silence. Denton's hands moved slightly. He closed his eyes, licked his lips, winced, coughed. And it was over.

At 7:09 p.m., Jefferson County coroner Havis Hester declared Denton dead.

Ruiz was having his last smoke about the time Denton died. An official came to tell him it was time. The tie-down team arrived at 7:42 p.m., and they began the long walk to the execution chamber a minute later. Guards placed the inmate on the gurney, put the straps in place and opened the curtains.

At the last, Ruiz had nothing to say.

At 7:56 p.m., the same witnesses watched as the lethal drugs snaked down the plastic tube into the inmate's arm. He coughed three times and tried to move his arm. Seconds later, Ruiz blinked, twitched and was gone.

Hester pronounced him dead at 8 p.m.

Wainwright was next.

Despite the big appetite he displayed earlier, Wain-wright refused his last meal. He visited with Taylor and attorney Craig Lambert, made his last phone call to Tisha Edwards and watched some television.

He paced the cell snapping his fingers and singing until 8:26 p.m., when officials came to get him.

"Let's do it," Wainwright said.

The tie-down team took him to the Death Chamber. The catheters went in at 8:31 p.m. A different set of witnesses entered the viewing room.

And the book went out the window.

A last-minute appeal to the U.S. Supreme Court put Wainwright's execution on hold, and the witnesses were escorted out of the room to await the final decision.

According to a prison log and Correction Department spokesman Dina Tyler, Wainwright lay on the gurney with the catheter inserted — on the frontier of death — for about an hour before word of the high court's denial came through.

The witnesses, including another Associated Press reporter and a representative of Prescott's weekly news-paper, returned.

At 9:36 p.m. Wainwright spoke his last words, recit-ing a poem titled, "The Embrace," that he'd written at Tucker Max.

"Now send me to my god," Wainwright said at the end of the poem.

The chemicals began to flow.

Wainwright appeared to laugh and tried to speak.

"Before he could finish that sentence, his eyes closed, his right hand relaxed," said the AP's Edith Paal. "And that was the last sign of any life from him."

—Arkansas Times, *Jan. 17, 1997*

On The Need For A State Dog

The state legislature has named the fiddle as the official state musical instrument. We have nothing against the fiddle — indeed the instrument is inexorably intertwined with the state's history and image — but we wonder if this business of naming official state things hasn't about exhausted itself. We started wondering this a few years ago when the Pennsylvania legislature solemnly debated a proposal to name the ball-bearing official commonwealth mechanical part. Alas, nobody spoke up for the mountain dulcimer as a possible competitor against the fiddle. Or — in honor of Scott Joplin of Texarkana — the pianoforte. Or the guitar, in honor of B.B. King's Lucille, or the one Jimmy Driftwood made out of a fencepost. Or the trombone.

By coincidence, our friend Seth Thompson of Waldron has notified us that he thinks Arkansas should have an official state dog. He's not particular about which breed it should be; he just thinks we should have one. Our opinion is that it shouldn't be Lassie, or a dachshund, or a Mexican hairless, and that it shouldn't be rabid or hit by a car and swole up by the side of the road. A bulldog, after the one the town of Hector was named for, would do. Or a blue-tick hound.

—Editorial, Arkansas Times, *1985*

"As God Is My Witness, You'uns..."

BY MILLER WILLIAMS

... I ought to mention here, while we're dealing with language, that in that endless search for a new plural "you" in English — something unfortunately lost to us in the Middle Ages — the flatland solution to the problem is only one of many solutions found in various regions of the country. In the metropolitan Northeast we find "youse." Throughout most of the Midwest we hear "you guys" applied to both sexes. In the mountains of the South we still hear, as I grew up hearing, "you'uns," or even "you'unses."

It is particularly notable here that of these four ways of re-inventing a plural you, only "you all" has gained currency in its region among the middle and upper middle classes and even in the very highest economic and socio-political circles. Scarlett O'Hara can say "you all" with perfect decorum; it is extremely difficult to imagine her saying "you'uns."

— Arkansas Times, *August 1985*

A Rumination On Gov. TR

BY O. F. BARTLETT

If Tommy Robinson is elected governor, I believe he will:

1. Not allow UFOs to land at the Capitol to abduct citizens or legislators.

2. Make women who chatter or speak out of turn wear signs around their necks saying: MAGPIE.

3. Harness magnetism as a cheap source of energy for high-speed flying trains to link all the state's major arts, crafts, commerce, and science centers.

4. Change the name of the Arkansas Razorbacks to the Melody Boys.

5. Ban proctoscopic examinations.

6. Jail all crooks/lawyers, slap them around, and pop them with wet towels.

7. Assess big fines for "low riders."

8. Refuse to permit "student leaders" at Arkansas Tech to take over Russellville and chant anti-government slogans.

9. Cut way down on whale obituaries, Nelson Mandela updates, and lesbian news on public radio.

10. Arm all seventh-grade and older males, teach them handgun safety and marksmanship, and create an award for the best shooter to be called the Golden Badge of Moguso.

11. Name "Shortenin' Bread" the new state song.

12. Stop skipping, hopping, jumping and other immature behavior at bank board of directors' meetings.

13. Enforce a strict two-minute time limit on nuts who call radio talk shows.

14. Oppose a Gay Truckers Bill of Rights amendment to the state Constitution.

15. Open free Houses of Fondue at border cities to welcome tourists.

16. Eradicate the serving of exotic cheeses at official Governor's Mansion functions.

17. Speed cafeteria lines by wiring old ladies with electric-shock devices.

18. Put Lake pipes or glass-pack exhausts on all executive branch staff cars.

19. Lure the world's fastest clarinet player to the state with a promise of lifetime free tickets to Travelers' games.

20. Assemble a choir of 1,000 trombones to play "Ruffles and Flourishes" at his inauguration (but no saxophones).

And those are the things I believe Governor Tommy will do.

—Arkansas Times, *1990*

Herein Hangs A Tale

A Brief History Of The Hangman's Noose In Arkansas

The bill in the current legislature to permit public hangings in Arkansas, House Bill 1307 by Rep. Tymothe Wooldridge of Paragould, revives a debate that started in the General Assembly more than a century ago.

It was the 1887 state legislature that passed Act 24 of that year, limiting attendance at Arkansas executions to just a few people. Before that law went into effect, all executions in the state — the legal ones, anyhow — were public hangings. More than that, they were one of the main public entertainments of that frontier era.

Most Arkansas counties had several of them a year, and they inevitably drew bigger and more enthusiastic crowds than political rallies and brush-arbor revivals, their principal competition.

Perhaps the most lurid of the hangings (but certainly not the only ones) were those occurring at Fort Smith, at the famous Western District federal-court gibbet where as many as 12 men could be hanged at once, though the record for a single execution there was six.

Those six-at-once were the first of 79 men hanged by federal Judge Isaac Parker, the "Hanging Judge," over a 20-year span, and the crowd that showed up to "bon voyage" them was not atypical of an Arkansas hanging crowd: it numbered more than 5,000 people.

That particular hanging was in 1875, and historian Glenn Shirley gives a sense of the festive air of such occasions with his description of another public hanging at that same site two years earlier:

"... *Two thousand sweating sight-seers packed the jail yard inside the grim stone walls of abandoned Fort Smith. Outside, the walls of the fort were lined with hacks, spring wagons, and saddle horses. Many had come on foot. Others had traveled hundreds of miles and had been in town as much as two days, camping on the ground and sleeping at the foot of the scaffold the night before to have ringside places. The whole population, it seemed, along the Arkansas River on the Arkansas border — all colors and sexes, from babes in arms to the halt and graybeard — had turned out to watch, with eager, morbid curiosity, the spectacle of the first human being to die on the newly erected gallows.*"

For some years, the enormous publicity generated by such scenes was considered positive and beneficial because it was thought to work against Arkansas's post-Civil War reputation as a place of murder and wanton violence. It showed that justice was being served here, that law and order finally were being affirmed.

But by the 1880s a reaction had set in and had become, in fact, the prevailing sentiment: that is, that such bloodthirsty spectacles actually contributed to the state's reputation as an uncivilized place where watching people die was a popular pastime.

This latter view led to the passage of Act 24 of 1887, and it's interesting that the rationale of those who voted for that law 108 years ago was precisely the opposite of that of Rep. Wooldridge and those who would bring back public hangings today.

Rep. Wooldridge argues that public executions would be a "great" deterrent to murder; the lawmakers of 1887, who were all too familiar with public executions, thought otherwise.

A newspaper account survives of the 1887 state Senate's debate on the bill that became Act 24, and one after another the senators told of people they knew who had been inspired by having witnessed public executions to commit violent acts — even capital offenses — themselves.

One of them, a Sen. Theo F. Potts, said a hanging he attended triggered a chain of violence that resulted in three other deaths — of one woman and two children — before sundown of the day on which the hanging occurred.

Another senator told of a group of young men among his constituents who saw a murderer hanged and came to admire and romanticize him because he had gone bravely to his death. Would they go so far as to emulate the deeds of the man that got him condemned, the senator wondered. He feared that they very well might.

A senator from Lonoke was a former sheriff, and in that former role had hanged men on two different occasions. The second man he'd hanged had served as hangman of the first, and the sheriff-legislator was convinced that the first hanging had left that second man deranged, to the point that he'd been driven to murder.

Several other senators concurred with the judgment of one of them "that public hangings have not had a moral effect upon the people" and in fact had had the opposite effect.

"Sen. McConnell ... attended the hanging of the train robbers at Clarksville," the newspaper account said. "He saw a woman stand [for hours] in the hot sun with her baby in her arms, and after the men were executed, she found her neglected child had died from the effects of the heat."

Other senators thought the spectacle attending public executions had become an offense against good taste, if nothing else. A Sen. Pettigrew told of a crowd in his bailiwick so disappointed by a last-minute stay of execution that it almost got up a mob to lynch the prisoner.

There were legislators who didn't share these sentiments, but in the end the proposal to restrict public access to executions passed both houses of the General Assembly by large margins. No more than 25 people could

attend a hanging thereafter, including the defendant's lawyer and his minister.

This law was amended in 1901 to allow public executions in certain cases of rape, but it's unclear whether any such execution ever took place. The law was changed again in 1911 to make electrocution the official method of execution, replacing hanging. Electricity was much in vogue then — as a novelty and as a "scientific" substitute for old-fashioned neck-stretching. It was actually represented as a much more humane way of putting people to death.

Even so, the legislature was still of a mind that more harm than good would come of allowing people to see wrongdoers in their final agony. The assembly that year restricted even more the number of spectators who could be present at an execution. Only the convict's lawyer and minister, the prison superintendent or his representative, and the prison surgeon could watch, the legislators decreed, "and a number of respectable citizens numbering not less than six nor more than twelve."

Those limitations are still in effect.

The 1911 lawmakers were so uneasy about the consequences of witnessing executions that they also wrote this provision into the statute: "No newspaper or person shall print or publish the details of the execution of criminals under this Act. Only the fact that the criminal was executed shall be printed or published."

Though it has been routinely ignored since the 1940s, this provision also is still a part of the law. A proposal to repeal it is on the legislative agenda this year.

— Arkansas Times, *Jan. 27, 1995.*

Mansion Spending: From A Dog House To Panty Hose

BY LESLIE NEWELL PEACOCK

Here is a sampling of the Huckabees' spending from the Governor's Mansion Account from August 1996 through May of 1997, taken from records kept by administrator Kamala Williams.

The expenses, though small individually, are important. The state Constitution prohibits expense reimbursements to the governor except for those related to official duties and then only for documented expenses. Previously, the Huckabee administration had said it had no underlying documents for expenses reimbursed to the Huckabees from the Mansion account, which is supposed to be used for operation and maintenance of the Mansion, including official entertaining. But Williams actually made records of the expenditures — information she says should still be on the hard drive of the Mansion computer.

Included are amounts the first family spent on meals outside the home, an expenditure that clearly seems outside the bounds of the Mansion appropriation, and a sample of other purchases that appear to be entirely personal for which the Huckabees, nonetheless, were reimbursed from the Mansion account.

As Huckabee office memos noted, Mansion spending is unaudited and, by statute, requires none of the documentation that must be submitted on reimbursements the governor is also allowed to file for official expenses in his office budget.

MEALS OUT

August 1996: Arthur's Cafe, $20; Denny's, $5; Pizza Hut, $5; Tia's, $20; Tia's, $20; Daytimer, $82.85; Casa Manana, $60; El Chico, $10; Taco Bell, $2.97; Breadbasket, $48.93; Casa Manana, $70.87; Grady's, $35.70. **Total: $381.32.**

October 1996: Red Lobster, $20; 4 pizzas, $38.58; Big Mamou, $36.45; Bowen's Restaurant, $40.05. To-tal: **$134.95.**

September 1996: Arby's, $13.71; Emerald Coast, $17.63; Tia's $25.43; Papa John's Pizza, $75.24 and $5.27; Chiquitos, $8.50; 10 pizzas, $87.55. **Total: $305.43.**

November 1996: El Porton, $53.19 and $8 tip; Kirby's, $88.50; Sonic, $3; Juanita's, $48.33; Way Out Willie's, $42.81; Big Mamou, $80.41. **Total: $324.02.**

December 1996: El Porton, $35.32; Steak and Ale, $154.12; Taco Bell, $8.56. **Total: $198.**

February 1997: Big Mamou, $70.74 and $12 tip; Tia's, $33.68 and $3.32 tip; Way Out Willie's, $19.01

98

and $4 tip; Kirby's, $36.21 and $7 tip. **Total: $185.96.**

March 1997: Cracker Barrel, $9, $2.78, $42.80; Chi's, $19.66 and $5 tip; El Porton, $40.50 and $6.50 tip. **Total: $120.46.**

April 1997: El Chico, $39.33 and $7 tip. **Total: $46.33.**

May 1997: Mexico Chiquito, $34.17 and $8 tip. **Total: $42.17.**

Total spending on meals out: $1,738.64.

PERSONAL ITEMS

George's Men's Shop, alterations, $450. (July 1996)

Hogman's Hogpen, 3 Razorback shirts, $56.95 each. (September 1996)

Kaufman Lumber, dog house, $45.99; dog house door, $13.99 (November 1996)

Linens 'n Things, shower radio, $9.99. (November 1996)

Tandy Leather, saddle tan, $8.98; satin sheen, $5.98. (November 96)

Parkview High School Drama Department, 10 tickets, $100. (No date)

Lakewood Gallery, framing of caricature of governor, $71.77; photo with Mrs. Bob Dole, $27; a newspaper article, $110.80; watercolor, $22.40; watercolors, $75.73; delegate pin, $52.76. (November 1996)

Time Magazine, one-year subscription, $29.97. (December 1996)

J.C. Penney, 9 pairs of panty hose, $2.99 each. (January 1997)

Bass Anglers membership, $20. (March 1997)

Chainwheel bike shop, ladies' shorts, $52.50; 3 helmet mirrors, $33.75. (March 97)

FLORAL GIFTS

Floral Express, candy gift with balloons for Sarah Huckabee, $25. (July 1996)

Garden of Eden, dozen roses to Brenda Turner, $65. (March 1997)

Garden of Eden, fresh arrangement for Vickie Boozman, $35. (April 1997)

Garden of Eden, sympathy arrangement to Mrs. Clare Bell, $100. (April 1997)

Garden of Eden, dozen roses to Diane Bray, $65. (May 1997)

Garden of Eden, sympathy arrangement to Will Clarkston, $100. (June 1997)

FAMILY GROCERIES

The mansion account also included itemized grocery receipts for which the Huckabees asked for reimbursement. Listed here are what the Huckabees' spent at the grocery store in a sample month, January 1997.

The itemized account shows that these are not bulk food expenditures, as would be expected for the mansion's official food needs. Included with the receipt figures are a few of the items purchased that suggest the expenditures are personal, rather than official. All purchases appear to be from Harvest Foods.

• $31.84 (Mountain Dew, pot roast, mushrooms); $98.33 (crackers, ribs, 1 pound carrots, Kraft marshmallows, cool whip); $40.34 (hot dogs, Tostitos chips); $108.84 (3 yogurts, 3 pints strawberries, 3 apples, head of lettuce); $32.23 (pasta and loaf of Italian bread); $73.88 (Pringles chips, Lifesavers, Velveeta loaf, 1 bunch grapes); $7.46 (cheese); $48.45 (Spanish rice); $41.86 (bacon, 2 heads of lettuce, steak). Total: $483.23.

—Arkansas Times, *Oct. 23, 1998.*

How Clinton Won In '96

A tiny worm of doubt wriggled across the scene one day last week, eight days be fore the election.

Several of those tracking polls, which for nearly a month had shown President Clinton with a steady lead of 15 points or more, now hinted of a turn in Bob Dole's direction.

Nothing drastic. The President's lead was still one of those double-digit rascals that politicians dream about — about 12 points — but the move in Dole's favor was inexplicable. Was it the beginning of a trend? Was it the fabled "late movement" in the polls that keeps underdogs hopeful? Would it close the gap down into the range of the genuinely suspenseful by election eve, as usually happens?

Republicans crossed their fingers.

SOMETHING SIMILAR HAD happened about a month earlier. For no discernible reason, support for Dole surged a little at the same time support for the president sagged, and for the first time in the 100-day history of these intensive surveys, the president had only a single-digit lead — 48 points to 39 in two of the national polls. Because his advantage had been so big and so consistent, now he suddenly looked vulnerable. On both sides, partisan eyebrows raised; foreheads knitted; lips pursed.

A wire-service reporter described the Dole campaign as "greatly energized" by this unexpected showing, and a campaign spokesman said the Republican nominee had moved "within striking distance ... for the first time." Pat Robertson, who had earlier called for divine intervention ("a miracle from Almighty God") to save the moribund Dole candidacy, crowed on his Christian News Network that "the momentum is now all in Dole's favor."

False alarms.

Each time the upshot was this: after a day or two, nobody knew why, the support lines on the tracking graphs moved back whence they had come. After the momentary bump and the hopeful buzz, the president resumed his daunting lead. Low to mid 50s to Dole's mid to high 30s. And each time, because time and options were running out, it actually became more daunting than ever.

SUCH VAGARIES AND fluctuations in the polls were hard to interpret because, for all the millions of dollars that the Democratic and Republican presidential campaigns were spending, neither was making any dramatic gestures, disclosures, claims, charges, or initiatives: neither was doing much of *anything* to make the numbers dance, or not much of anything *noticeable* — the Clinton campaign because it didn't have to; the Dole campaign because it didn't know how.

Dole certainly tried to seize those rare opportunities — with every poll bump, he declared a fresh start, a new beginning, a change in direction, a new line of attack. The Dole campaign "has become famous for its multiple starts," the New York Times reported on Oct. 6, enumerating five of them to that point (and there would be at least two more). But despite all those launchings and relaunchings, the paper reported, "the president's lead in most polls has been unchallenged for at least six months." Despite all those launchings, or *because* of them.

The state Republican Party chairman in Ohio — the one state that the presidency hasn't been won without in the 20th century — said despondently on Oct. 22 that there hadn't been a scintilla of change in the polling picture there in 75 days. That same day, a New York Times/CBS Poll measured the results of the latest of those "multiple starts" — what the Times called Dole's "sustained two-week assault on President Clinton's ethics." That particular " new line of attack" had backfired, the poll showed — to the point that for the first time ever voters now considered Clinton to be more ethical and more trustworthy than Dole.

The next day, a Los Angeles Times Poll showed Clinton with a commanding 20-point lead in California,

whereupon Dole committed to spending several days in a row campaigning there. The result: zippo. California pollster Melvin Field summarized a week later: "Clinton is now headed for as big a win as Reagan had in '84, as Nixon had in '72, and Johnson had in '64."

Every move Dole made seemed to be one behind the right one. He took a moment from proclaiming himself the most optimistic man in America to sigh: "Maybe there is no interest in politics. Maybe nobody cares."

THE 1996 PRESIDENTIAL race was a waiting game, to a great extent. The Clinton camp was poised to respond to any bold stroke the Dole apparatus might make, but the Dole effort couldn't (or didn't) sustain an initiative long enough or intensely enough for the counter-campaign to kick in. It lurched one way and then the other. Even at the end, Dole's 96-hour marathon vote-quest had the look of trying to make up for not knowing how to campaign simply by doing more of it than anybody else.

Because of this harum-scarum nature of it, the '96 campaign was one in which the style became the substance, or as close to substance as there would be, and it

was as if the two principal candidates had got their styles reversed somewhere along the way. This gave the latter-stage politicking a curious sense of bassackwardness. The president, an able barnstormer, opted for a low-key, understated campaign that almost ignored the Republican challenge—a rope-a-dope strategy, it came to be called; and ironically Dole, possibly the worst platform speaker since Herbert Hoover, gave old-fashioned podium-pounding oratory a go, with a heavy regimen of whistlestop and stump speeches attacking the president's record and character — a style at which he proved to be smashingly ineffective. Columnist Tony Snow, a Dole sympathizer, said Dole making a speech looked and sounded like a disgruntled postal worker.

This made for some surrealist campaign scenes: as when, the day after he got that poll-gap down to single digits last week, Dole turned up in California for one of those diffident, scattershot speeches, with three recognizable characters on the stage with him — the asylum escapee U.S. Rep. Bob Dornan, the confused oldtimer Admiral James Stockdale, and the actress Bo Derek, rather drastically depreciated from her days as a 10. It was a lineup that characterized or personified the Dole campaign better than any other gathering of the season.

These dignitaries commiserated with each other, and with several other washed-up and washed-out old entertainers and pols, over the persistent foolishness and intransigence of American voters in not having already enlisted as Dole supporters. The tone of the gathering could have been described as, "What's *wrong* with you people?" That could almost have been the theme of the Dole campaign in the three climactic weeks before the election, as the candidate himself became increasingly querulous about the voters shunning him, the press favoring his opponent, and his opponent refusing to respond to his taunts and gibes. "Where is the outrage?" he would shout, and then he'd shout it a second time and a third time, and there was no answer. And it wasn't clear who he was demanding an answer from. David Letterman said Dole's campaign slogan might be, "Hey America! Bite me!"

THE PRESIDENT'S campaign this year could hardly have been more different from the 1992 campaign. James Carville and the Arkansas War Room were gone, and with them the provincial piquancy of the campaign, the flying-by-the-seat-of-its-pants quality, the notion of it being the political equivalent of the Clampett family tootling along in their open ancient pickup piled high with all their belongings, furniture, critters, and kin.

The techniques were still out of the Carville book — the rapid-response mentality, the incredibly sophisticated spotting of the campaign advertising — but this was a different operation: faceless, rich, smooth-running, operating out of Washington, D.C., managed by taciturn people like Harold M. Ickes, the sphinx-like deputy White House chief of staff. Even with the president, Little Rock had resumed its status as a kind of frontier outpost in a state electorally inconsequential.

The Arkansas Travelers were back again but they seemed a superfluity this time, or an anachronism, because people across the country knew now who Bill Clinton was, and knew a good deal about what he wanted them to know about him — that is, his presidential record — and didn't need a swarm of Arkies gadding about telling them what a swell president their former governor would make.

The '96 Clinton campaign was a carefully understated beast, almost exquisitely so, its intention not to cultivate new support but to hold on to what the president had already gathered and nurtured over the preceding two years by way of his political positioning on hundreds of issues. His task four years earlier had been to make himself known; now it was simply to reinforce the generally favorable impression of his first-term job performance. To keep his support, much of which was "soft," from eroding. To shore up his reputation wherever, whenever, and however the ubiquitous polls indicated that it needed it.

Dole inadvertently and catastrophically gave him his campaign theme when, at the Republican convention in early August, he imagined that bridge to a past that never was. Clinton, at the Democratic convention soon after, built his own bridge going the other way, into the 21st century, and it turned out to be a devastating metaphor — really the only image he would need to secure his re-election.

He never quite believed it, though, couldn't bring himself to trust what those polls had been telling him since the spring, until a point in the second debate with Dole on Oct. 16 at San Diego, when the suspicion stole over him that Dole just didn't have what he knew it would take to beat him. He realized he no longer had to answer anything Dole said; he didn't even have to try. He had rehearsed that line, Clinton had, about how ad hominem attacks on him didn't educate a child, didn't feed a hungry face, didn't give hope to someone in despair, but now he'd be able to say it without it coming across as an evasion, and without feeling inside his own self that it was an evasion. It was the one soliloquy in the debate and in the campaign that impressed the president's admirers and made those who think he's a phony want to gag. You could probably have taken a true measure of the final vote then and there.

Thereafter, the president campaigned with new confidence, and with a freedom that let him range into offbeat campaign territory. An example of his creative venturing out was his pausing during a handshaking binge in Louisiana for that serious impromptu tete-a-tete about partial-birth abortion with the emotional young woman who disagreed with his opinion on that matter. It was a riveting scene, and provided a better look at his political talent than all the debates he'd ever been in and all the flatbed speeches he'd ever made.

His solid standing in the polls in many of the key electoral states freed him in the last weeks of the campaign from the traditional obligation to scurry from strategically important state to strategically important state, rationing campaign appearances according to the relative amount of electoral-vote reward he could expect from them. Unthreatened in California and the industrial midwest, he could, instead, move about the country bearding Dole in the deepest, darkest Republican dens — Texas, Florida, Arizona, along the Redneck Riviera — and doing whatever other geographical mischief caught his fancy. Rarely can you use scheduling to show wit, but the president did it in late October, as he dawdled in New Orleans and stomped like Davy Crockett through Texas. One of his schedulers called it "poetry" that the '96 campaign could conclude (New Hampshire back to Little Rock) as the '92 campaign had commenced (Little Rock on to New Hampshire), completing a kind of definitive presidential-campaign circle.

—Arkansas Times, *Nov. 8, 1996*

A Taste Of Silver-Tongued Oratory

BY GEORGE SEXTON PEASE

A paragraph in the special section of the Arkansas Gazette celebrating Arkansas's 150th birthday noted the 1924 visit to Little Rock of William Jennings Bryan, the "silver-tongued orator from the Platte," and the Democratic Party's seemingly perpetual and consistently unsuccessful candidate for president.

I was a Gazette reporter in those days. J.N. Heiskell, the distinguished editor of the paper and the co-owner along with his brother Fred, the managing editor, assigned me to spend the day with the famous visitor. I was not only to report on all his activities, but also was to secure an interview for a human-interest feature for Sunday's paper.

The assignment resulted in a grueling day's work. A Democratic Party breakfast and speech at 8 a.m. Public luncheon and a second speech at noon. Private dinner for party bigwigs and another speech at 6:30 p.m. Public appearance and a fourth speech in the old revival tabernacle on south Main Street.

Bryan agreed to the interview.

"I always nap after lunch," he told me. "I'll leave my door unlocked. Come in at 2:30. I'm a very heavy sleeper, so squeeze my shoulder and speak loudly until I wake up. We can visit while I dress."

I followed orders. Indeed, Bryan was hard to rouse, but once awake was quite alert. A consummate actor, he dressed to fit his chosen role as protector of the common man: long johns; black socks held up with garters; congress gaiters (ankle-high, black shoes with elastic sides); white shirt with iron-hard bosom, to be pulled on over the head; low, detachable stiff collar; black string tie; baggy black pants, low-cut black vest, black frock coat.

His old-fashioned apparel, his strange addiction to radishes, and his gargantuan appetite (pancakes, steak, hash browns, and radishes for breakfast; an elaborate meal and radishes for lunch; the banquet —also with radishes — at 6:30 in the evening; and supper, with more radishes, at bedtime) provided a feature story so good that Fred Heiskell slipped me a ten-spot. At $40 a week, that was big money.

Bryan left the next day for Dayton, Tenn., to tangle with the formidable Clarence Darrow at the famous Scopes Trial over the teaching of evolution. After the trial, which Bryan had won, technically, but at which he also had been humiliated and reduced to bumbling rages by the clever Darrow, a reporter from the New York Times sought an interview. Just as he had with me, Bryan suggested that the reporter awaken him after his midday nap. Accordingly, at 2:30 p.m., the reporter entered the room, squeezed Bryan's shoulder, spoke to him, shook him, then shouted in his ear — to no avail.

The Great Commoner was dead.

— Arkansas Times, *May 1986*

The Chronicles Of Weed

BY BOB LANCASTER

Here's the smoking article. Call it "A Treatise on Butts" or "That Old Devil Weed." A Tale of Two Guys. All the time I was working on it, the old song "Smoke Smoke Smoke That Cigarette," was playing on a car radio somewhere in a back corner of my mind. With the line about telling St. Peter at the Golden Gate he'd just have to wait while your immortal soul had just one more drag. So round, so firm, so fully packed. Also, I kept hearing Winthrop Rockefeller the time I asked him just how many Picayunes he smoked in a day. These were nasty old Louisiana cigarettes made of perique tobacco rolled in reptile dung and battery acid. Or so they tasted and smelled. Mr. R. admitted to five packs a day.

But he died and we turn our attention elsewhere, to others.

Okay.

1. About the old guy.

One time he smoked 300,000 cigarettes.

Give or take a few.

50 a day on the average for more than 20 yrs.

First thing he reached for on waking in the a.m.; the cherry Viceroy fire what he saw last every night.

Wake up in the small hours sometimes, out to the patio, look at the stars, listen to the owls, have a smoke.

Light up between courses of the slower-paced meals.

Many people he knew lived the same story and some died it. (He would come to die it himself after a fashion.)

Drug addicts one and all.

One time he thought: 300,000 cigarettes placed end to end would reach from here to the moon. Well, no they wouldn't, but nearly to Conway, which is almost as impressive, and, come to think of it, pretty much the same thing. A cigarette you couldn't see the other end of for the curvature of the earth.

And further: 300,000 cigarettes might make you wish you were dead, but usually takes nearly twice that many to kill a human person. Half a million to get the cancer nicely, terminally rooted.

Tobacco poison had killed most of the men in his family who had died in his lifetime: His Daddy, his Uncle Red, Mr. Claud, Lee, Al, Henry Joe, Don. Or it was what was called "a contributing factor." It drove the getaway car. The hearse.

He remembered this: In the last days his Daddy would cough up this godawful brimstone corruption washpansful at a time, literally, and soon as he got his feeble breath back first thing he'd use it for would be to ask for a cigarette.

Lucky Strikes were what his Daddy smoked.

Luckies.

Lucky, lucky.

Just about all the people he knew who had smoked 1,000,000 cigarettes were dead, or worse off than dead. One of them on the list above had passed just recently.

That one particularly gruesome but that horror story lost on people now. Everybody has his or her own harrowing cancer tale. It's a cliche. You don't ignore it exactly, but put it off to the side so you see it but don't see it, it exists but it doesn't, like surgeon generals' warnings.

2. New Guy Goes to the Capitol.

In a corridor at the state Capitol one day recently, the new guy (that's ol' moi) ran into longtime acquaintance, a former legislator, now a lobbyist whose clients include one of the big tobacco companies.

Tobacco Lobbyist No. 1.

This was outside a legislative committee room in which, I learned later, some lawmakers were met to review a proposal to add a couple of pennies to the state tax on cigarettes, the money to be used for breast-cancer research.

Legislators were there to offer personal testimony about their experiences with breast cancer — themselves or wives — but people don't listen to those stories anymore either. By now we've all lost to the oncologist's whackers a bosom dear to us. Breasts running third behind lungs and rectums as cancer's favorite haunt. So many chopped off every day that a few more flung on the big pile aren't going to sway anybody's vote on a tax bill.

Bleeding-heart sentiments (or bleeding whatever) politically out of fashion now anyway. Here in the era of the Contract.

A coincidence I should bump into him, I told Tobacco Lobbyist No. 1, because I'd just got in mind to do this article you're now reading. He said he'd be glad to help, in the way that lobbyists help, with data, statistics, printed material: what sort of article, exactly, did I have in mind?

"Uh," I told him, at a loss how to describe this.

A Treatise on Butts. The Chronicles of Weed.

"I'm hoping it'll be, er, wide-ranging."

"I'm sure it will," he said politely.

Tobacco Lobbyist No. 1 was one of at least three tobacco-industry lobbyists working that one corridor when I happened down it. All of them heavy hitters.

Since No. 1 shills for only a single tobacco, he passed me along to No. 3, who represents the tobacco industry as a whole in legislative matters arising in the Arkansas capitol. No. 3 is a woman. She was crushing out a butt in the hallway ashtray when I was introduced to her.

Said she hadn't seen the big *60 Minutes* tobacco-lobbyist meltdown a few nights before — interview with one of the industry's top guns, confessing his sins. His forte had been working state legislatures, helping stymie proposals to discourage smoking or make it costlier. He'd made a long career of this, and suggested the secret of his success was a kind of humongous shamelessness. He knew tobacco was killing people, and every day turning thousands of young people into drug addicts, but he was an old pro at denying those facts, affecting to refute them, changing the subject when their inescapability got uncomfortably close. Lies and evasions his stock-in-trade. His art throwing up smokescreens, so to speak.

He'd help bury a lot of anti-smoking bills. Reason he was 'fessing up here at the end was he'd got throat cancer — three guesses what caused it — and wanted to unbur-den afore he died.

Get it off his chest, so to speak.

Clear the air, so to speak.

Lucky, lucky.

STATE SEN. JIM KEET OF Little Rock told me later he'd had to "run a gauntlet" of tobacco lobbyists to get to a legislative hearing on the smoking-restriction bill (SB 379) he put in the hopper at the start of this legislative session. Actually more tobacco lobbyists in the corridor outside than legislators who made their way through them into the hearing, he said.

I asked Rep. Pat Flanagin of Forrest City how many lobbyists he knew of who'd been working the Capitol on behalf of the principal pro-smoking bill of the session — HB 1952 by Rep. James C. Allen of Hot Springs. He named four before he got to the ones I've ciphered already, and we'd both neglected the Skoal man, the specialist in smokeless protectionism.

A gauntlet, to be sure.

And it doesn't mention the slicks for the Arkansas Hospitality Association, the restaurant and tourism people, who got their big shoulders behind HB 1952 and helped muscle it through to passage.

Tourism and tobacco teaming up, like Blifil and Black George. It almost suggests a new slogan for our brochures: "Arkansas Is Cancer-Friendly: Come Visit."

Flanagin said I might mention that the other side in this debate, the Not In My Face Lobby, had zero lobbyists working the legislature this session, and in fact doesn't exist.

I think that cigarettes are Evil — that the Devil uses them to get into people's brains — and what I was out there to ask all those professional cigarette pushers was: Does it ever trouble your conscience to be using your life, your talent, your good name, to promote this evil, to help these death merchants merchant their death?

But I didn't do it.

Maybe out of chagrin they'd be clever enough to turn the question back on me. *How many publications have you worked for, tubby, that paid your giant salary with the proceeds from cigarette ads?*

A standoff before we even got started.

And so I wound up mostly just listening to the other side's stock-in-trade.

For instance, the crying need for legislation to "balance the rights of smokers and non-smokers."

The tobacco lobby blowing smoke.

3. Blowing Smoke.

HB 1952, this legislature's homage to butts, pretended to be legislation to *restrict* smoking.

Ho, ho.

Title of the bill, in fact: "An Act to provide comprehensive smoking restrictions and to prevent youth access to tobacco ... and for other purposes."

Them "other purposes" are always the killers.

Elsewhere in its text the bill claimed to have been created "in order to protect the health and welfare of the citizens of this state." To have been necessary to protect the public health and safety of the people. H-, h-h-.

(The sound of one lung laughing.)

Buried 4 pages and 147 lines deep into HB 1952 was the only part of it that meant very much. Or that meant much other than the opposite of what it said. It was there you came upon the infamous uniformity clause.

"Section 8: Statewide uniformity.

"The General Assembly finds that it is necessary and proper to prescribe a single, uniform standard of conduct statewide regarding the field of tobacco regulation, and the General Assembly hereby occupies that field. In occupying that field, it is the intent of the General Assembly that all regulation of the sale, distribution, promotion and use of tobacco products shall by this Act be made uniform throughout the state, and that this Act, as the means of such regulation, shall be uniformly enforced throughout the state ..."

Here in one swell foop we declared it "necessary and proper" that Arkansas have a statewide smoking policy — how come? who says? — and nominated the legislature to formulate that policy.

The idea was to cut off individual towns, counties and other communities and localities that might have wanted to devise their own policies to restrict smoking in their public buildings and public places. Couldn't be having any of that.

The tobacco lobby can handle a legislature as a rule. Anyhow can hold its own with one. But a thousand unruly town councils and quorum courts, each with its own notion of what's necessary and proper in a smoking policy, might strain even the tobacco lobby's long reach and tight clutch.

A uniformity clause to cut them off.

An idea the tobacco lobby borrowed from the gun lobby, which used it early in the session to cut off comparable prospective local say-so over guns.

The state of Arkansas guaranteeing your right to get shot, if the Marlboro haze doesn't kill you first.

A tough tussle lasting the entire session, each side using just about every parliamentary trick in Robert's book — "a real civics lesson," Keet called the experience — but in the end smoking was about where it was when the contest started.

The cigarette lobby with its dragon's breath blew away SB 379, while knights-errant Keet and them ripped some lethal holes in HB 1952, including a big one through which they yanked out its uniformity clause and stomped that sucker flat.

4. A Visit to the Leper Colony.

Two ways of looking at this.

One, the tobacco industry, on the run until recently, is resurgent—with tobacco-friendly Republicans back in control of Congress, with new smoking starts among children more than offsetting the cravenly swearing off or dying off of their elders, with major propaganda advances like the movie industry's renewed commitment to glamorizing smoking, and with aggressive political initiatives like little HB 1952 coming after a period of general defensiveness: all of which is said to be turning the tide loosed against the industry in recent times by all these meddlesome surgeons-general, health fanatics, do-gooders, free-breathers, lung-lovers.

The other view: the industry really isn't making advances, it's just getting some ties for a change — some draws, holding some ground, successfully defending some status quos. And in these tilts and tussles, you hear it wheezing. Corporate giant doomed by the growing malignancy in its own breast.

With smoking have lost its respectability and continuing to lose even its acceptability, you can just sense the great vorpal blade out there beginning its terrible descent.

I don't know.

I think probably the former, but the second view, the

hopeful one, is bolstered by a phenomenon that's become a commonplace just in the last year.

That's the spectacle of all these little covens of smokers gathering outside public buildings, office buildings, malls, factories, schools. To perform their 10-minute suck-and-blow ritual and then hurry back inside. Huddled against the rain, the cold, the gloom of tornado watch, the approach of panhandler and mad dog — suck and blow and hurry back in, eight or 10 or 20 times a day.

STATE SEN. WAYNE DOWD of Texarkana (Merit Ultra Lights) compares it to being put in a pen, or put in jail, where regular people then come by and gape at you. They come by and look at you — with scorn, or with pity, or with no particular emotion, as they might look at a criminal in the stocks or a baboon at the zoo.

Fumigatus americanus: Look at the strange critter, boys and girls. See him suck and blow.

If the anti-smokers had their way, Dowd says, "we'd have to go outside the building and go off the grounds and go off somewhere on down the street."

He's funny about this but it's a humor spiked with wormwood. Look at one of the covens and you can see that vaguely resentful quality looking back at you. Sometimes defiant, sometimes abject. A sense of exclusion, of have been identified as an offender and sent away.

One of these covens — at Arkansas Tech University at Russellville — call themselves the Leper Colony.

"What's this sect that shuns people — the Amish?" says English Prof. B.C. Hall. "That's how those of us in the Leper Colony feel: shunned."

The Lepers — students, faculty, administrators; never more than a dozen at a time — have developed a compensatory camaraderie, a sort of fellowship of the despised. It's an egalitarian group, no officers, no membership requirements, come as you are.

"We talk about literature, philosophy, psychology, and horses," Hall said. "It's turned into one of the best learning venues I've ever experienced." He recalled that in the world's first great school, the students of Plato strolled about outdoors in the groves of Academe, and that some of them in the urn renderings can actually be seen to be smoking Chesterfields or Old Golds.

Sometimes the Lepers even talk about the devil that draws them all together. "You know, the greatest irony of the modern age might be that Duke University is now a smoke-free campus," one of them opined not long ago. "That tremor you feel in the ground over there is ol' Buck Duke twirling in his grave."

Hall started smoking in 1956 at age 19 at the Pepsi-Cola plant at Blytheville, the better to cope with the onset of the dual anxieties of having to operate a forklift and trying to get a girl named Elaine to think of him as a stud duck. He took up Kents and has hung with them.

Kents with the Micronite (little trademark symbol) filter.

"Where I come from," I told him politically incorrectly, "Kents were the cigarettes that homos smoked."

"I know," he said. "The homosexuals smoked Kents and the black people smoked Kools."

"And everybody else smoked Winstons," somebody said.

That was true. Winstons tasted good like cigarettes should.

Except girls, who as a rule didn't do enough smoking then to be associated with a particular brand. And now they have the lesser cancer rate to show for it.

They knew Winstons stank, but didn't tell us.

5. In the Land of Honilee.

The Lepers and Sen. Dowd and all these other addicts will quit cigarettes sooner or later.

Either by an act of will or an act of expiration.

Dying may be the only real escape from nicotine addiction.

It's the route I took.

I mean that metaphorically but just barely.

The addiction was stronger than I was; I couldn't ever have conquered it; and to escape from it I had to sacrifice myself to it, to die in a way, and come back as somebody else.

This was one day in the Salem spring of 1984. Vertiginous from chain-smoking away a tense morning, I put my head on my desk, closed my eyes and said, like Roberto Duran, *No mas*, and the me who'd been me, like Gen. MacArthur, faded away. Old guy: a reeking old chunk of tar and regret, farewell.

Well, actually, the transformation took some time and occurred in stages — two weeks, then two months, then four or five years. (They say it takes seven years to clean your system of the residue.) But it was indeed a new creature who slowly took shape (lamentably the shape of Mr. Peanut): somebody whose mind worked different, whose habits were those of a stranger, whose prose was suddenly this pile of Coke-bottle fragments and broken runic stones, whose signature suddenly looked like Chinese.

To quit cigarettes, you have to be willing to give up who you are and take your chances on who and what you'll become.

The new guy might not be a better person; might not be one the old guy would've wanted to be or would've given the time of day; might be a bad swap all the way around. But you can count on him being different. Somebody else.

One thing the new guy had that never troubled the old guy was a big void in the middle of his being. A big hole somewhere inside him. Causing him little fits of grief, anxiety, and longing, mystifying because they were irrational. They came and went. They might last two seconds and yet cause major desolation. Ten years after, he still had them.

New guy figured this hole might've been in the old guy too, but old guy kept it filled with cigarette smoke: magic smoke with the tranquilizing power to let him pretend it wasn't there.

Puff the magic dragon.

This calm that really wasn't, this placidity of self-deceit, had been the payoff he got from his brain for supplying it with the drug.

Addicts duped, manipulated, jerked around and put through hoops by their own brains.

Knowing your own brain is smarter than you are. And knowing it's trying to kill you.

Quitting means going to war against your own brain, knowing you're outgunned. Your brain even more devious and calculating in this struggle than the tobacco lobby.

You have to run a different gauntlet.

Longer than from here to Conway.

I had to enlist some religious terms and symbols to have a chance against my own devil brain. One of these was that metaphor about the old guy dying, with such tyrannies of the flesh as the nicotine addiction dying with him, and the new guy emerging from the baptismal waters reborn, a different person.

Deliver us from Evil. The evil being your own brain, under the seductive power of the drug, beseeching you to poison yourself by sucking down all these old gasses and slime. Ordering you to. Furious and despondent and pathetic. Smarter than you are, weary sinner, and stronger than you are. And finally you just have to let it have the old guy, like Jaws getting the old skipper, and watch his torment with pity till he expires.

And give the new guy to know he simply has to keep clear of this old dangerous craziness. Can't be flirting with it, entertaining notions of "cutting down," "tapering off," or "just one after breakfast to kill the taste of the eggs."

Those just preludes to another fall. They'll kill you again, and next time maybe your body too.

Just a couple of hundred thousand more will probably do the trick.

—Arkansas Times, *April 7, 1995.*

God Didn't Pull That Trigger

The first questions occasioned by such monstrous events as the Jonesboro school shooting last week are philosophical or religious. You can count on the earliest network reporters jetting into the scene to declare that the one question haunting the stunned community is "why?" (Gov. Huckabee, in his Saturday radio address: "At a time like this, all Arkansans ask one question: Why?")

Also inevitable, when there's great carnage involving children:

How could a merciful God allow such a thing to happen? It's a question that edges the abyss, easier to head off than to answer, and usually headed off by declaring the Lord's ways mysterious and by calling for prayer to Him for the victims and the bereaved. Vice President Gore and Gov. Huckabee were among the first to ask people to remember the people of Jonesboro in their prayers, and here is Huckabee again: "Let us pray for the injured, the grieving, and yes, even the accused, knowing full well that God is loving and just."

A main theme in at least two of the Jonesboro funeral sermons was "God didn't pull that trigger" or "Don't blame God for the Devil's handiwork." These were a way of answering a question no one had asked, or a way of avoiding the observation that if God didn't pull the trigger, he also didn't find it in his will to keep someone else from pulling it. At least 27 times.

Only one child at Jonesboro had the courage to come right out and say that the killing of his classmates brought some religious doubts unbidden into his heart. He was quoted by the New York Times as saying, "In times like this, I question God's judgment. It's hard to see what good will come from this."

But this boy promptly "asked for forgiveness" for entertaining the momentary doubt.

And meantime others saw the hand of God at work in the shooting, and no irony that it worked so selectively. The mother of one of the girls who was shot — the one whose "breakup" with 13-year-old Mitchell Johnson was said to have triggered the shootings — told reporters:

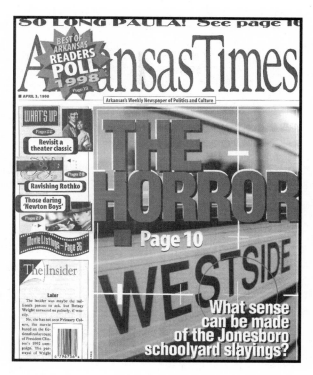

"My daughter took a bullet to the right side. It hit a rib and that saved her life. God turned her the right way."

God turned her the right way.

Some of the others He didn't.

The mother of a boy who survived thanked God for having "put a shield" around her son — unthinking how such a sentiment might sound to those parents whose daughters didn't survive. The father of the most seriously wounded survivor thought she lived only because "God had his hand on her the whole time." Parents of another boy who was spared thought God might have stayed the entire episode if the school had given Him a little more attention. "If they hadn't taken prayer out of school," the father of 14-year-old Brandon Hazlewood said, "this never would have happened."

—*From the* Arkansas Times *cover story, April 3, 1998*

An Unruly Woman

The Unsinkable Susan McDougal

BY JAN COTTINGHAM

The worst thing that happened to Susan McDougal was being forced to strip naked in the Pulaski County Jail and then being sprayed with a delousing agent.

That, she says, was worse than being handcuffed and shackled and led away in front of TV cameras. It was, apparently, worse than male prisoners masturbating in front of her.

None of it — not cells full of insects, cells where one had to relieve oneself in view of a bench full of drunken college boys, alleged harassment of her family — was bad enough to get the effervescent McDougal to talk to Kenneth Starr.

Obstinate, defiant, rebellious and unmanageable are some of the words that have been used to describe McDougal. They all come down to the same quality: disobedience — the sullen, stubborn, willful disobedience of a naughty little girl.

It's hard not to believe the prosecutors and pundits who describe McDougal this way haven't deliberately chosen these words to portray her as something less than adult, to diminish her stand against Starr and the Office of the Independent Counsel, to reduce actions many see as heroic to something silly.

A little vignette illustrates that non-pundits view her differently.

After a reporter and McDougal have lunch in Ashley's at the Capital Hotel, where the staff, from bellman to busboy, restaurant hostess to waitress, greets McDougal warmly and enthusiastically, McDougal walks off to get her car. As the reporter pays the check, the hostess and waitress talk about the night a few weeks ago when an Arkansas jury decided that Susan McDougal wasn't guilty of obstruction of justice.

"She kept saying to all these people coming up to her and congratulating her, 'Thank you, thank you, thank you.' I wanted to say to her, 'You thank yourself, Sister,'" the waitress tells the hostess. The waitress utters "Sister" in a tone indicating solidarity, approval and deep admiration.

The hostess, who earlier had requested and received a hug from McDougal, nods. The hostess' sister is also a fan; she'd sent McDougal a congratulatory bouquet after her acquittal.

SUSAN MCDOUGAL, LIKE Bill Clinton, gives great hugs. A tall, voluptuous woman, she wraps her arms around you firmly. She's earthy and sophisticated at the same time. She likes to laugh and eat and jokingly warns a hovering server not to remove her plate, she's not finished yet.

McDougal twice refused to answer questions before a federal grand jury investigating Whitewater, despite a grant of immunity. She says she refused because the Office of the Independent Counsel, led by Kenneth Starr, wasn't concerned with the truth but was, instead, seeking any material damaging to President Clinton or First Lady Hillary Clinton.

After McDougal's first refusal to testify, in September 1996, federal Judge Susan Webber Wright sent her to jail for 18 months — the maximum — for civil contempt. She also spent three months of a two-year sentence in prison for her 1996 conviction with her ex-husband, Jim McDougal, on fraud charges in the Whitewater case.

Earlier this month, Susan McDougal was acquitted in Little Rock on a charge of obstruction of justice stemming from her refusal to testify before the grand jury. A jury deadlocked on two other criminal contempt charges, and the judge declared a mistrial on those counts.

She says she never reads articles about herself, and yet it's hard for some not to believe she doesn't revel in the limelight. Associate Independent Counsel Julie Myers told jurors during McDougal's criminal contempt trial that McDougal "craved the spotlight. She enjoyed the attention."

Susan McDougal, like Bill Clinton, is, indeed, an extrovert. She is "a people person," a cliché that rings true when she uses it to describe herself. She draws energy from others.

She is also a woman of large and incautious gestures. She has threatened to kick Starr's ass in court. (Of course, she, with the help of Los Angeles lawyer Mark Geragos and fiancé Pat Harris, eventually made metaphorically good on those threats.) She finds humor in situations others would find frightening, perhaps because she has had to.

Writers are almost always introverts, and Susan McDougal is everything that the people who write about her tend to distrust. Seeing McDougal through a prism of introspection, some have portrayed her as theatrical and calculating.

Indeed, the very traits that make Arkansas-raised Susan McDougal warm, fascinating and human, the traits that have allowed her to stand firm, have also caused her to be misperceived by many.

She's well aware of this.

She says the biggest misperception is that she enjoys the celebrity resulting from the Whitewater investigation that has snared so many.

"I used the media for what I thought I could get across about Starr," McDougal says. "And my entire goal during my time in jail was to talk about Kenneth Starr and what I knew about him. I wanted people to know what that man was about.

"Every failure that he had, every setback that he had, every negative article about him, I read it. I kept up with it. I wanted to know about it. Because it was what helped me a little to see an end to what I knew was wrong. I really thought it was as bad as the McCarthy era in America. It didn't ruin as many lives, but it ruined lives effectively."

If any picture illustrates the madness that was Whitewater, it will be the one of McDougal, then 41,

being led away in shackles Sept. 9, 1996. The effect of that image was opposite of what was intended. What was certainly meant to convey McDougal's humiliation and powerlessness before the might of the Independent Counsel instead became a picture of the abuse of power.

But even there, what some people commented on instead of McDougal's harsh treatment or her determination was the fact that she wore a short skirt, maybe a little too short.

Consistently, the criticism of McDougal has seemed to focus more on her defiant, sometimes apparently even light-hearted demeanor than on the actual meaning of her actions.

McDougal also agrees she's not willing to be submissive. She's not an easy client for a lawyer, she says. She's not an easy girlfriend.

McDougal admits that since her troubles began "I have become a lot harder to deal with. I don't sit still. That's one of my problems in court. I didn't sit in jail for 20 months waiting to tell my story to be told to shut up in court."

MCDOUGAL SAYS HER lawyer has received overtures from television producers interested in her story. She says HBO has expressed interest. Writers want to write her story. She says that, even though she's broke, she's not interested in any of that.

McDougal says she'd like to do something to help women in prison, get them the drug and alcohol counseling that is lacking, particularly in county jails, get them more legal and financial aid.

Cynics, and that includes most in the press, wonder why McDougal took the position she did, why she endured so much — in their minds — unnecessary suffering. McDougal herself notes that a puzzled federal prosecutor called her "complicated" several times.

"I don't think they can figure it out," McDougal says. "It doesn't mean that you're complicated that one day you say to yourself, 'This just isn't right and I'm not taking one step further.' In fact, it takes a pretty simple human being to do that.

"I don't have a lot of other thoughts than just a person without asking for it got dragged into the middle of something that was totally wrong and said, 'I won't be a party to it,' a simple Arkansas woman.

"And I think anybody would do the same thing. I do."

—Arkansas Times, *April 4, 1999*

The Fall Of A Governor

BY DOUG SMITH

Public service has not been an appealing career choice for quite some time. Term limits, single-issue fanatics, bloodthirsty media and a growing meanness in American politics dissuaded people from entry. What happened to Jim Guy Tucker should scare off a lot more.

Tucker has been convicted of a couple of felonies, may go to prison, and is resigning the governorship because of improper business dealings from a decade ago, when he was a private citizen. Another set of criminal charges hangs over him. How many businessmen thinking of public office will take the plunge knowing it could bring a special federal prosecutor down on them? Special prosecutors have millions of dollars, and legions of lawyers and investigators. People who stay in the private sector don't attract this kind of unwanted attention, no matter how many corners they cut.

The Tucker case is even scarier because he was pursued not for his own political activities, but for those of another — Bill Clinton, who dared be president. Tucker is something like the baseball player who is plunked by the pitcher because the batter in front of him hit a home run. The pain may be especially sharp considering that Tucker and Clinton, though teammates in a way — both Democrats and Arkansans — have been more rivals than friends over the years. But here is Tucker dying for Clinton's alleged sins, and having to drag himself from the courthouse while Say McIntosh jabbers insults at him. Then he has to turn the governor's office over to Mike Huckabee, whom he dislikes personally and who is a member of the political party that did Tucker in. It doesn't get much worse than this. Make a tape of the Jim Guy Tucker story, show the thing to enough people, and nobody'll run for public office again. Even voting may be considered unsafe.

(In fairness to Arkansas Republicans, they didn't cause Tucker's agony, and both Huckabee and state Chairman Lloyd Stone of Conway were graciously sympathetic Tuesday.)

Why Tucker was in the courtroom was the bigger story — and easier to understand — than what happened after he was there. For a good part of what was a long trial, Tucker seemed bound for acquittal. (And Susan McDougal even more so. James McDougal, who faced the most charges, was always most in danger.) The charges, conspiracy and bank fraud, were complicated; the prosecution's star witness and some of its other witnesses were sleazy sorts themselves, and the jurors appeared to look more kindly at the defense table than the

prosecution. Appearances can be misleading, obviously, and jurors' appearances especially. The jurors indicated they were persuaded by the hundreds of documents the prosecution introduced as evidence — the smoke-and-fire thing. Maybe they understood the charges better than people expected, or not as well. Either conviction or acquittal could result from understanding or misunderstanding; this is the kind of uncertainty that gives the justice system a good or bad name. Obviously they were not overwhelmed by President Clinton's videotaped testimony for the defense, but no native expected they would be. Arkansans vote for Clinton most of the time, but they're not overwhelmed by him.

Maybe the jurors were unfavorably impressed by Tucker's not taking the stand to testify in his own behalf, a decision surely made by his lawyers and in which he acquiesced, as good defendants should. It is not Tucker's way to sit quietly when he has a chance to talk back to his detractors. After the verdict Tuesday, he was asked if not testifying had proved unwise. He shrugged and said speculation was pointless: "It might have made a difference, and it might not have. You never know what goes through a juror's mind." True enough, although lawyers are paid to guess.

The first sitting governor to be convicted of a felony, or charged, Tucker was thus the first to face the choice of resigning or trying to hold onto the office while strug-gling through an appeal. He chose to resign, and that is not really his way either. He will put up a fight, sometimes rashly, as he's shown with some of the issues he's backed as governor. (Did he really engage a monstrous football player in physical combat during his law school days? It's a story they used to tell about him.) There were extenuating circumstances. Word had circulated privately in recent days that lawyers researching the legal question had decided the answer was clearer than anyone had been willing to say publicly, and the answer was yes, the state Constitution did rather clearly require removal of the governor upon conviction of a felony. Resistance, in this case, would be embarrassing for all concerned — the state, the party, Tucker and his family. Tucker and his family had been under great strain already. Besides, Tucker expects he's going to lose the appeal — the appellate courts are stacked with partisan justices.

Quitting was hard, though. "I love this job," he said in his resignation announcement, and there was no doubting the sincerity of that. Probably somebody will always love it, and somebody will always want it, even knowing what a Kenneth Starr can do to them. But they'll think longer and there'll be fewer and they may be only the kind of people who can live down to Starr's standards. That's the worst thing about this mess.

— Arkansas Times, *May 31, 1996*

Prying Into Paychecks
The *Times* Explores Relative Worths

Herewith we present a list of personalities and just plain folks and how much money they make. Some told us after a little hesitation; others said no, and we had to dig in the public records. The figures are for salary only and do not include any outside personal income from investments and property. We started our search with a call to a small-town banker.

Burton George, president, the First National Bank of Berryville: "Well, it's about $36,000."

William Bowen, board chairman and CEO of Commercial National Bank of Little Rock: $106,306, including salary, fees and bonuses.

Hall McAdams, executive president, Union National Bank of Little Rock: $75,000, salary.

Frank White, governor of Arkansas: $35,000.

Sonny Simpson, Little Rock police chief: $37,387.

Bill Williams, patrolman, Little Rock Police Dept.: $16,100.

Anchorman/TV personality: A performer like Tom Bonner on Channel 4 earns, according to sources in the TV industry, $60,000 minimum annually from salary and "talent fees." Salaries for anchormen like Roy Mitchell of Channel 4 and Steve Barnes of Channel 7, so we are told, are in the range of $35,000 to $50,000.

Craig O'Neill, disc jockey KKYK radio, Little Rock: $19,500 salary.

Bill Strait, lawyer, Morrilton: $17,000.

Richard B. Adkisson, chief justice, Arkansas Supreme Court: $36,253.04.

Attorney, Little Rock, who asked not to be named: $100,000.

Bill Simpson, chief public defender, Pulaski County: $33,264.

Fenton Adams, dean, UALR Law School: $62,000.

Tommy Robinson, Pulaski County sheriff: $27,000.

Carol Hurley, Traskwood police chief: $100 a month, part-time.

Sheffield Nelson, president and CEO, Arkansas Louisiana Gas Co.: $274,033.

Jerry Maulden, president, Arkansas Power & Light Co: $127,000 (includes salary, fees, commissions).

David Joslin, AP&L lineman, Morrilton: $25,000 with overtime.

"Johnny," part-time drug dealer, Fayetteville: $25,000.

Air traffic controller, Pine Bluff: $26,605.

Air traffic controller, Little Rock: $35,023 (with 21 years service).

William Penn, American Airlines test pilot, Perryville: $100,000.

Lou Holtz, Razorback football coach: $55,804 in line-item salary.

Dr. James Martin, University of Arkansas president: $69,050.

Larry Frey: mail carrier, Little Rock: $20,500.

Merrill Lynch stockbroker, Little Rock: $75,000-$100,000.

Mahlon Martin, Little Rock city manager: $46,255.

Ken Parker: Texarkana city manager: $28,500.

Mike Davis, Cammack Village trash collector: $9,770.

Bill Lancaster, state House of Representatives information officer: $30,800.

Lloyd McCuiston, West Memphis, House speaker: $10,000 plus allowances.

Reporter, Arkansas Democrat (experienced reporter, top salary): $17,420.

Alan Leveritt, publisher Arkansas Times: $18,000 including bonuses and commissions.

Carl Grimes, publisher Clarendon Sentinel: "About $20,000."

Phyllis Nash, bus driver, Little Rock, $15,037.

Joe Jones, private investigator, Little Rock: $25,000.

Bruce Weigel, assistant English professor, UALR:

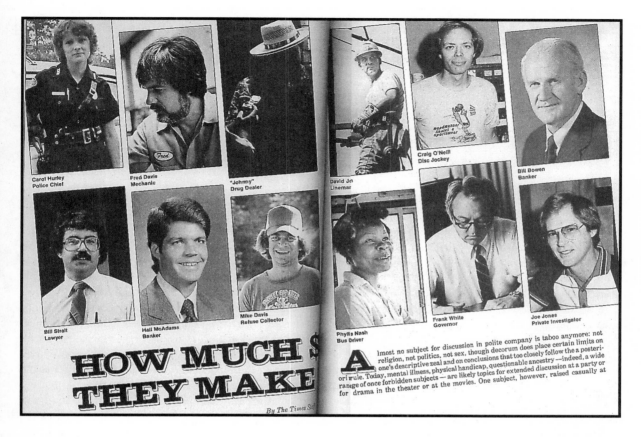

Carol Hurley
Police Chief

Fred Davis
Mechanic

"Johnny"
Drug Dealer

Craig O'Neill
Disc Jockey

David Jo
Linemar

Bill Bowen
Banker

Bill Strait
Lawyer

Hall McAdams
Banker

Mike Davis
Refuse Collector

Phyllis Nash
Bus Driver

Frank White
Governor

Joe Jones
Private Investigator

HOW MUCH $
THEY MAKE

By The Times S...

Almost no subject for discussion in polite company is taboo anymore: not religion, not politics, not sex, though decorum does place certain limits on one's descriptive zeal and on conclusions that too closely follow the a posteriori rule. Today, mental illness, physical handicap, questionable ancestry — indeed, a wide range of once forbidden subjects — are likely topics for extended discussion at a party or for drama in the theater or at the movies. One subject, however, raised casually at

$20,000.

Dr. Harry Ward, UAMS chancellor: $62,667 salary, with $18,000 in allowances.

Gynecologist, Little Rock: "...between $150,000 and $160,000."

Surgeon, Little Rock: $650,000.

Registered nurse, Little Rock: $15,000.

Bill Becker, president, Arkansas State AFL-CIO: $26,180.

Rt. Rev. Herbert A. Donovan, Episcopal bishop of Arkansas: $42,270 (includes housing and allowances).

Robert K. Bennett, Walnut Ridge Presbyterian minister: $16,776.

Lon McDonald, Arkansas Best Freight truck driver, Fordyce: $35,000.

Plumber, Little Rock: $25,000.

Jim Riggleman, player coach, Arkansas Travelers: $13,800 for the 6-month season.

CPA, Little Rock: $99,000.

Tricia Tyran, Cheer's waitress, Little Rock: $4,500 a year (for 25-hour week).

Phyllis Blumenfeld, Arkansas Rep actress: $8,400.

Col. Dan Freeman, wing commander, Little Rock Air Force base: $38,800 (including flight pay).

—Arkansas Times, *August 1981.*

On Moving To The Country

Rules For Living

BY MARA LEVERITT

If you've ever thought of moving out beyond the reach of city services or taken aimless "just-looking" drives to where the egrets graze, there may be something in the following list for you. If you've already surrendered your lease and put down money on some sweet place way out with a rutted driveway and a big wood-burning stove to feed, you may want to read ahead quickly. The tips that follow are the kinds of little, crucial things you may not have thought of at first. We didn't.

1. *Never buy a chainsaw in a city, or worse, in a suburban mall.* All chainsaws look big at first. It's only when you have to cut up real trees, regularly, that you begin to notice the difference between your wimpy little backyard buzzer and your neighbor's gas-powered model. The comparison becomes more acute around sunset, when you're still sputtering over what might be a week's worth of wood, while he's putting the finishing touches on a stack as big as a boxcar. The thing to remember about chainsaws is that all of them are dangerous, so you might as well get the meanest one you can live with.

2. *Start stockpiling candles.* I once asked why the power seems to go out ten times more often in the country than in town, and was told that, as with so many things, blame goes to the squirrels. It seems hunters are all the time shooting up wires when they're trying to shoot up the squirrels on the wires. Stupid squirrels.

3. *Buy boots.* Not pointy high-heeled things made out of lizard skins, but rubber boots; the tall, black ones they sell at discount stores. One thing you learn is that there's a lot of mud in the country. You can either go crazy, scraping and cleaning your life away, or you can buy each member of the family a six-dollar pair of boots. You think they're not very pretty at first, but after a while you love them.

4. *Be good to your feed-store owner.* Come summer this is the person who will teach you about insecticides. Send him a card on his birthday and a basket of fruit at Christmas.

5. *Avoid shock.* Say the pipes have frozen, there's no brunch for 30 miles, and you can't make coffee in your own kitchen. Don't do anything rash. Don't, for instance, plug together all the extension cords in the house, attach a glowing electric strip heater, and take the whole, humming thing outside *through the snow* to get at the pipes under the house. Take the heater under the house if you must, but make sure it stays unplugged until you come back inside. It's a little thing, but the alternative could be even worse than the plumbing bill you've got coming.

6. *Be willing to adopt.* It is commonly agreed that no place with a rural route number address is completely legit unless it has two or three dogs and cats hanging around — that's two or three of each. You need the cats as mousers and the dogs as announcers. The dogs' job is to make sure no automobiles or possums approach the homestead without an adequate commotion. But don't start worrying about how you're going to find these helpful animals. The wonderful thing about the country is that you don't find them, they find you. They come right to your door. They ask to be taken in. In fact, the supply usually exceeds the demand.

7. *Join the volunteer fire department.*

8. *Keep a fully loaded emergency shelf.* You never know when the bridge will get too icy to cross, or the kids will go off with both cars, leaving you stranded. Or the electricity will go out at 8:30 p.m., in the midst of a

tornado warning. For such moments we keep a bottle of Scotch and a flashlight handy.

9. *Buy rocking chairs.* A subtle thing happens to you when you leave the city. Definitions change. "Slave labor" becomes "chores." "Rocking" is no longer what you do till dawn, but what you settle down to after chores, in the rocking chair. And sometimes they all run together, as when you relax in the rocking chair with 15 pounds of peas to be shelled in your lap. Once that might have been "boring"; now it's "contentment."

10. *Be sure to cap the chimney.* Every house pulls its own pranks, and every owner has his or her foibles, so, overall, a list like this is probably pretty useless. You'll find your own ways to spend money, waste time, overexert, do and undo, and otherwise enjoy yourself in the country. But if you take nothing else said here to heart, at least be sure to cap the chimney. If you don't, as sure as there's a God in Heaven, one day you'll wake up and find a 12-pound duck in it.

— Arkansas Times, *October 1985.*

A Place Called Talk

BY JO MCDOUGALL

I couldn't know it until I left it, but I know it now. After eight years away from Arkansas, the thing I most miss in my sojourn here in the Midwest is not Arkansas as a place, as in trees and mountains and swamps and bayous; it's not even that white, humid summer light that hangs over the rice fields I grew up knowing in southern Arkansas or the lemony haze fingering the pines and dogwoods along the pig trails of the Ozarks. What I miss most about Arkansas is the talk.

When Arkansans talk, they display an inborn need to dramatize, to keep an audience—even if it's only a flop-sprawled hound. They have a need to connect, and they will reel you, friend or stranger, into their worlds. A few months ago, as I was unloading the trunk of my car at a Fayetteville motel, a middle-aged couple who had parked beside me, also unloading their stuff, engaged me in conversation. In three minutes I heard the circumstances of the incredible amount of luggage in their trunk (the wife's fault); I heard about the man's sister-in-law's asthma; I learned where the couple had been that morning and the arguments they'd had and what they had eaten for breakfast. A third of it might have been true. It didn't matter. For a few moments strangers were kin, walking around in each other's stories. I knew then I was home; I knew then I'd been away too long.

But it's more than human connection that Arkansans seek when they talk. Most of the time, even in the most idle of conversations, they're aiming to enter into myth. One of my most memorable experiences of such alchemy occurred a year or so ago as I sat with dear friends, a man and his wife, as dusk made its dreamy way onto their sun porch. The man told a story of somebody who had just moved into this neighborhood of wide lawns and ferny porches that morning and had, that very evening, parked his pick-up in the front yard and facing the street. What that action said to the rest of the enclave (Arkansans all) was that this newcomer had transgressed a ritual, some social, primal agreement, and was seemingly oblivious to it. They would have to set him straight. Myth from simple acts of life; on that porch, as the sun went down, I'd been in the presence of ancestral voices.

Talk, and the way they do it, is, I think, the difference between Southerners, and especially, Arkansans, and the rest of the world. Most people talk, much to their credit, to share ideas. Arkansans talk to make themselves and their listeners feel good; they talk to hear the old, shared stories.

This community of nonsense and alchemy and myth can include the stranger, though, if one is willing to listen. The telling of a story even when there's not much of a story to tell is typical of the Arkansan, who, soon or late, will tell it to you, the visitor, in the parking lots, the small cafes, the filling stations across the state. If you listen you will hear almost any Arkansan above the age of 3 transform with talk the drab and ordinary of happenstance into mystery and shimmer, while wanting—indeed, almost commanding—you, stranger or friend, to enter there also.

— Arkansas Times, *Sept. 15, 1995.*

How Much Okra Is Enough?

BY JOHN CHURCHILL

I couldn't know it until I left it, but I know it now. After eight years away from Arkansas, the thing I most miss in my sojourn here in the Midwest is not Arkansas as a place, as in trees and mountains and swamps and bayous; it's not even that white, humid summer light that hangs over the rice fields I grew up knowing in southern Arkansas or the lemony haze fingering the pines and dogwoods along the pig trails of the Ozarks. What I miss most about Arkansas is the talk.

When Arkansans talk, they display an inborn need to dramatize, to keep an audience—even if it's only a flop-sprawled hound. They have a need to connect, and they will reel you, friend or stranger, into their worlds. A few months ago, as I was unloading the trunk of my car at a Fayetteville motel, a middle-aged couple who had parked beside me, also unloading their stuff, engaged me in conversation. In three minutes I heard the circumstances of the incredible amount of luggage in their trunk (the wife's fault); I heard about the man's sister-in-law's asthma; I learned where the couple had been that morning and the arguments they'd had and what they had eaten for breakfast. A third of it might have been true. It didn't matter. For a few moments strangers were kin, walking around in each other's stories. I knew then I was home; I knew then I'd been away too long.

But it's more than human connection that Arkansans seek when they talk. Most of the time, even in the most idle of conversations, they're aiming to enter into myth. One of my most memorable experiences of such alchemy occurred a year or so ago as I sat with dear friends, a man and his wife, as dusk made its dreamy way onto their sun porch. The man told a story of somebody who had just moved into this neighborhood of wide lawns and ferny porches that morning and had, that very evening, parked his pick-up in the front yard and facing the street. What that action said to the rest of the enclave (Arkansans all) was that this newcomer had transgressed a ritual, some social, primal agreement, and was seemingly oblivious to it. They would have to set him straight. Myth from simple acts of life; on that porch, as the sun went down, I'd been in the presence of ancestral voices.

Talk, and the way they do it, is, I think, the difference between Southerners, and especially, Arkansans, and the rest of the world. Most people talk, much to their credit, to share ideas. Arkansans talk to make themselves and their listeners feel good; they talk to hear the old, shared stories.

This community of nonsense and alchemy and myth can include the stranger, though, if one is willing to listen. The telling of a story even when there's not much of a story to tell is typical of the Arkansan, who, soon or late, will tell it to you, the visitor, in the parking lots, the small cafes, the filling stations across the state. If you listen you will hear almost any Arkansan above the age of 3 transform with talk the drab and ordinary of happenstance into mystery and shimmer, while wanting—indeed, almost commanding—you, stranger or friend, to enter there also.

— Arkansas Times, *Sept. 15, 1995.*

Lucky Lindy Lands In Little Rock

Oct. 1, 1927. Fifty years ago. Bad weather, part of a massive cold front moving down from the Great Plains with tornadoes that had killed 88 in St. Louis the day before, had been in the state for two days, and skies in Little Rock were cloudy when a single-engine airplane flew low over the Veteran's Hospital at Ft. Roots, dipped its wings, circled North Little Rock and the capital city and landed at the Little Rock airport, known to many in those days as "the flying field."

The pilot of the plane was Charles A. Lindbergh. Four months earlier, "Lucky Lindy" had been the first man to fly the Atlantic Ocean alone, having landed his "Spirit of St. Louis" at Le Bourget Field in France on May 21. In Arkansas that day he stepped from the plane to be greeted by a crowd of dignitaries and cheering admirers in a time when Little Rock was a city of 80,000, nickel cups of coffee and 5-cent streetcar rides.

The newspapers of the period were filled with stories about aviation: stunt-flying, plane crashes, and accounts of transatlantic crossings by plane. Since Lindbergh's landing in France, 17 attempts to fly the Atlantic had been made and only eight had been successful. The people of Little Rock were worried that something might happen to Lindbergh because of the stormy weather. After he had landed safely here, one newspaper reported that "Lucky Lindy's luck has held."

With the concern there was tremendous excitement and anticipation. The lead paragraphs of the Arkansas Gazette on Oct. 1 said:

"Welcome Lindbergh!"

"Thus today speaks the spirit of Greater Little Rock."

And in the same story, the paper wrote: "Little Rock and North Little Rock are dressed up for the occasion ... and the most elaborate precautions ever have been taken to protect Lindbergh." A special fence had been erected around the landing area to keep back the crowd, and six units of the Arkansas National Guard were on duty to watch over the heroic flyer. A football game between Little Rock High School and El Dorado that had been set for that afternoon had been rescheduled not to interfere with Lindbergh's arrival.

That Oct. 1 was called "Lindbergh Day" and the memory of it for all the dignitaries has passed on — for such men as then Lt. Gov. Harvey Parnell, who welcomed Lindbergh to the state; Pulaski County Judge C.P. Newton; Acting Mayor Joe H. Bilheimer Jr.; Alfred G. Kahn, then president of the Little Rock Chamber of Commerce; and Methodist Bishop H.A. Boaz, who gave the invocation at a supper honoring the flyer that night.

Lindbergh, too, is dead, buried at Kipahula, Maui, Hawaii.

But there are some who remember not only that day but having a conversation with Lindbergh, shaking hands, exchanging stories. One of them is Louis E. Throgmorton, a retired insurance man and former wholesale grocer who was 30 and working in Stuttgart at the time. Now 80, Throgmorton is a nervy gentleman who considers himself something of a "gate crasher," admitting that had it not been for his "forwardness," he wouldn't have met the man.

"I came over from Stuttgart," he says, "with one purpose, that of meeting the famous flyer. I barged in on him at his hotel suite in the Marion and introduced myself. I knew the hotel clerk and he gave me his room number, and I went up to his room. I had no official capacity. I was just forward. Anybody who was notable like that, I would go to meet them. I did the same with Francis X. Bushman when he came to Little Rock in 1914."

Recalling his conversation with Lindbergh at the Marion, Throgmorton says: "I remember that he was very likeable, and I was surprised. You'd think anyone with that much fame would be kind of conceited but he wasn't. He called me Louis like he'd known me all my life. We talked about his flight, and I noticed that he kept using the word 'we' whenever he mentioned the flight.

The 'we' meant he was flying with God. He told me God was never out of his mind on that long journey.

"Then he told me an amusing story about his audience with King George of England. I had asked him about that audience and what took place, if they had talked about serious matters. Lindbergh said that one big laugh had come out of the meeting. It had come about, he said, after the king asked him what he had done to relieve himself during the crossing. Lindbergh said he told him that he kept a bottle on board for that purpose and that he 'opened the window just enough to empty it.' Lindbergh said the king quickly replied: 'Why didn't you save it, and I would have placed it in the British Museum.' "

Lindbergh arrived in Little Rock at 2 p.m. from Muskogee, Oklahoma, after flying over Ft. Smith and dodging thunderstorms on the way down. The Arkansas Democrat described him stepping from the plane as "a slim and very tanned young man with windblown hair and not a trace of disdain in his face for the attention he would receive." Throgmorton recalls that rain had been forecast but didn't materialize. "There was a tornado that day in El Dorado, but it didn't dare rain on Lindbergh's parade."

A parade, of course, was part of the ceremonies. The cars, mostly Model Ts filled with people, assembled at 18th and Broadway about 2:45, came down Broadway across the Broadway Bridge and traveled to the Clendenin School grounds in North Little Rock and returned to Little Rock via the Main Street Bridge, ending at the state Capitol.

Lindbergh rode in the fifth car in the caravan, and, according to newspaper accounts, stood most of the way waving to an estimated 75,000 people lining the streets. The politicians rode with him, and they played a little politics. While the motorcade was in Little Rock, acting Mayor Bilheimer rode in the back with Lindbergh but gave up his seat to North Little Rock Mayor Ross Lawhon on the north side. Lindbergh's car, according to the Gazette, was "piloted" by one T. Gilroy Cox.

Throgmorton can't recall why Bilheimer and not Mayor Charles E. Moyer welcomed Lindbergh, nor why Lt. Gov. Parnell stood in for Gov. John Martineau at the state Capitol. But there is evidence that Parnell choked in assuming his role as chief dignitary, for when he introduced Lindbergh to the crowd, he failed to get his name right. Says Throgmorton: "I never will forget Harvey's mispronouncement of the colonel's name. He pronounced it Lindenberg, evidently thinking of Von Hindenberg of Germany."

—Arkansas Times, *October 1977.*

The Black Iron Skillet

BY JACK BUTLER

I've been around black iron skillets all my life without thinking much about them. In fact, that phrase, "black iron skillet," is redundant. I can't remember saying it before about 1975, which is a comment on the sad decline of modern standards. All you really ought to have to say is "skillet." But I'm getting ahead of myself.

A black iron skillet is made of iron. Black. Iron. Aluminum will not do. It's too dry. It won't take oil the way iron will, so you can't cure it. It doesn't conduct heat the way iron does. That's the point of the copper-bottomed stuff, I know. Mate a highly conductive metal and a highly durable metal, and have the best of both. High technology trying to approximate the virtues of old reliable iron. Why bother? And you can't cure copper worth a flip, either.

I presume you understand that Teflon is out of the question. But you're worried about your heart, your intake of low-density lipoproteins, all that grease you have to use with a black iron skillet. Now you know better than that. It's not the skillet's fault. Just don't put so much in your *mouth*, hey? And really you don't have to use that much grease. Once you get the skillet cured, less than half a pat of butter will set up just fine for a delicious one-yolk three-egg omelet.

OK, so we've got the question of materials settled. Iron, and nothing else. Let's talk workmanship. Nowadays, there are a lot of iron skillets showing up in the housewares sections of supermarkets and in the various X-, Y-, and Z-Marts. But it doesn't mean you can just grab something off the rack and walk straight into skillet heaven. Many of these are quickie jobs, rough-cast and unevenly cooled, which means they're liable to cracking, and even if they don't crack, to patchy cooking. You can tell these ripoffs because they seem lighter and cleaner, and because their surfaces are minutely pebbled and pitted. The outside of a good iron skillet should be a nice, smooth matte. The inside, the cooking surface, should be smoother, about the texture of a watermelon that has just been washed down with cold water from a garden hose.

If you're buying your skillet new, it won't be black, of course. *Yet.* Curing and cooking and history is what turns it black. It'll be, well, iron-colored. If it is black already, they've painted it. Don't buy it. But I don't recommend buying your skillet new. Your skillet ought to be roughly as old as you are, in my opinion.

So where do you get a good old black iron skillet? Flea markets, probably. You take your chances there. Every now and then you buy a skillet that has a hairline crack. The crack's invisible, but when you try to cook, oil seeps through and sets the gas flame to flaring yellow, or smoke to billowing off the electric coil. And black iron skillets are becoming collectibles, so the prices are going up.

So anyway, you've found your skillet, taken it home, and rubbed the oxidation away with kitchen cleaner and steel wool. It's time for the cure. I've mentioned it a couple of times, and maybe you're puzzled. But there's nothing mysterious about it. Take out a couple of table-spoons of oil or solid shortening, a good soft cloth. Rub the skillet with the grease inside and out. Make sure you get every bit of it. Make the black *shine*. Then put the skillet in the oven and bake it slowly, 250 to 300 degrees, for a couple or three hours. You may have to do this several times. What are we up to? Iron is friendly to lipids. It seems to have pores. It seems to absorb the slippery stuff, and that's how you get your famous smooth nonstick surface.

Now try cooking. Start with something simple like pancakes. If they stick, clean the skillet with a plastic scrubber — no steel wool this time! — and hot water, and cure it again. Now this is very important. You must never — *never* — clean a black iron skillet with soap and detergent. It will strip your cure, and you will have to start all over.

What else can you cook in a black iron skillet? Better to ask what else you can't cook. Gravy. Soups. Soups do wonders in a black iron skillet. (It should be deep-shouldered, of course.) Casseroles. And chili. Spaghetti sauce. I love to make crusts.

And quiches. You make your quiche in a black iron skillet, you won't be getting any snide remarks about not being a real man. Or if you do, you can bonk the offender.

Pot pies. Chicken pot pies, with dill, rosemary, garlic, carrots, mushrooms, and dumplings, baked till the criss-cross strips on top are golden brown.

It's dark outside now and I'm getting hungry. Talk to you later. Time to be thinking of supper. Don't know what I'll cook, but you can guess what I'm going to be cooking it *in*.

—Arkansas Times, *February 1992.*

Just Who Is The Average Arkansan?

A Pollster's Definition

BY JIM RANCHINO

If you think the typical Arkansan is 30 years old, has two kids, is married in a relationship where the husband works and the wife stays home to mend his socks, then guess again. That description is a once-upon-a-time profile of the average Arkansan and his family and now fits only about 12 percent of all households in the state. If you're looking for a picture of the average Arkansan, look for someone who is a bit of a stick-in-the-mud, tight with the dollar, better versed in Biblical than current events but who, faced with such temptations as premarital sex, pot, and the grass-is-greener syndrome, is beginning to loosen up. The Arkansan of today is as much in a state of flux as formerly he represented a state of mind.

In the majority of Arkansas households today, women work at outside, paying jobs. Moreover, the number of households without male adults present has been growing phenomenally, having quadrupled in recent years. Part of the reason is that men in Arkansas and the nation as a whole are not as responsible to the family as they once were and divorces are easier to get. Divorces continue to ravage marriages in Arkansas just as they do across the country, and if a marriage begins for a couple, aged 18 to 21, the chances are about even that it will fail. The new sexual freedoms that allow for togetherness without a legal, formal marriage relationship actually keep the divorce rate from going even higher. Other mores have disappeared for the average Arkansan these days. Premarital sex, the use of marijuana, unfaithfulness to marriage vows are becoming more the rule than the exception.

Socially, the swinging lifestyle still awaits fulfillment for most Arkansans. Habits of early to bed (after about 3 hours of boring TV) and early to rise still dominate the profile. While most families will eat out once or twice a week (they prefer hamburgers to chicken and beer to liquor), the active social life that shows up in the form of going out to sophisticated night spots does not appear in Arkansas, not even in Little Rock. A number of citizens express discontent over the entertainment alternatives, but the simple fact is that Arkansans would prefer seeing a $2.50 Grade B movie to a night out on the town, complete with dinner, dancing and drinking.

Politically, the voters love Dale Bumpers, like David Pryor, are split evenly on Anita Bryant, and worship the Democratic donkey. Republicans win in the state only by luck, disease, or when the Democrats make fools of themselves (which they do, but unfortunately for the Republicans, only on an irregular basis). If you want to run for office in the state and lose, then simply be a woman, a black, a Jew, or a Republican — in that order.

The voters are no fools and are discerning of the differences among candidates. They lean towards the not-so-intense, candid, intelligent, joyful kind of candidate. Demagogues can't get far in Arkansas politics of the 1970s. And while these voters believe in issues deeply (oppose gun control, hate busing, love their country passionately, don't trust unions, etc.) they seldom support a candidate because of his position on an issue.

Liberalism and conservatism, which are nice catchwords, have less significance in the way a person votes to Arkansas than in almost any state in the Union. In fact, liberalism and conservatism in Arkansas are best defined (at least among white people) by a voter's view on racial matters. A liberal likes blacks, but doesn't want them in his neighborhood. A conservative doesn't want them in his town.

For information, the Bible is still read more (and followed less some wags would say) than Time, Newsweek, and U.S. News & World Report combined. The mother paper, the Arkansas Gazette is read almost daily by a third of the people in the state, and the editorials are cursed by about twice that many. Television news is the chief source for information about the state and is 2-to-1 more believable than newspapers. A key insight into the Arkansan's taste is that Tom Bonner, a handsome, smooth, smiling weathercaster, remains the single most popular local television personality in the state. With his looks and poise, he would make a good political candidate.

Psychologically, Arkansans are troubled by a strong belief in their own inferiority. It's a curse that strangles many a southerner—paranoia, some would say. But the citizens of the state have listened too long to Northerners who talk of "backward," "country" Arkansas. Even the intelligentsia and leadership of the state are often trapped by the feeling. When a recent NBC television story on the state portrayed Arkansas as hillbilly heavy, the guardians immediately overreacted to their own sensitivities and defended their homeland in such a way as to document their feelings of inadequacy. Some hide their feelings by making heroes of the redneck image; others "liberate" themselves by blindly imitating their critics and building pretentious suburbs and crime-ridden cities. Still others attend and support the social and literary arts, not quite sure what it all means, but it does provide a badge of identification that say's we're not like we once were.

The character trait that saves the Arkansan from his paranoia is his fiercely independent quality for survival. From the Ozark hills to the eastern Arkansas flatlands, an almost cavalier spirit exists that says Arkansas is on the threshold of something good. It is not yet a fully flowered optimism, but a strange, dogged conviction that our time is coming.

—Arkansas Times, *September 1977*

Overlooked Heroes

BY MELBA PATTILLO BEALS

"It is a natural instinct for a mother or father to protect their young. But when we nine black students attended Central High School during the 1957-58 school year, our parents had to watch us go to school each day, knowing we would be hurt and they could do nothing to protect us," says Jefferson Thomas.

Thomas recalls the story of the sacrifice made by his parents. It is typical of what the other families suffered.

"My father was a part-time salesman for International Harvester. He was only allowed to sell to blacks. Only the white sales boss was permitted to write the sales tickets. He took half dad's profit. My father was also a part-time janitor with the company, arriving early each morning to open up and clean up."

On the edge of tears, Jefferson tells how his father, Ellis Thomas Sr., was called into his boss' office one day and fired. "We're getting too much grumbling from the community," the boss said. "We have to let you go."

The International Harvester executive offered Mr. Thomas an option. He could work for the company in Chicago. But he had to take Jefferson with him. Mr. Thomas refused.

The resulting money crisis meant that Jefferson's mother, Jessie Thomas, had to find work to keep the family going while Mr. Thomas began doing odd jobs for his dentist.

"One great thing," Jeff says, "is that my dentist, a white man, showed compassion for us. He called two of his friends, one an attorney and another business owner who used by father for odd jobs and cleaning."

Despite the difficulties, Jefferson Thomas returned to Central for a second year in 1959-60 to earn his diploma after the 1958-school year closure by Gov. Orval Faubus.

Like Thomas, Carlotta Walls LaNier is a two-year veteran of the battle to integrate Central and a graduate. Her father, Cartellyou Walls, also lost his job because she was a student there. He was a bricklayer in 1957, working jobs doled out by white contractors. The usual length of a job might be two or three months. But when bosses learned that Mr. Walls had a kid trying to integrate Central High, they'd fire him after a week.

"The financial pressure was evident in the lines on my mother, Juanita's, face," says Carlotta. "I watched her age and her hair quickly turn gray as my father was forced to leave town to find work. He would go to Los Angeles or St. Louis for say three weeks, and return home for a week. And through all the coming and going, my mother kept an even keel within our household, trying to run it as normally as possible."

Throughout that first year at Central, despite the turmoil and the financial pressure, Carlotta's parents stood firm and encouraged her to stay the course.

"My folks have always said if you see a gold ring — an opportunity —grab it. And they have always told me to keep my commitments," she says.

Even when Carlotta's front porch was bombed, her family did not relent — she deserved the opportunity to go to Central to better her education.

"I feel bad about the fact that the FBI detained my father 48 hours questioning him about the bombing because he wasn't here at the time. He was working in a restaurant that night, trying to earn the money he couldn't earn as a bricklayer because I was his child and I was in Central High."

If she has any regrets, it is the attention the Central High crisis focused on her. She fears it may have detracted from the nurturing and energy her sisters deserved.

The first black graduate of Central High, Ernest Green, says his mother, Lothaire Green, was courageous despite the fact that his father, Ernest Green Sr., had died the year before.

WARRIORS DON'T CRY

*A Searing Memoir of
the Battle to Integrate
Little Rock's Central High*

MELBA PATTILLO BEALS

"She kept me focused," Ernie says. "She pointed to the goal saying how important it was for me not to give up. Certainly there were times when I thought about leaving—about what it would be like not to have to face the daily grind of being taunted and physically abused, but she would help me see beyond that to graduation and my commitment to what we had set out to accomplish."

Ernie also points to the support he got from his aunt, Treopia Gravelley, a teacher at Dunbar Junior High, and his grandpa, Eugene Scott. "These people were always there for me, listening to what I needed and encouraging me to take it one step at a time, one day at a time."

Thelma Mothershed Wair remembers that as she attended Central High, her parents, Hosana Claire and Arlevia L. Mothershed, encouraged her to keep her commitment. "At times they were undaunted by what they read in the newspapers because I didn't talk much

about what they did to me. They would question me and seem really stressed by what they learned, nevertheless, they would not make demands of me."

The Mothersheds' attitude is notable considering that Thelma had a serious heart ailment. During her walks along Central High's long hallways, she would often kneel to catch her breath.

"What I remember most is that my mother and father always kept calm and kept my feet on the ground," Thelma says.

All of the nine said their parents' most agonizing moments were television reports of violence or hearing at midday that there had been more problems inside the school. They had to wait until 3:30 p.m. to know for certain whether their children were safe. The wait was sometimes made harder by segregationists' cruel telephone pranks.

For example, Dr. Terrence Roberts' mother, Margaret, was called at home in the middle of the day and told her son had been beaten unmercifully inside Central High.

"Mother was told she had better get to school if she wanted to see him before he died. Rushing through traffic with her heart pounding, she made it to school where a Central High vice principal assured her the report was incorrect. Of course she insisted on seeing me for herself. She peeked through the glass insert in the door, but she didn't let me see her. She carried that burden inside for quite some time before she told me."

Terrence says he was most grateful that his father, William, and his mother always told him they supported him whether he chose to go to Central High or not.

Minnijean Brown Trickey says her parents, Robert and Emma Jean Brown, felt the same way. They always conveyed to her that her value or well-being didn't depend on staying in Central. So when she was forced to leave in January 1958 after the now-famous "chili incident" (she dumped a bowl of chili on a white male tormentor), she went on to a productive and successful life without a defeatist attitude. Rather, she knew she had done her best.

Minnijean says the most important gifts from her parents were her father's sense of humor and her mother's way of reassuring her that all was well. "She kept the home fires burning in a way that let me know we could survive no matter what," Minnijean says.

Gloria Ray Karlmark says her mother, Julia Ray, lost her job as an instructor and was blacklisted across the street. For a time, she cleaned houses to keep things going.

"That tragedy would eventually break up our family," she says. "We had to take an offer from a relative in Kansas City so my mother could find decent work.

But even during that period, Gloria remembers that her mother and father, Harvey Ray, were determined to keep her concentrating on academic excellence and productive habits that would give her comfort.

"They kept me to my routine, encouraged me to study and minimized the destructive aspects of our Central High experience. I will always be grateful to them for the strength they gave me and because they allowed me to make the decision to go to Central on my own."

Elizabeth Eckford, the girl who walked alone to face a jeering mob and hostile militia that first day, would also suffer the tragedy of her father Oscar's job loss because of her efforts. Her mother, Birdie Eckford, taught laundry work at the Arkansas School for the Blind and Deaf for blacks. She had four sisters and brothers dependent on that income.

"A calm facade and day-to-day assurance that I could go to school and make it work was most valuable," says Elizabeth. "Like several of the others, my parents were called to school to check on my probable demise. Of course, it taxed them terribly."

Elizabeth's father often drove some of the nine back and forth to Central. She especially remembers a cold afternoon when he arrived and he and four of the nine were trapped amid flying snow balls filled with rocks.

"It devastated him that he could do nothing to protect us as the police and school officials stood looking on. Nevertheless, he kept his dignity about him and that enabled us to keep ours."

As I prepared this article, I was saddened to realize what a collective price we had paid. And, at that, it is but a scratch on the surface of a deep loss.

Like the others, my mother, Dr. Lois Pattillo lost her job. She had been a school teacher with a good record for 14 years. Just after telling her she had done an excellent job, the superintendent of the North Little Rock schools told her he could not renew her contract for the year 1958-59. It was a terrible thing to do because she was supporting me, my brother Conrad and my grandmother, India Peyton.

I watched day after day as Mother's and Grandmother's health deteriorated. Worry lines took over my face. I heard them whispering late at night about our alternatives. But Mother was determined not to allow such an outcome. She would not be deterred by people trying to deny her equality, she said.

My home had been my sanctuary. It was taken away by this problem that plagued us day and night and in every way, down to the fast-disappearing morsels of food we had left to eat.

Drastic circumstances called for drastic measures. After trying every avenue we knew without response, we turned to the media — the same newspapers that covered our Central High attendance now listened to our story and printed it on the front page.

Within days, mother got her job back. But things were not the same. We knew now that predators not only could shoot into our home and attack us physically, they could take away our very foundations. Where then could we turn?

Today as I visit my mother in her nursing home, I bow to kiss this brilliant woman on her forehead. At age 84, after four strokes, she no longer recognizes me. But I can't keep myself from wondering how much different her life might have been had I not been one of the Little Rock Nine; had I not risked life and limb and the well-being of myself and my family.

And then I am comforted to remember that she would have had it no other way. Over and over again, she and my grandmother India would say, "Above all else, Melba, you are an American citizen with all the rights therein. You must always see and be seen as equal!"

— *Arkansas Times, Sep. 19, 1997. (Beals was a high school junior when she was one of the Little Rock Nine who desegregated Central High School. She graduated from Central in 1960.)*

The National Car Of Arkansas

BY JAMES MORGAN

I love Arkansas with the deep true belief of the adoptive son. I was born in Mississippi but I chose Arkansas, and in many ways I'm able to feel that Arkansas chose me. I love how Arkansans don't march in lock-step. I love the way they get their backs up and hold grudges. I love how utterly indomitable the women can be. I love the texture of the land. I love the way everybody knows everybody else. I love, at least in theory, the lean no-nonsense ear that produces names like Joe Don, and Jim Bob, and Bill Jack. I love how Arkansans say things like, "I told him how the cow ate the cabbage," and "I appreciate you." I love the way they say "How yew."

Having said all that, I have to confess that I've never—ever—felt any affection for pick-up trucks.

Though my home state of Mississippi has always had its share of pick-ups, I spent a lot of years outside the pick-up belt. After stints in Miami, Kansas City, and Minneapolis, I moved to Arkansas directly from the north shore of Chicago, where the local version of the pick-up truck was the Mercedes station wagon. When I got to Arkansas in 1986, I immediately noticed two things: An unfamiliar phenomenon I labeled "Arkansas Tree Deaths" (people running off the road and being killed by smashing into trees—the newspaper reported occurrences of it several times a week), and an astonishing number of pick-up trucks. I haven't paid much attention to the Tree Death tally (my gut tells me it's been superseded by drive-by shootings), but what I have noticed is the increasing preponderance of pick-ups, even in my non-rural community. A few years ago, Texas Monthly proclaimed the Suburban as "The National Car of Texas." I believe the Pick-Up Truck is the National Car of Arkansas.

Try this: Stand practically anywhere and close your eyes. Then suddenly open them and see if, within your 360-degree field of vision, you don't spot a pick-up truck or two. It's possible not to, but not very often. I live in Hillcrest in Little Rock, and as I'm writing this I can look out my window and see two pick-ups, one of them owned by a lawyer.

That tidbit is important, actually, but hold that thought for a minute. In fact, pick-up truck sales in Arkansas are on the rise, and have been since the beginning of this decade. Dealers attribute this, on part, to the fact that pick-ups are now as comfortable to drive as cars, and they're even more versatile. Donna Jones of the Arkansas Motor Vehicle Department tells me that, in 1990, there were 508,363 pick-ups registered throughout the state; in 1991, the number went to 517,201; in 1992, 530,191; in 1993, the last complete year for which the Motor Vehicle Department has records, the number increased to 539,186. That's compared to a little over a million cars registered each year.

"The pick-up," says Jimmy Snap, who runs the Ford dealership in Walnut Ridge, "is now the Arkansas car dealer's biggest volume item." Joe Morgan of Service Chevrolet in Little Rock agrees. "It's become the Arkansas second car," he says. "In a two-car family, you'll now have one car and one truck."

As usual, though, the real story goes deeper than mere numbers. The attraction of the pick-up in Arkansas is more complex than soft seats and a nice stereo. This has traditionally been an agricultural state, and the pick-up has long been the country boy's workhorse. But as the country boy has migrated to town to work, the actual utility value of the pick-up has been superseded by something to do with image. A bunch of those new trucks are being bought by lawyers and other professional people, including women. These are people who could, in one lawyer's words, "buy the biggest Mercedes-Benz they'll sell to non-Arabs." Instead, they prefer to drive a truck.

But change inevitably produces, and sometimes reveals, conflict. Arkansas is a state that puts a premium on not getting above your raising—but also on pulling yourself up by your bootstraps. When something as rooted in country values as the pick-up becomes "trendy," the result is a funny little class war: Arkansas wrestling with itself over what it has been—and what it fears it might be becoming.

Truck people tell me there are four categories of pick-up trucks in this state:

• The 4-Wheel-Drive Deep-Woods Hunting and Fishing Truck. You can recognize it by the two fan-shaped designs on the windshield; every other inch of the truck is covered with dried red mud.

• The Everyday Down & Dirty Work Truck. It's the one with the plywood hanging too far out the back, and the rubber boots stuck upside down between the cab and the bed.

• The Country Cadillac. Two-wheel drive, extended cab, very clean. Not made for hunting or traditional labor, it's instead the rural family car. In small towns all over Arkansas, it sits side-by-side with others of its kind in front of every business on Main Street.

• The Junior League Truck. Extended cab, leather interior, carpeting, phone. Increasingly found in the ritzy Chenal Valley area of Little Rock and in Pulaski Heights. (The Heights' even has a couple of required colors: black or emerald green with khaki interior.)

The everyday work truck and the country Cadillac aren't all that pertinent to this discussion. They've always been here, and always will. But between the other two classes, one of which is new, there's a polar reaction.

Let me introduce you to two Arkansas pick-up truck drivers. The first one I'll call Joe Don, the second Jim Bob. They're real people, not even composites, and some of you may even recognize them before you finish reading this piece. Joe Don, age 48, is a printing salesman in Little Rock. He grew up on a big farm in the Delta, and he's an avid hunter and fisherman. He's college educated. Jim Bob, 42, is a personal-injury lawyer who also lives in Little Rock. He grew up poor

in the southwestern quadrant of the state, but he put himself through school and has made an enormous amount of money. He wants people to know it.

On weekend hunting and fishing trips, Joe Don drives what he calls "the classic Arkie pick-up." It's a '76 four-wheel-drive Chevy, oxidized red, with sprung hood, right rear fender rusted half off, broken CB antenna, and the driver's side mirror dangling from an encounter with a tree. It has big-tread tires and a short bed, which means better suspension over the ruts and ridges. Red mud is splattered over the body like a Bill Jack Pollock painting. Inside the cab, wadded camouflage clothes spill off the torn cloth bench seat onto rubber floor mats. The odometer shows 227,880 miles, but then this is the truck's second motor.

"The classic Arkie truck," Joe Don adds, "has to have a Ducks Unlimited sticker and an N.R.A. sticker. I have a M.A.D.D. sticker on there, too, just to ward off evil spirits." He loves that touch. He's positioned the M.A.D.D. sticker on the rear window of the cab, just above the crushed case of empty Busch cans in the bed.

Like Arkansas pick-up owners of all categories, Joe Don is happy to talk about his truck. Truck talk is just another dialect of Golf Talk or Fish Talk. What they have in common are good humor and exaggerations bordering on lies. The engine in this truck, Joe Don explains, is a "stroked three-fifty." "It doesn't get good gas mileage, but it's sure got power. It'll pull the set screws out of hell through a crawdad hole."

It used to be that the definition of a new truck was one that still had all the window handles. Those days are long gone. To a guy like Joe Don, Jim Bob's truck—a black 1992 Chevrolet Silverado extended cab four-wheel-drive with a Z71 off-road package—is a joke. He calls such trucks "Junior League trucks" because "most people who own them are married to Junior Leaguers. The husband wants a four-wheel drive to go hunting, but he has to compromise with the wife, who wants something fancy to drive to the club. What you get is a truck that's not suitable for either job well." Joe Don tells the story of a man he knows who wanted to take his new truck to deer camp. "He spent two weeks out in the woods before deer season trimming back trees just so he could go without scratching it."

Jim Bob, who's no longer married to anyone, much

less a Junior Leaguer, is undaunted. "I'll take my truck anywhere," he declares. "I've got a detailer." He will admit that his girlfriend persuaded him to add certain flashy features to the truck, such as the black bug guard across the front and the clear plastic rain protectors over each window.

The differences between Joe Don and Jim Bob show up most readily in their truck stories. Joe Don loves to tell about the time a friend of his was clearing land at a cabin in Northwest Arkansas and his tractor got stuck in a gully. Joe Don backed his old truck down the steep hill, hooked the tractor to the hitch, then pulled his buddy up the muddy slope with no trouble whatsoever. Then, at the top, instead of stopping, he hit the gas and dragged his hollering friend and the mud-covered tractor at 40 miles per hour in front of the cabin, all the time honking his horn so the rest of the guys would come out and see. In Joe Don's world, getting stuck is total failure. Pulling somebody out is total victory.

Jim Bob's stories are different. Oh, he can spin macho tales such as the one about how he dumped 42 landscape timbers in the street in front of McClard's in Hot Springs at lunch hour during racing season. The point is, his truck is so almighty powerful that when he floored it, it took off like something out of a Road Runner cartoon, leaving those timbers—which were sitting on a slick bed liner—hanging there in mid-air.

But his most-cherished stories deal less with performance than with image. "The first weekend I got my truck, I went to a friend's cabin," he says. "It snowed, and that white snow on the gleaming black truck looked great." The next week, he and his girlfriend drove down to New Orleans. "I drove right down the middle of the French Quarter," he says, savoring the memory. "On either side of me, I noticed people getting out of the way."

But nothing tops the time Jim and a buddy stopped at the Tiger Mart in Mount Ida. When they'd bought what they needed, they came back out to find the truck surrounded by teen-agers. "All the local teens, especially the girls, were hovering around just touching that big black truck."

Joe Don and Jim Bob remind me of the pair of magnetized toy dogs I had as a child. One was black, one white, and when you put them a certain distance from each other, the magnetic fields would set up an invisible barrier and the dogs would stay apart. If you got them a tiny bit closer, though, the dueling fields would magically evaporate, and the dogs would slam together as tight as Siamese twins.

Joe Don seems to be lamenting the twilight time of a certain traditional Arkansas macho. Ironically, Jim Bob seems to be driving a pick-up precisely because it is macho. The problem, for Joe Don, is that Jim Bob's truck is now generic, the way so many other things that once were wonderfully peculiar to this state have come to be. In that, he's right. "There used to be such a thing as a non-pick-up market," says Joe Morgan of Service Chevrolet. "That's no longer true. In fact, one of the reasons we don't have the supply we used to have is that GM has to send so many trucks to places like Boston and New York City."

Like the TV commercial says, "New York City?!"

Not only that, but California, too. "Everything originates in California," says Jimmy Snapp of Snapp Motor Co. in Walnut Ridge. "The pick-up that people seem to like, the one with stripes and psychedelic colors, started in California and has now spread across the country."

Be that as it may, Joe Don and Jim Bob aren't nearly as far apart as each may think. They've both got that kind of off-road street smarts that so many people here in Arkansas have. And they're both responding to the world from an Arkansas perspective. Coastal Johnny-come-latelys be damned, a pick-up truck has always parked pretty close to the heart of this state. The pick-up is what generations of Arkansans not only first drove and first worked, but what they first hunted and fished from, first drank in, first made love in ("You know what redneck foreplay is don't you?" says Jim Bob. " 'Get in the truck.' ") It's the vehicle they went to weddings in, baptisms in, funerals in. Somewhere in the history of this state, there must've been somebody whose casket was driven to the cemetery in the bed of the family pickup.

"I'm a truck kind of guy," says Jim Bob. "To me, that means somebody who's relatively unpretentious—a country person at heart." Both Joe Don and Jim Bob grew up with trucks. Joe Don's father managed a huge Delta farm, and from the fifth grade on, Joe Don lived in the country—hunting, fishing, driving pick-ups around the farm even before he had a driver's license. Jim Bob learned to drive in a 1957 Willys, forerunner of the Jeep. Back in the 1970s, when he was in college, he owned a Ford V8 pick-up for a while. It was powerful, but it drank fuel, and he couldn't afford to keep it. Joe Don admits his "classic Arkie pick-up" isn't very fuel efficient. "I tell people I get 20 miles a gallon," he says. "Eight in town and twelve on the highway." Jim Bob's Silverado gets 15 mpg.

Joe Don and Jim Bob are both conservatives, and Joe Don says he believes most Arkansas pick-up truck owners are. "Not necessarily Republicans," he clarifies. "When you move up to expensive Cherokees, that's Republican." Also, both are solidly American-Made men—neither would own a Japanese truck. "I intentionally drive up to see my clientele in a truck, and one that's Made in America," says Jim Bob. "There's not one of my peckerwood clients that doesn't lust after it."

The two also just generally prefer Chevys over Fords, which seems to be a regional thing. Ford is big in the Memphis area, says Joe Morgan, but Chevy has always been stronger in Arkansas. Both admit that, if you really want to be macho, you drive a GMC, the clear choice of the truck purist. "Troy Aikman drives two of them," Jim Bob says admiringly.

In the end, the Arkansas attraction to pick-ups has to do, as so much in this state does, with attitude. It's an attitude of macho, yes, but it's more elementally Arkansas than that. Sitting up high in the cab of a pick-up, you convey a subtle message of independence, of I-can-take-care-of-myself, of defiance even. I know one Arkansas woman who now lives just outside New York City. She drives a 1994 teal extended cab Ford Ranger. Before, she had one without the extended cab. When her parents came to visit, she would meet them at LaGuardia in the truck and drop them off at the exclusive Sherry Netherland Hotel, where the doorman would pop the tailgate and helps the driver's father out. Later the daughter would pick them up again, the father riding in the truck bed, and they would all head out to Le Cirque for dinner. Don't tell me that's not attitude.

And don't tell me it's not Arkansas. For Arkansas, who can't bear to lose the old oxidized, sprung hood and dangling mirror part of their souls to the rush of homogenization, a pick-up truck is the only vehicle to drive. Jim Bob knows. "Although I love both quiche and sushi," he says, "I drive my truck down and pick it up to go."

—Arkansas Times, *Feb. 6, 1998*

Sponsors

Business And History In Arkansas

The fur trade carried on by French hunters in the 18th century was the first
known business enterprise of the Arkansas region, and a salt works in southwest Arkansas was the first commercial venture by American settlers. The
commercial development of the state was retarded for a century after the statehood era by a lack of capital and credit, the result of foolish and corrupt early
financial policies.

Only in the 1940s did Arkansas begin to realize some of its business potential. The period of the state's greatest industrial growth and expansion began in
the 1960s, when the giant international firms like Wal-Mart and Tyson Foods
began to flourish.

Most of the Arkansas business firms, large and small, profiled in this section evolved during this definitive commercial efflorescence, or they came to
prominence and had their most notable success in this period. They're entering the 21st century in the middle of one of the nation's strongest-ever business surges, and altogether their contribution to that surge has been a significant one. They've played an important part in the latter-day commercial and
industrial development of Arkansas, and their advertising made the publication of this book possible.

ALLTEL
Making Communication History

Brothers-in-law Hugh Wilbourn Jr. and Charles Miller quit their jobs with Southwestern Bell Telephone Co. in 1943 with the notion that they could pool their skills and knowledge of the phone business and hire themselves out to the 100 or so tiny companies that provided phones to small towns across Arkansas. Wilbourn was a splicer, testman and switchman and Miller an outside plant engineer. They capitalized their venture with $35 in tools and a $25 one-ton truck bought at a bankruptcy sale.

It seems like naive ambition for the young men to have offered themselves as "engineering consultants" to struggling family businesses that had no capital and serving areas still flattened by the Great Depression. For a time Wilbourn and Miller realized how foolhardy it was. Their only taker was a woman in Mulberry who needed someone to set telephone poles. But they wound up rebuilding her little system, strung out over Ozark mountainsides, and then entered the management and ownership of rural exchanges themselves.

Now they look like prophets. The little business they founded is now a global communications and information services company, both the sixth largest wireline company and wireless company in the country and a world leader in information services with clients in 54 countries and territories.

The founders passed the torch to the next generations long ago, but the basic premise and business strategy that made their enterprise one of the leading regional telephone companies in the country makes it one of the fastest-

For more information:
ALLTEL
One Allied Drive
Little Rock, Arkansas 72202
501-905-8000

growing, technologically advanced and profitable communications companies in the world today.

The company's phenomenal growth the past 15 years is a tribute to Wilbourn's and Miller's business strategy: follow a policy of aggressive but shrewd acquisitions, stay abreast of technological advancement, practice sound financial policy and supply what your customers want. The present company's nearly 8 million communications customers are the result of 260 acquisitions and mergers.

Wilbourn and Miller had more modest ambitions when they set up shop on Kavanaugh Boulevard in Little Rock's Hillcrest neighborhood as Allied Telephone and Electric Co. One of their clients was W. R. (Witt) Stephens, an investment banker who owned a little company that served Sheridan and the surrounding rural Grant County areas including his family home at Prattsville. They told Stephens one day in 1947 at his office on Little Rock's Main Street that they were making no money managing his telephone exchange, which was comprised of 275 hand-cranked phones, a magneto switch board and lines strung under pine trees along the country roads of Grant county. As they were leaving Stephens followed them to the sidewalk and asked, "How would you boys like to buy the company?" They did, on credit provided by Mr. Stephens, and thus was Allied Telephone Co. born.

Allied quickly began buying other small exchanges, first in southern and western Arkansas, then across the state, and modernizing the antiquated equipment. In 1961, Allied converted Fordyce to dial service, linking it with the outlying towns of Bearden, Sparkman, Thornton and New Edinburg and creating the first entirely automated dialing system for both local and long-distance calls in the United States.

In 1968, Allied began acquiring independent telephone companies in other states, eventually moving into Missouri

ALLTEL's Riverdale campus houses the Corporate and Telecommunications headquarters. A fifth building is currently under construction and scheduled for completion in 2000.

and Oklahoma, then Kentucky, Tennessee and Texas, and into other communications ventures. In 1970 it acquired Southern Telephone Supply Co., which had sales offices in Atlanta and Memphis. That company, now ALLTEL Supply, would become a leader in communications equipment, marketing telecommunications, network, data and videoconferencing products in all 50 states.

The pivotal development came in 1983 with Allied's merger with Mid-Continent Telephone Co., to form ALLTEL Corporation. The Ohio company was a Midwestern mirror of Allied. Weldon Case, who had begun as a summer line crewman, founded Mid-Continent with five small independent companies and by strategic acquisitions created one of the largest independents in the country. The union created a telecommunications company with 847,000 customer lines in 19 Midwestern, Eastern and Sun Belt states and a nationwide equipment marketing network.

Wilbourn began phasing into retirement in the 1970s. His son-in-law, Joe T. Ford, who had started with Allied in 1959 as a yellow pages salesman, became Allied's president in 1977. After ALLTEL's formation Wilbourn retired as chairman emeritus. Ford became president of the new company in 1983 and its chairman of the board in 1991.

The new responsibility required scrapping a political career. Ford had been elected to the state Senate in 1966 and served four terms—a 16-year span through five governors.

ALLTEL's creation coincided with the onset of breathtaking changes in the communications industry—deregulation, sweeping mergers and consolidations, and dramatic technological innovation. For Ford and ALLTEL, it was the perfect environment. In the decade after the merger, the company nearly doubled the number of telephone access lines it served, from 847,000 to 1.6 million.

But the new environment was not without anxieties. No one was exactly sure in the mid-1980s that the new cellular telephone technology would actually work or whether the market could be profitable, but the company took the risk and applied for wireless licenses as ALLTEL Mobile. Its first cellular market was Charlotte, N.C., closely followed by Little Rock in 1985.

To prepare for heightened competition in the industry, ALLTEL began to reposition both its wireline and cellular service areas to achieve greater efficiency, selling or exchanging its interests in slower-growing markets for a larger presence in the growing Sun Belt. In 1993, ALLTEL purchased GTE's telephone properties in Georgia. It sold its telephone operations in eight states to Citizens Utilities, moving out of areas where it had a small presence. During the decade after the merger, ALLTEL invested more than a billion dollars in fiber optics and other capital improvements and converted all its access lines to digital switching centers.

ALLTEL was one of the first in the industry to foresee the convergence of voice and data. In 1990, it entered the information services business with the acquisition of Little Rock-based Systematics, which provided information processing and software to the financial services industry. The company quickly merged its own data processing and billing operations into Systematics (ALLTEL Information Services) and made a number of strategic acquisitions and alliances. It acquired Virtuoso, the industry's premier cellular billing, customer service and information management system. In 1992, ALLTEL added Computer Power Inc., the nation's largest provider of software and processing services for the mortgage industry.

Today, 18 of the top 25 U.S. banks rely on ALLTEL for account processing, and its advanced loan system is the retail lending application used by more of the top 100 U.S. banks than any other vendor. More than 34 percent of the dollar volume of outstanding consumer loans and 57 percent of all outstanding mortgages in the country are processed on ALLTEL's software applications. Business Week recently ranked the company 49th among the top 100 best-performing information-technology companies in the world.

The federal Telecommunications Act of 1996 opened the communications market to another level of competition. It spurred a reorganization of ALLTEL's operations to offer customers a broader and more economical array of services and a new round of acquisitions and mergers.

Joe Ford's son, Scott, an acquisitions expert, joined ALLTEL in 1996 as executive vice president with responsibility for ALLTEL's communications businesses and corporate staff functions. Ford had been assistant to the chairman of Stephens Inc., where he spearheaded the company's acquisitions in the media and communications industries. Ford had previously worked in the corporate finance and merger and acquisitions areas of Merrill Lynch Capital Markets. The younger Ford would become president in 1997 and Chief Operating Officer the following year.

In 1998, ALLTEL completed a merger with 360° Communications Co., and gained 2.6 million wireless customers in 15 states. The $6 billion transaction expanded ALLTEL's wireless presence and improved its ability to deliver bundled communications services across its markets. Connecting ALLTEL's 10,000-mile fiber-optic network with 360°'s contiguous markets in the Midwest and Mideast produced dramatic savings in transport costs as well as economies in purchasing, network operations, information technology and administration.

Continuing its push into less populated areas with fewer competitors, ALLTEL purchased Aliant Communications in 1999 for $1.63 billion in stock and assumed debt and added 285,000 wireline access lines and 290,000 wireless customers in Nebraska.

In the fall of 1999, ALLTEL completed a $600 million merger with Liberty Cellular, a privately held communications company that provides wireless, paging, long-distance and Internet services in Kansas.

ALLTEL maintains headquarters for its operations at Little Rock, where the fifth building of its campus on Allied Drive in the Riverdale area is nearing completion. As the No. 1 high-tech employer in the state, ALLTEL now employs more than 4,100 people in the city and occupies more than 1.3 million square feet of office space in greater Little Rock.

ALLTEL's communications customers have swelled from Wilbourn and Miller's 245 in Grant County in 1945 to nearly 8 million in 25 states. More than 1,000 businesses in 54 countries rely on its information services and products. It operates 825 retail stores and produces and markets telephone directories for more than 100 independent companies across the country in addition to its own. The company's revenues have swelled to $6 billion annually, its assets total $10 billion and it employs more than 24,000 worldwide.

In addition to customers and employees, shareholders in the publicly-traded firm have benefited from the company's growth. In 1998, ALLTEL's Board of Directors approved the 38th consecutive annual dividend increase, and the compounded annual return on the company's stock has been 24 percent for the past 10 years.

It is now a far different company than the founders' hand-cranked phone system—except for their basic business doctrine of practicing sound financial policy, and keeping abreast of technology to enrich the lives of customers and the well-being of shareholders.

Arkansas Capital Corporation Group
Building On A Historical Foundation

The Arkansas Capital Corporation Group is unique in the United States. This is because the 42-year-old "granddaddy" of the group, Arkansas Capital Corporation (ACC), was an Arkansas idea that was put together by Arkansans solely to meet the needs of their state in a way that would fit its character. Put another way, ACC is a private, nonprofit company that has 2.5 million shareholders who happen to be all of the residents of Arkansas.

ACC makes loans to create jobs or to save those at troubled Arkansas businesses on which banks and other lending institutions have determined they cannot take a chance. Until recently, ACC had one affiliate—Arkansas Certified Development Corporation (ACDC), which was founded in 1989 to provide small companies with 10- to 20-year loans for fixed assets such as equipment or real estate to expand or start up through the U.S. Small Business Administration's 504 guarantee program.

Though ACC was quite sound financially, it operated so quietly that few outside the state's banking and industrial circles even knew it existed. This changed eight years ago when Little Rock native C. Sam Walls became ACC Executive Vice President and Chief Operating Officer. At the time, Walls knew that at least one change was going to take place: "We believed we had an excellent product, and we were going to market ACC," he said.

But the changes haven't stopped with marketing. Seventy five percent (75%) of all the transactions in the history of both companies have been made in the last eight years. Then ACC was comprised of Walls and two

other staff members; now there are a total of 20 employees. ACC's corporate office is located in Little Rock, but has Regional offices in Springdale, Fordyce and Jonesboro.

In the last two years, three new affiliates have been created and added to the list of services available under the ACC umbrella. These additions resulted in the official name change to The Arkansas Capital Corporation Group. Capital—money to invest with the expectation it will make more money—is the common thread among the five companies, though their funding sources are different.

Arkansas Capital Relending Corporation (ACRC), the third entity in the ACC Group, was organized last year to provide maximum 15-year fixed-rate loans of up to $150,000 for working capital and fixed assets in rural areas and in municipalities with fewer than 25,000 residents.

When Walls became ACC's leader, it and ACDC had about $8 million in managed assets. Now the company and these two affiliates have in excess of $90 million in managed assets, which is a whopping growth rate of 1,100 percent. Specifically, in the last eight years, ACC approved 303 loans, of which it put up $81,708,438 of the total project costs of $146,587,248. (Sometimes ACC teams up with banks or other institutions that are willing to fund part of a loan.) ACDC in the last eight years approved 96 loans; its portion was $37,515,659 of the total project costs of $101,117,660.

In August, Gov. Mike Huckabee and Lt. Gov. Winthrop Paul Rockefeller helped ACC announce the formation of another affiliate, Diamond State Ventures (DSV) as Arkansas' first for-profit venture capital fund or Small Business Investment Company (SBIC) and the fourth entity in the ACC Group. At the time, 41 banks, 3 individuals and Stephens Inc. already had become part-

For more information:
Arkansas Capital Corporation Group
225 South Pulaski Street
Little Rock, Arkansas 72201
1-800-216-7237
E-mail: acc@arcapital.com   www.arcapital.com

ners in the new affiliate, according to Joe T. Hays, its managing partner. Walls is forbidden by U.S. Securities and Exchange Commission (SEC) regulations to mention Diamond State's worth, but he does say it has the potential to be a $60 million entity.

A key difference between the venture capital that Diamond State Ventures will provide and traditional lending is that instead of collateral to secure a loan, the venture capital firm itself will become part owner of the entrepreneur's business and provide management assistance. The money the fund will invest is called patient capital because the business will be given several years to show a profit before it has to start repaying DSV. Banks and other lending institutions usually require loan recipients to begin paying interest and repaying capital within a matter of months.

Unlike a bank or other lending institution that makes money off the interest charged, DSV generally will recoup its investment through increases in its share in the business as it prospers. If the business fails, however, the fund loses the money it invested. "One of the common misconceptions is that if people only had money, they'd be successful. That's a straight untruth, and it gets a lot of people in trouble," Walls said, adding, "One of the values of Diamond State Ventures is that not only do we provide capital, we participate in management development."

Wall's said, "DSV's real objective is to stimulate the creation of a venture capital industry in Arkansas...activity begets activity. By doing this, we are raising the profile of venture capital and stimulating other people to participate." Because DSV is the first of its kind, "it's extremely important that we be successful," he added.

Quarterly profit and loss reports drive Wall Street, but not ACC or its affiliates. "We are not about today," Walls declared. "We are about tomorrow. We have a long-term mentality."

Capital Resource Corporation (CRC), organized early this year and the fifth entity in the ACC Group, is described as an educational vehicle. However, its full vision is to also proactively seek capital anywhere in the world for Arkansas entrepreneurs. From the educational perspective, CRC will help build the Arkansas Venture Capital industry by educating both entrepreneurs and individual investors regarding the venture capital pro-cess. This will be accomplished in a variety of ways including formal courses, mentoring and investment forums. In addition, CRC expects to foster regional investment funds consisting of 'angel' investors to aid in the formation of startup companies in Arkansas. Wall's says, "individuals called 'angels' are the single greatest source of capital for start up companies".

Unlike ACC and its other affiliates, CRC is not restricted to operating in Arkansas, and Walls has been intensely busy recently building relationships with potential venture capital sources in other states to benefit Arkansas.

Because decades went by without Arkansas history being taught in the public schools, many residents today are unfamiliar with the circumstances and the events that made and kept Arkansas poor and undercapitalized, starting with the establishment and the crashes of the State Bank and the Real Estate Bank shortly after statehood in the 1830s. The Civil War and internal civil strife immediately afterward retarded recovery and development. During the first half of this century, Arkansas was almost exclusively an agricultural state that was in bondage to one cash crop—cotton, a situation that was exacerbated by the Great Mississippi Flood of 1927, in which a third of the state was under water; the drought of 1930—the second worst on record, which occurred at a time when farmers did not irrigate their crops; and the Great Depression.

With other Southern states, Arkansas began a drive under Gov. Orval Faubus in the 1950s to attract industries from the North with a promise of cheap labor and other resources. The Arkansas Industrial Development Commission (AIDC) was established by the 1955 legislature as a vehicle to accomplish this. Faubus was aided in his campaign by a future political foe, Winthrop Rockefeller, who had moved to a farm he bought on Petit Jean Mountain and who had decided to devote a substantial part of his wealth and energy to developing his adopted state.

Two years later, the General Assembly enacted legislation allowing the formation of development finance corporations to provide financing for Arkansas firms that could not get funds from banks or other lending institutions. The result was First Arkansas Development Finance Corp., which had capital of $923,725 contributed

C. Sam Walls, Executive Vice President and CCO.

by 43 utilities that purchased preferred stock, and 124 individuals who bought $109,500 in common stock, the equivalent of nearly $7,000,000.00 in today's dollars. The individuals included some of the best-known names in the state at the time—Rockefeller, Herbert Thomas Sr., John Ed Chambers, James Penick, R.A. Lile, and J.A. Riggs Jr.

All of this money was raised in one afternoon in 1957 at a barbecue at Rockefeller's farm. Essentially, all of the money was donated because even though they received "stock" in the company, no dividends have ever been paid. If the corporation were ever dissolved, the stockholders would receive only their original investment, which is valued now at more than $6.7 million. All the remaining assets would become the property of the state.

What makes ACC unique is that it is not part of state government, but it is the only non-public entity in which the state is allowed to invest funds through the Board of Finance.

ACC repays with interest the money it borrows from the state Treasury. "You could argue easily, in my opinion, that this one of the best investments in economic development that the state makes, because no one else generates those double returns [interest and jobs] like we do," he said.

Walls himself has an entrepreneurial background—a man with ideas who thrives on performance. After putting himself through the University of Arkansas at Little Rock (UALR), he went to work for Dillard's in 1969 when the retail giant had only 14 stores. There he participated in the development of the company's renowned computerized MIS system which fueled a desire that burns even now to provide ACC, its affiliates, and the staff with state-of-the-art technology. Walls became an entrepreneur himself in 1976 and has spent 25 years finding the necessary capital to "help put deals together;" he became acquainted with ACC as a funding source and then was offered a job with it. Walls said his wife has told him " this was the job he had prepared for all his life."

Wall's believes that the ACC Group has an excellent opportunity to build on its historical foundation provided by visionary Arkansas citizens. "During the last few years our Board, as well as our Staff, has focused on looking at the horizon and determining opportunities for us to provide leadership and resources." Our Board in particular has given us the freedom 'to be our best, and we believe in aiming to be the best'. We believe this to be a continuation of our founder's commitment.

ACC's Board members are George E. Campbell of the Rose Law Firm at Little Rock; David H. Shindler, Bank of America, Senior Vice President, Little Rock; Bert M. Mullens, Chairman, First National Bank of Russellville; H. Glenn Rambin, Simmons First National Bank President, Pine Bluff; William T. Staed of Subiaco Abbey; Sherry H. Stringer, CPA, of Jonesboro; Gary E. Garton, President, The Bank of Fayetteville; Joseph B. Ford, President, The Capital Bank, Little Rock; Donald H. Henry of the Mitchell, Williams, Selig, Gates & Woodyard law firm in Little Rock; Don Pattillo, President/CEO of Farmers & Merchants Bank, Stuttgart; D. Patton Rudder, CEO, The Peerless Group, Little Rock; Carl E. Baggett, Chairman, First National Bank of Rogers; and these three heads of state agencies who were added ex-officio in 1985—Barbara Pardue, Arkansas Department of Economic Development (ADED) (formerly AIDC); Rush Deacon, Arkansas Development Finance Authority (ADFA); and Dr. John Ahlen, Arkansas Science & Technology Authority (ASTA).

The Arkansas Financial Group, Inc.
Financial Planning With A Team Approach

Because they designed it this way, Rick Adkins and Cindy Conger know the financial planning firm they founded nearly 15 years ago is different from the typical business in their profession and is the only one of its kind in Arkansas.

The Arkansas Financial Group, Inc., of which Conger is president and Adkins is CEO, doesn't stop at suggesting ways clients can invest their money but emphasizes a comprehensive approach to financial advice. Issues such as tax reduction, cash flow strategies, insurance needs, and estate planning are integral to their holistic approach. In this respect, The Arkansas Financial Group "is the only game in town," Conger said, adding, "We don't do modular planning," which is analogous to making decisions in a vacuum — a dangerous approach to financial planning.

No one person can know "everything about everything," however, so the company uses a team approach in which clients interact with several planners as their game plan is developed. Naturally, individuals within the firm have developed areas of expertise which helps assure clients they will have someone who understands their situation and can answer their questions at all times. Additionally, "we refer clients to other specialists when that's appropriate," Conger said.

For example, if a client's "game plan" shows he (or she) needs more insurance, The Arkansas Financial Group refers the client to agents in that business. Referrals are also made to lawyers when the client needs

For more information:
The Arkansas Financial Group, Inc.
225 East Markham
Little Rock, Arkansas 72201
501-376-9051
www.ARfinancial.com

assistance with wills or trusts. Conger can and does handle the tax aspects because she is a Certified Public Accountant as well as a Certified Financial Planner.

The Arkansas Financial Group's services differ from those of stockbrokers and other financial advisers in that they aren't paid for selling any product to clients. Payment for services is on a fee-only basis, which means they receive no commissions from any transactions their clients make. This helps eliminate the conflicts of interest that clients have with other advisers.

Many financial planners talk about long-term investing, but Adkins and Conger really mean it. "People put their lives in our hands and we take that seriously," she exclaimed. Conger and Adkins are so conscious of this she said, that they realize when they hire new employees that "we're hiring our replacements and they need to be around for 20 years" to know and serve the needs of clients if the two founders decide to retire decades from now or if, heaven forbid, something happens to either or both.

Relationships are what The Arkansas Financial Group values and what makes it thrive. "They [our clients] place a great deal of trust in us. We don't have a lot of barriers between our clients and us. They can talk to us about almost anything."

The Arkansas Financial Group, Conger continued, seeks clients "who value long-term professional relationships, who appreciate the worth of high quality, objective, professional advice and service, and who are willing to work with us as we develop sound, long-term solutions rather than a 'quick fix.'"

Because The Arkansas Financial Group is concerned about the long-term, saving is built into almost every plan, particularly for its younger clients. "We want saving to become an unconscious (automatic) action for clients and spending to be something they do consciously,"

Conger explained. Clients are routinely surprised at how much money they save when it becomes a habit.

Conger had just completed her MBA at the University of Arkansas at Little Rock (UALR) in 1983 and was looking for a job that was more "people-oriented" than the usual work a CPA does when she came across a "blind ad" in a newspaper. She responded, and as she sat waiting for a job interview in Connecticut Mutual's Little Rock office, "out walks this little boy" and puts on his suit coat. "I remember thinking, 'I can't work for a child!'" but the more she learned about the man with an MBA from the University of Mississippi and the more he talked about his vision of the future, "Well, we just clicked," she recalled.

Conger worked as a commissioned agent for Adkins for 15 months, during which they found they had complementary personality and character strengths. For example, Adkins is the more analytical of the two, but she is the better manager. In December, 1984, Connecticut Mutual closed its Little Rock office, forcing Adkins and Conger to act on the plans they had been discussing and their shared vision by founding The Arkansas Financial Group, Inc. as a registered investment advisory firm with the U.S. Securities and Exchange Commission.

Financial Planning as a profession was in its infancy at the time and Conger and Adkins found that, unlike today, there was little comprehension or appreciation of the need for it. As one staff person "held down the fort," Adkins and Conger fanned out into the city, educating those who might benefit from long-term, comprehensive financial advice and building a client base.

When a potential client contacts The Arkansas Financial Group, the first step is for the planners to get a clear picture of the client's goals and situation. After a careful review of the client's important documents an estimate of the cost of services is provided. "We learned a long time ago that people don't like surprises, particularly where money is concerned," Conger said.

In addition to doing mathematical analysis of ways to achieve client goals, the firm gauges the client's Risk Tolerance and calculates the client's Risk Capacity. Risk Tolerance is how much risk a client can take and still feel comfortable; Risk Capacity is how much risk would be prudent for a client to actually take based on their life situation.

Cindy Conger, CPA/PFS, MBA, CFP and Rick Adkins, CFP, MBA, ChFC.

AFG planners gather and analyze all of the information — the client's current situation such as assets, liabilities, existing insurance coverage, investments, and current tax strategies. Then they measure the client's goals, Risk Tolerance and Risk Capacity against what could and should be done to reach his or her goals.

Once this is done, the planners sit down with the client, explain options that can be taken, and make recommendations about what could be done to reach individual goals. The rationale behind recommendations is explained so that any concerns expressed by the client can be factored into the ultimate solution.

The "nitty gritty" comes next with the development of a list of tasks, a description of how recommendations will be carried out and a timetable for implementation. Depending on the circumstances, AFG planners may carry out the recommendations for the client or merely serve as a coach, coordinating the process between clients and

(Clockwise from top left) Karron Hofmann, CFP, John Kelley, Dinah Soderling and Kristina Arundel, CPA. Not pictured: Sean Barron

other professionals such as attorneys or bankers.

AFG does not leave its clients to twist in the wind after the game plan has been written. It monitors the client's progress toward his goals and provides quarterly reports on investments. Planners know that life is not static - that a person's situation can change, which is why reviews are done regularly and recommendations adjusted, if needed.

True to his analytical nature, Adkins said there is a scientific approach to investing money. The Arkansas Financial Group uses "Modern Portfolio Theory" that classifies investments by their behavior patterns, determines the appropriate mix of investments for a client and calculates the likely return and risk for the portfolio. By using this approach, The Arkansas Financial Group, can customize a portfolio for clients rather than placing them into a "cookie cutter" portfolio.

Since The Arkansas Financial Group is not a brokerage firm, it places orders for stocks, bonds and mutual funds through discount brokerage firms, acting as a client's agent (for which AFG receives no commissions). Relationships have been developed with various investment firms such as Fidelity Investments, Charles Schwab & Co., Vanguard Funds and Federated Investments, all of which treat AFG clients in a "special way" that is normally reserved for large institutional clients.

From 1988 to 1998 Conger said Adkins gave her the freedom to work nationally with organizations in the financial planning profession. "He was very supportive," she said, which allowed her to serve from 1994 through 1998 on the board of directors of the International Association for Financial Planning (IAFP) after having served on the organization's Registry Advisory Council where she chaired the Registry Admissions Task Force for four years. In 1994 she also chaired the IAFP's Conference for Advanced Planning (CAP) held that year in Washington, D.C., and was on the task forces that planned and carried out the IAFP's 1996 and 1998 annual meetings.

"Now it's Rick's turn to work with national organizations," Conger said. He has been serving on the Certified Financial Planner Board of Practice Standards for the past two years and was recently elected to Chair the Board for the year 2000. This Board develops the manner in which CFP licensees around the world provide services to clients. He also chaired the IAFP's Conference for Advanced Planning in 1999, making the firm the only one in the country to have two members chair this prestigious meeting.

Both Adkins and Conger have established local, state and national reputations. A former adjunct professor of finance at UALR, Adkins created the Risk Capacity IndexSM that is featured in the text and software versions of Practitioner Publishing Company's Guide to Investment Advisory Services, now in its third edition. He also co-authored two of the books in PPC's Financial Advisor series for CPAs.

Magazine, newspaper and journal writers frequently use Adkins and Conger as sources. He has been quoted in such publications as The New York Times, Business Week, USA Today, Kiplinger Personal Finance and Money Magazine, among others. Authors have quoted

Conger in such publications as Physicians Financial News, Medical Economics, Elle and Working Woman, to name a few. She recently has become an oft-quoted source for syndicated financial columnist Jane Bryant Quinn.

None of this national exposure helped The Arkansas Financial Group's growth more, however, than recognition by two prestigious publications, Conger said. In 1997, Adkins was the only Arkansan to be included in Worth magazine's list of the "250 Best Financial Advisers" and Medical Economics magazine's list of the "120 Best Financial Advisers for Doctors." This is appropriate, Conger explained, because The Arkansas Financial Group built its practice serving young doctors, and two-thirds of the firm's clients today are physicians. For the past two years both Adkins and Conger have been listed by Worth as the Best Financial Advisers in America.

In spite of this national exposure, Adkins and Conger feel their company remains relatively unknown in their home state, calling it "one of Arkansas' best kept secrets."

Even so, "We have grown immensely in the last five years," Conger said, noting that as late as 1994, the company still consisted of only her, Adkins, a Paraplanner and a secretary. Today, there are two additional professionals and four support staff. And from a firm that began from scratch, it has grown into one with over 100 clients and $100 million of assets under management.

Conger attributed much of this success to The Arkansas Financial Group's participation three years ago in a "study group" made up of planners from nine firms around the country who are similar in size and mission. "We pick each other's brains...and serve as a board of directors for each other; we no longer have to do it all by ourselves," she said. When one company has a problem and is looking for advice, "we use our meetings or e-mail to discuss it." In 1996 she recalled, the firm needed to hire another professional. Adkins and Conger were hesitant, unsure that the firm's revenues would support this move, but they took the advice of the group. Hiring that additional person has more than paid off in allowing the firm to grow and serve more clients. There has to be something to this networking business because "all nine firms have grown rapidly and become much more efficient over the past three years," she reported.

Speaking of e-mail, the company has positioned itself for the 21st Century by creating a site on the Internet that allows people to become acquainted with the firm, its officers and employees (biographies of all AFG principals and financial advisers are included). Browsers can also click on a "link" that provides explanations about financial markets and how they operate, market news (without being bombarded with bulletin board ads) and helpful financial calculators. Clients are able to use this site to obtain an update on their portfolio information.

Adkins and Conger said their clients typically have certain characteristics. "They're bright, affluent, goal-oriented, busy, demanding people who appreciate service and expect value." That's why the company's slogan has remained "Helping Busy People Make Smart Financial Decisions."

Bank Of The Ozarks

Branching Its Way To Number One

In 1979, 25 year-old George Gleason bought control of Bank of Ozark, a $28 million bank with branches in Ozark and Altus. While owning a bank might satisfy most young men, Gleason had a bigger vision — to build Arkansas' premier banking organization.

In the past 20 years, Bank of Ozark, now renamed Bank of the Ozarks, has achieved numerous milestones. In May of this year, Bank of the Ozarks accomplished yet another piece of Gleason's vision when it became the largest state-chartered bank in Arkansas. With $757 million in total assets, the bank now stands atop the list of the 145 state-chartered banks.

In the process of growing 27-fold in 20 years, from $28 million to $757 million in total assets, Gleason and his management team have seen it all. From the ultra high interest rates of the early 1980's to the current record setting economic expansion, they have been successful. The bank has successfully navigated through the oil bust, the savings and loan crisis and the real estate collapse of the turbulent 1980's. The bank has thrived in the midst of the mergers, acquisitions and industry consolidation of the 1990's. Through it all the bank has maintained a steady course and now stands ready to enter the age of Internet banking.

The bank's success has come from a combination of hard work and its commitment to three simple principles: provide customers great service, give them the products they want, and offer them competitive pricing. It is a strategy that has made Gleason and Bank of the Ozarks a hit with customers, but often unpopular among competitors.

De Novo Branching Strategy

By 1994, Bank of the Ozarks had grown to five offices — in Ozark (two), Altus, Jasper and Western Grove. At that time, the bank embarked on an aggressive growth program through a de novo (to start anew) branching strategy. With the anticipated wave of bank mergers and statewide branching looming on the horizon, Bank of the Ozarks believed it could build an Arkansas franchise that could compete with the largest competitors in the state. While many banks chose to expand through buying other banks, Bank of the Ozarks determined that with good locations and experienced management they could implement a de novo strategy and expand rapidly and efficiently. This strategy has worked amazingly well. As of September 1999, the bank had successfully expanded into 15 communities with 21 locations in western, northern and central Arkansas. The locations stretch from Little Rock north up Highway 65 to Harrison and west along Interstate 40 to the western edge of the state in Fort Smith.

The bank is continuing its growth and de novo strategy with plans to open five additional offices in the near future. Two new offices were to open in 1999 in Clinton and on North Hills Boulevard in North Little Rock. Three new locations are planned for 2000, including Yellville, a second Fort Smith branch and a branch in the Otter Creek area of

For more information:
Bank Of The Ozarks
12615 Chenal Parkway
Little Rock, Arkansas 72211
501-978-BANK (2265)
www.bankozarks.com

The Bank of the Ozarks Corporate headquarters has been recognized by two city groups for both its design and site development.

Little Rock.

Upon completion of these planned offices by year-end 2000, the bank will have 26 offices serving 17 communities in 11 counties. The bank already has the largest market share in three of those counties. Beyond this the bank expects to continue its expansion strategy, entering new markets with additional offices for years to come.

Community Bank Service

Despite its rapid growth, Bank of the Ozarks remains a community bank dedicated to excellence in customer service. The management and staff of each of its 21 offices are committed to serve the town or neighborhood in which they are located.

While the bank has been able to attract seasoned professionals from large competitors, it also has some key management people who have been with Gleason from the beginning. Danny Criner who is President of the northern division has 23 years experience with the bank and knows the economy and people in the bank's northern division better than anyone in the area. The staff in this region is

well known for their customer service skills and Criner has insured this by hiring the best bankers in the area.

Mark Ross joined Gleason a year after he originally bought the bank and has been involved in managing all the operations of a fast track company. Ross has become President and is in charge of making sure the operational systems and policies are fully up to speed to support the rapid growth the bank has experienced. Ross knows that providing excellent customer service involves making sure the front line people have the systems in place to give them the ability to perform their best.

At Bank of the Ozarks, the employees frequently know the names of the people who bank with them. They know what is going on in their lives. And when someone applies for a loan, that applicant is not just another number. According to Gleason, the majority of branch managers are experienced lenders and have the authority to make decisions on most of the loan requests they receive. It's not like some banks where a clerk takes an application and faxes it out of state for approval.

The loan is approved and made by people who work and live in that community and know the customer. This sort of autonomy is the reason why so many experienced managers and lenders from other banks have come to work for Bank of the Ozarks. It's simple — they're allowed to take care of their customers and make decisions rather than having a corporate committee make them for them.

A good example of acquiring experienced management from a much larger organization is Jim Patridge who joined Bank of the Ozarks in January 1998 as Vice Chairman and head of lending. Patridge was in charge of lending at Worthen Bank for many years and helped Worthen rebound from some difficult loan problems. He was excited to have the opportunity to join a local bank after going through two bank mergers in a relatively short period of time. His expertise has been valuable as Bank of the Ozarks has expanded into more metropolitan markets with larger customers and increased demand for local lending expertise.

"There is no substitute for friendly, personal customer service," says Gleason. "In each market, we strive to hire local managers with deep roots in the community. As we continue to grow, Bank of the Ozarks promises to preserve this best ingredient of hometown banking - fast, friendly service and local decisions."

Advanced Banking Products

"While we continue to provide the friendly hometown service of a community bank, we offer our customers the same services as the big banks. That's a powerful combination," Gleason says. "Bank of the Ozarks can truly take care of the needs of just about any customer. Whether you're a large commercial customer with dozens of outlets and 100,000 deposit items per month, or a retiree dependent on your social security check as your sole source of income, Bank of the Ozarks has the products to fit your needs."

For consumers, the bank offers such customer-friendly products as totally free checking, 24-hour telephone banking, Check Cards, a worldwide ATM network and a broad selection of mortgage, con-

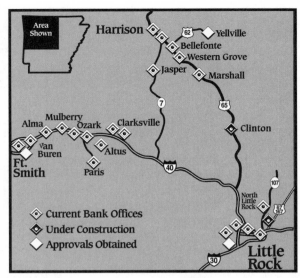

This map illustrates the bank's expanding coverage of the state.

sumer and home equity loans. For commercial customers, the bank offers a comprehensive range of deposit, loan and cash management services. The bank's cash management services include lock box services where the bank collects and processes a customer's receivables depositing them directly to the customer's accounts. In addition, the bank offers sweep accounts where customers earn interest on the investable funds in their account each day, and cash consolidation services where the bank consolidates customer's deposits made in multiple banks across the country into a single account in one location.

Bank of the Ozarks also offers a comprehensive selection of trust services including personal trusts, estate planning, investment management accounts, corporate trusts and a full range of employee benefit plans.

To build and manage a first-rate trust operation the bank knew it had to attract experienced and talented people. The bank was fortunate to get Aubrey Avants to return to Little Rock where he had previously managed a trust operation for a large bank that has since been bought out. Avants started recruiting other experienced trust

The Bank of the Ozarks sign is currently seen at 21 locations around the state—soon there will be one near you.

professionals including Ernie Farquharson who was in charge of Employee Benefit Plans for one of the state's largest trust departments which has also been acquired by an out-of-state bank. This kind of proven trust expertise is hard to find and crucial to building a successful trust department. Bank of the Ozarks wants to continue to attract the type of experienced bank officers who share the bank's philosophy on customer service.

Bank of the Ozarks is also gearing up to offer Internet services, simplifying the process of banking. Customers will be able to get their account balances, perform transfers, initiate payments, check all their account activity and pay bills. Customers will also be able to apply for a variety of loans on the bank's Internet site.

Aggressive Pricing

"We strive to give our customers excellent personal service and great products, but customers also expect great rates," Gleason said. Bank of the Ozarks has a reputation for aggressive pricing that often rankles competitors. Bank customers at some offices were surprised earlier this year to find both a special CD product paying 5.9% and an introductory rate on a home equity line of credit at 5.7%. While this anomaly is an extreme example, it reflects the bank's aggressive nature in offering special rates and pricing, giving its customers real value.

A Winning Formula

While many banks are being purchased by larger banks, that's not expected to happen to Bank of the Ozarks. Over 40 percent of the Company is owned by executive officers and directors and much of the remaining 60 percent of stock in the public's hands is owned by bank customers. Gleason says with that level of ownership the bank can stay the course, providing Arkansans the type of banking services that they deserve.

In the past 20 years, Gleason and his Bank of the Ozarks' team have seen plenty of change. With the rapid advances in technology and Internet banking, they expect the rate of change to accelerate in the next 20 years. But Gleason is confident that Bank of the Ozarks will continue to be successful if it sticks to its simple formula - give every customer great service, great products and great pricing. When executed by Bank of the Ozarks' local managers, this formula seems to be a winner whether you're in a small town like Jasper nestled in the mountains of the Ozarks or working in a high rise in metropolitan Little Rock. It is why Gleason and his growing team call their bank "the Right Bank at the Right Time" for Arkansas.

Baptist Health
Providing All Our Best To Every Patient

It would be difficult to walk down a street in just about any small town or city in Arkansas, begin a conversation about medicine and health care, and not find someone who has been affected by Baptist Health. Health care has changed and evolved, as the history of Arkansas has unfolded. Baptist Health has continued to lead the way with medical technology, innovative treatment options and dedicated physicians and caregivers.

It all began on Nov. 12, 1919 when the Arkansas Baptist State Convention recommended that "a great, modern, scientific hospital" be put into operation in downtown Little Rock. In November 1920, at the corner of 12th and Marshall, Baptist State Hospital opened with 80 beds.

The mission of Baptist Health was born with the opening of that very first facility and remains the same today. A belief that health care is not just a business, but a healing ministry and personal witness of Christian faith. This strong focus combined with incredible leadership helped create a huge following of patients and families that continue to look to Baptist Health for prevention, diagnosis and treatment services.

In 1921, Baptist Health realized the importance of educating future health care professionals and opened the Baptist School of Nursing.

In 1925, a new hospital with 300 beds was built on the original site, in downtown Little Rock. Baptist extended its arm of health care North of the river when it joined with the city of North Little Rock to pass a bond issue and build Memorial Hospital, which opened in 1962. Phenomenal

growth continued with the ultimate relocation of the original hospital to West Little Rock where Baptist Health Medical Center-Little Rock is now located.

Since opening, Baptist Health has impacted the state of Arkansas unlike any other health care organization. Baptist provided many firsts in medicine for Arkansans including, the first open heart surgery performed in 1961; the first intensive care unit, established that same year; the first use of cobalt for the treatment of cancer and the first complete eye treatment center. On Friday morning, Nov. 10, 1989, Mary Wilson of Jacksonville became the first heart transplant in Arkansas history. It was an event that drew statewide media coverage.

Today Baptist Health is the state's most comprehensive health care delivery network, with more than 80 points of access. Major facilities include Baptist Health Medical Center-Little Rock, Baptist Health Baptist Memorial Medical Center, Baptist Health Rehabilitation

Today Baptist Health is the state's most comprehensive healthcare delivery network, with more than 80 points of access, including major medical centers, free clinics, therapy centers and community wellness centers.

For more information:
Baptist Health
9601 I-630, Exit 7
Little Rock, Arkansas 72205
501-202-2000

The Baptist State Hospital opend with 80 beds in November 1920 in a small, wood-frame building on a square block bounded by 12th, 13th, Marshall and Wolfe streets.

Institute, Baptist Health Medical Center-Arkadelphia and Baptist Health Medical Center-Heber Springs. Other facilities in the Baptist Health system include physician offices in Arkansas Health Group (a Baptist Health affiliate), Parkway Village, Healthline, schools of nursing, free clinics, home health and hospice care, therapy centers and community wellness centers.

"The first class care we provide to the citizens of Arkansas would not be possible without the trustees, employees, physicians and volunteers who have been the guiding force in the rich heritage of Baptist Health. They have made Baptist Health what it is today, and what it will become tomorrow," said Russell D. Harrington, Jr., president of Baptist Health. The history of Baptist Health is marked with progress, growth and expansion, but the real history lies in the faces and stories of the people who have felt the compassionate care given on a daily basis. Baptist Health continues to stand by the promise of providing all our best to every patient and every family.

Construction began in 1921 on a 300-bed, five-story brick building, which formally opened Jan. 1, 1925.

Baptist Health

The New Baptist Memorial Medical Center

In 1959 Baptist Health was selected by the North Little Rock Municipal Hospital Commission to operate Baptist Memorial Medical Center.

Over the past four decades the hospital has grown and developed into one of the finest urban community medical centers within the state and region. The original hospital opened with 118 beds. In 1965, the facility was expanded to add a physical therapy department. In 1969, to meet an increasing demand, 30 beds were added. A major expansion in 1978 increased capacity to 260 beds and provided new space for the intensive care and coronary care units, a new emergency department and additional surgical and diagnostic testing facilities. By the mid-1980s, a major shift in health care had begun. New technologies, many of them the result of the computer, allowed procedures that once required overnight stays to be performed on an outpatient bases. To respond, in 1988 Baptist Memorial Medical Center opened a 16,000-square foot outpatient services facility with four surgical suites and special room equipped for treatments. The facility was expanded in the 1990s, including space for the GI lab, the cardiopulmonary lab and MRI.

In the early 1990s Baptist Health began investigating a unique opportunity, to consider the purchase of land and construction of a new facility. Extensive efforts were placed on researching the health needs of Arkansans and then designing programs and services to meet those needs. Countless hours of research and talking to numerous people, resulted in the concept of a more futuristic

hospital, designed with patients and family members in mind. In 1996, ground was broken and construction began.

The result is a $110 million health campus whose centerpiece is a 320,000-square-foot medical center which provides easy access to outpatient services and "patient-focused care," a term used to describe the concept of bringing diagnosis and treatment services to the patient, with not only their health but also their comfort in mind as well. The new facility will open with 135 beds, and due to flexibly planned construction, can quickly have in operation approximately 170 beds.

The campus is easily accessible by Interstate 40, yet provides a secluded and peaceful atmosphere, with trees, a lake and paths for walking. Each patient room has a unique view of the inviting surroundings. A 60-foot tall, glass-enclosed atrium provides the entry an incredible amount of natural light as you enter the facility. "This new campus is a physical expression of Baptist Health's vision to provide comprehensive, excellent, personal care for our patients and their families," said Harrison Dean, senior vice presi-

In 1962, Baptist Memorial Medical Center opened with 118 beds.

For more information:
Baptist Memorial Medical Center
3333 Springhill Drive
North Little Rock, Arkansas 72114
501-202-3000

The new Baptist Health Baptist Memorial Medical Center, located just off Interstate 40, is a futuristic, state-of-the-art facility which will provide the people of North Little Rock with the most advanced healthcare services available.

dent and administrator of Baptist Health Baptist Memorial Medical Center.

The new Baptist Health Baptist Memorial Medical Center continues to provide the people of North Little Rock with the most advanced healthcare services available including, complete cardiac care, comprehensive services for women and children and emergency care services. Every physician, each caregiver, and employee of Baptist Health Baptist Memorial Medical Center is committed to providing these services with each individual patient in mind.

Barton Coliseum
Home Of The State Fair And Much, Much More

There are a handful of buildings and structures in Arkansas that most residents recognize immediately as signature locations in their state.

Most Arkansans, for example, have mental pictures of and know the significance of Old Main at the University of Arkansas at Fayetteville, Bath House Row and Oaklawn Park in Hot Springs, and the Capitol, the Old State House and War Memorial Stadium in Little Rock.

Barton Coliseum is one of those signature locations, and though rock and other music concerts, tractor pulls, horse shows, basketball and ice hockey games and numerous other events routinely draw thousands to this building, it is associated primarily with the annual State Fair and Livestock Show that is in its 60th year.

The fair as Arkansans know it today began in 1938 with the organization of the State Fair and Livestock Show Association. To be sure, an occasional state fair had been held before, starting in 1906, at locations from Fair Park in Little Rock to Oaklawn Park in Hot Springs, but Arkansas was too poor and travel too difficult for them to succeed. In addition, most of these fairs were held before radio and obviously before the advent of television, so the principal entertainment was politicians and public officials making stump speeches.

Conditions had improved slightly in 1937, but Arkansas and the rest of the nation were still mired in the Great Depression in 1938. Many among the state's leaders had begun to realize that if the standard of living was ever going to improve in Arkansas, the stranglehold of "King Cotton" had to be broken by diversifying its agricultural base. The University of Arkansas said they should look to livestock raising as an answer. A group of business, civic, agricultural and education leaders met to discuss how it could foster diversification by promoting livestock raising—an endeavor in which Arkansas farmers had shown no interest before. They approached Lion Oil chief Colonel T.H. Barton of El Dorado to lead the effort, and the Arkansas Livestock Show Association, which later became the Arkansas State Fair and Livestock Show Association, was incorporated as a nonprofit organization on Feb. 12, 1938. Its mission was to raise farm income by improving the quality and quantity of livestock, dairy products and poultry, and rebuilding the fertility of the soil, among other moves.

Barton and his followers concluded Arkansas needed an annual livestock show at which farmers could learn about the best animals to raise and become acquainted with the latest methods to "grow" and market them. They wasted no time, and the association held the first Arkansas State and Livestock Show from Nov. 9-13, 1938, at 5th and Smothers Streets in North Little Rock. Apparently someone forgot to consult the Farmer's Almanac or had forgotten about Arkansas' highly variable weather, however, because rain and snow kept the crowds at bay. Only 17,000 people showed up, and the event was a financial disaster.

Barton and his fellow business/industrial leaders personally assumed the $23,000 loss, but they did not give up, and in 1939, the fair was scheduled in the more predictable month of October. They also brought in an up-and-coming young Hollywood singer destined to become the "King of the Cowboys," the late Roy Rogers, as the principal entertainer. Rogers and his wife, Dale Evans, would return to the Arkansas State Fair many times over the years, the last being in the early 1970s.

For more information:
Barton Coliseum
2600 Howard
Little Rock, Arkansas 72206
501-372-8341

Barton Coliseum around 1949 awaiting outside walls, roof and permanent seating at the north and south ends.

Barton Coliseum today, home for many events throughout the year, including the State Fair.

Joining Rogers as entertainers at the 1939 fair were The Blenders Quartet, billed as the finest group of its kind in Hollywood; The Dell Sisters; elephant acts; and roller skating by the Six Skating Marvels. This time the fair was held under 15 mammoth tents representing 240,000 square feet of canvas, but barns and other buildings later replaced much of this. One of the fair's most remarkable features (to today's patrons) was that a bottle of beer cost only 15 cents!

The day after the State Fair ended in 1942 at its North Little Rock site. Fire swept through and destroyed the buildings. With this site in ruins, the State Fair moved to Pine Bluff in 1943 with the help of Barton and others. The government had restricted the use of gasoline and barred moving animals across county lines because of World War II, forcing cancellation of fairs in 1944 and 1945. As the war was ending, the Little Rock Chamber of Commerce stepped up and donated several acres on Roosevelt Road as a permanent home for the fair, and the 1945 General Assembly appropriated $250,000 over two years to help the association get back on its feet. Modern brick beef cattle, dairy cattle, and swine barns were built first. Through the years, the fair has expanded its home on Roosevelt Road so that it now consists of 135 acres, 96 of which are used. The 1946 fair was the first held at the new location, and in just five years, attendance grew to more than 220,000.

Construction started in 1948 on the fairgrounds' crown jewel, Barton Coliseum, and was completed in stages as funds became available until it was dedicated

formally on September 30, 1952. The structure originally was an open rodeo arena with ascending seats on both sides. A steel-beamed domed roof was placed over the arena in 1949, and then bricklayers went to work erecting the walls. For a time, Barton Coliseum had the largest seating capacity of any arena between St. Louis and New Orleans. A substantial renovation of the Coliseum took place in 1974, and improvements are made to it almost every year. Today the Coliseum has permanent seating for 7,152, but if the arena floor is used as well, the building can hold up to 10,551 persons.

Huge tents were used to house exhibits at the State Fair until the Hall of Industry was constructed in 1966 to accommodate up to 135 displays (or 1,500 dogs when these annual shows sanctioned by the American Kennel Club are held). The Association has 20 full-time employees who, in addition to organizing the State Fair and Livestock Show, make arrangements for the concerts and other events held throughout the year at Barton Coliseum and the other buildings.

Some Arkansans have voiced concerns about the future of Barton Coliseum now that Alltel Arena has opened across the Arkansas River in North Little Rock. Will Barton continue to be used as a major entertainment center other than during the fair? Not to worry, say experts in the entertainment industry, who point out that many "name" stars and groups and other events will continue to favor Barton Coliseum rather than trying to fill Alltel's 18,000 seats. Still others have faith in the capabilities and innovative drive of Yell County's Jim

Pledger, the Fairgrounds' general manager, who demonstrated these traits as director of the Arkansas Department of Finance and Administration under Govs. Bill Clinton and Jim Guy Tucker. Pledger realizes that in a time of fierce competition for people's attention, the fair must deliver top entertainers and some new features every year, though some attendees would be furious if such standard performers as The Fox Brothers and The Robinson Family failed to show up.

To some, the fair is a once-a-year excuse to gorge themselves on corn dogs, cotton candy, funnel cakes, barbecued turkey legs and an array of other "eats" as well as taking wild rides and testing their eye-hand coordination at games on the Midway. But the State Fair is still dedicated to the serious business of education and competition, made possible by the participation of several different departments and outside organizations. Arts and crafts became a major component of the fair in 1965, but was not established as a department until in 1977, the same year the Arts and Crafts Building was added to the Fairgrounds to house exhibits of needlework, sewing, crafts, art, photography, plants, fruits, vegetables, and canned preserved foods during the 10 days of the annual fair. Organizations that are major participants in the fair include the Future Farmers of America, 4-H Clubs, and the Farm and Ranch Club. A State Fair Rodeo Queen and a State Rodeo Queen are crowned each year from among contestants who come from throughout the state to compete. The first Youth Talent Show was held in 1958, and horse judging was added to the Livestock Show the next year.

Special exhibits are arranged annually. This year's show featured an Artmobile displaying works normally seen at the Arkansas Arts Center and a Cultural Booth that demonstrated and explained many of the cultural differences among and between the highlands and lowlands of the state. An Animal Specialties Exhibit offered hands-on cow milking demonstrations, chick hatching, egg-producing hens, pony rides for the children and plenty of animals to pet. The art, science, and tradition of brewing great beers was explained at the Budweiser Beer School, and participants received a lesson in physics at the Air Glory, which pulled two or three persons at a time to a height of 75 feet for a smooth but harrowing flight after a quick release mechanism is pulled. (Some

who tried it said they imagined it was like being on a huge pendulum.)

Roy Rogers and Dale Evans were frequent celebrities at the rodeo through the 1950s, though Tim Holt, Gene Autry, Tex Williams and Arkansas' own Johnny Cash also made appearances. By the 1960s, Arkansans wanted to see the stars of some of their favorite television westerns, and they were not disappointed with visits from Dennis Weaver (Chester) and Amanda Blake (Miss Kitty) of "Gunsmoke"; Irene Ryan (Granny) and Max Baer Jr. (Jethro) of "The Beverly Hillbillies"; Dan Blocker (Hoss), Lorne Green (Ben) and Michael Landon (Little Joe) of "Bonanza"; and Fess Parker, also known as Davy Crockett. In May 1962, pop singer Pat Boone performed at a three-day charity horse show. Ever mindful of Arkansas' whimsical weather, the Arkansas Livestock Exposition hired Major Homer Berry to "prevent" rain over the Fairgrounds during the show, promising to pay him $500 if he "succeeded." No rain came until eight hours after the show ended, and Berry had his $500!

Some of the biggest stars in the country music galaxy have been featured at the fair since the 1970s, including Arkansas native Glen Campbell, Tanya Tucker, George Strait, Reba McIntyre, Tammy Wynette, Roy Clark, Hank Williams Jr., Waylon Jennings, Charlie Rich and Charley Pride. The up-and-coming group, 98 Degrees, opened this year's fair, and superstar singer Vince Gill with special guest Jo Dee Messina thrilled the audience the next night.

Community and business support of the State Fair and Livestock Show has grown noticeably in recent years. All three of Little Rock's network affiliate television stations usually send their weather personalities and reporters to broadcast live from the Fairgrounds, and Channel 4 (KARK) sponsors a discount Ride-Orama day. Power 92/ UPN38/ KOKY sponsor Midway Day. Affiliated Stores is the outlet for special advance gate admissions and discount ride coupons.

Before the Arkansas State Fair and Livestock Association was organized in 1938, the only certainty about a state fair was the uncertainty that there would even be one. Those who may have missed the food, fun, and learning at the 1999 show—and those who didn't—can count on there being a 61st version of the fair in 2000.

The Capital Hotel

"I can think of no name more appropriate than 'Capital Hotel'"

"The Capital Hotel is to Little Rock what the 'St. Charles' is to New Orleans and the 'Galt House' to Louisville, viz., it is the one hotel the mention of which suggests at once the name of the city of which it is a leading feature, and on whose register is written the names of people of taste and means who travel, and are bound to have the best accommodations wherever they may be....'The Capital' has 101 elegantly appointed guest chambers, large office, hot and cold baths, barber shop, bar, news stand, large and cheerful dining room, and the cuisine and general service is that of the highest class hotels in the land."

This was written about 100 years ago, but the general description of The Capital Hotel as the utmost in accommodations for discerning travelers to Little Rock is as true today as it was then. And it was extremely accurate then.

The brick structure with cast iron facade at Markham and Louisiana Streets that would become The Capital Hotel was built speculatively in 1872, not as a hotel but as a three-story building called the Denckla Block that had shops on the ground floor, professional and business offices on the second level, and "gentleman's quarters" or bachelor apartments on the top floor. William P. Denckla, one of the state's wealthiest men, and a partner had bought two city lots for this building venture from former Arkansas Supreme Court Chief Justice George C. Watkins, whose family regained ownership of the improved property in 1874.

For more information:
The Capital Hotel
111 West Markham
Little Rock, Arkansas 72201
501-374-7474   1-800-766-7666
www.thecapitalhotel.com

In mid-December 1876, Little Rock was reeling because fire had leveled its premier hotel, the Metropolitan. "Wanted — A First Class Hotel", screamed a headline in the old Arkansas Gazette. With prodding like this, the Metropolitan's manager, Col. A.G. DeShon, wasted no time, and in seven days, he and Maj. John D. Adams had persuaded the Denckla Block's reluctant agent to evict its current tenants and lease what the Gazette called "the prettiest and most commodious building in the city" to them to be renovated into a hotel.

The first task was to find a name for the hotel-to-be, and Mrs. Morehead Wright is credited with having done this when she wrote Maj. Adams that, "I can think of no name more appropriate than 'Capital Hotel,' as it is a capital enterprise located in a capital building, which will do honor to the capital city, which I trust will prove a capital success to yourself and major [sic] DeShon."

DeShon was in St. Louis purchasing "a full outfit of first-class furniture" for the new hotel as the Watkins family was having the building's windows repaired and calcimine, a kind of whitewash, applied to the plaster walls. The Capital Hotel opened for business on Jan. 21, 1877. Although DeShon wanted to add two wings to the hotel, only one was built along Louisiana Street in the hotel's first year, and in 1878, "water closets" housing indoor plumbing were built in the guest rooms. (Yes, before that, guests used outhouses behind the hotel.) Electric lights gradually replaced gas and oil lamps, and in 1895, ceiling fans were added to the guest rooms. The fourth floor was added in 1890.

From the first, the hotel attracted well-known individuals, but none was more famous than President Ulysses S. Grant, who visited Little Rock and stayed overnight at the Capital on April 15, 1890. There's a story that the hotel persuaded the state prison warden, who bore a strong resemblance to Grant, to stand and greet the public while the exhausted President rested upstairs.

Joe Rantisi, the hotel's current manager, related that the city held a parade in honor of the President that was to pass in front of the hotel. Grant did not know that a group of Southern women planned a protest because of the President's role in leading Union troops to victory in the Civil War. Unlike today's in-your-face protesters, the Southern women silently turned their backs on the President en masse during the celebration.

One of The Capital's most memorable features in the 1800s as well as in its current restored state is an elevator that measures 6 feet 6 inches by 12 feet — the size of some offices today — and has two benches. One story about the elevator, albeit an unlikely one, was that it was "built large" so it could transport Grant's horse to his room, Rantisi related. A more likely explanation for the elevator's size is that the upper class fashion-conscious women who would be among the Capital's clientele wore hoop skirts in the 19th century. Another probable accommodation to the hoop skirt, Rantisi said, was that the women entered the hotel through an oversized side door while the men used the standard-sized front entrance. A hydraulic system has replaced the series of pulleys that originally were used to raise and lower the elevator.

The Capital Hotel is about one block east and across

Since opening in 1876, The Capital Hotel has been a prominent fixture in downtown Little Rock. At the turn of the century, trolley tracks ran in front of the hotel allowing guests easy access to the entrance.

Markham from The Old State House where the General Assembly met from 1836 when Arkansas became a state until the legislators occupied the current but then unfinished Capitol in 1911. The hotel was their favorite retreat, and it is here that the state's movers-and-shakers made their deals. "The laws were made there [in The Old State House], but the deals were made here," Rantisi said. After World War II, most of the lawmakers shifted both committee meetings and their deal-making to a building that no longer exists—the Marion Hotel.

The Capital Hotel, which underwent another major renovation in 1908, was Arkansas' most prestigious social center, the scene of lavish dances and parties during World War I and the "Roaring Twenties." One debutante who attended dances at the hotel during school breaks that were given by units at Camp Pike, was impressed with The Capital's comfortable furniture and plants. The hotel, she wrote, "was decorated with palms in large urns all around the room, and paper duplicates of the tiger, the university mascot, hung on the walls. Between dances and at intermissions, couples sat in overstuffed leather chairs on the mezzanine or strolled on to the balcony which overlooked the entrance. The Bordeaux Drug Store in the downstairs corner of Markham was full of couples. The music at these dances was usually jazz." Her quote can be found today on The Capital Hotel's Web site on the Internet.

From its beginning, The Capital Hotel housed a billiards parlor, and this tradition continued into the 1950s and 1960s with Brunswick Billiards, which was located where Ashley's At The Capital is today.

Almost all buildings, particularly hotels, go through cycles for reasons that defy easy explanations, and The Capital Hotel was no exception. It began to decline and finally could be said to be in "disrepair" in the 1960s. Finally, it joined the ranks of other downtown hotels that had closed. Plans were developed in the 1970s to destroy The Capital Hotel so that a parking deck could be built. Prominent Little Rock architect Ed Cromwell stepped in, however, and led a campaign that put The Capital on the National Registry of historic places in 1974. This put an end to any plans to demolish the structure.

Cromwell also worked to restore the structure, which was accomplished, and a grand reopening for the unique hotel was held in 1983. Rantisi pointed out there are no

Guests may relax and take advantage of the comfort and elegance of The Capital's magnificent lobby. The mosaic tile floor, marble walls and staircase in addition to the hotel's crowning jewel — its original stained glass skylight — transport visitors back to a time of grandeur and luxury in the South.

steel structural beams in The Capital Hotel because this is not how buildings were constructed in the 1800s; the beams are of wood. Architectural historians continue to be fascinated by the Markham Street cast iron facade of pleasingly repetitive arches and columns. The front of the building was designed, cast, and then shipped to the Little Rock site where it was bolted into place on a masonry wall that had been built to receive it. Stories still circulate that the facade was cast in Europe, but historians consider this unlikely because such facades were "a uniquely American phenomenon," and numerous examples still exist throughout the country, includ-

ing the California State Capitol at Sacramento as well as the U.S. Capitol dome in Washington, D.C.

Rantisi said that when workers were in the basement during the restoration, they found the original stained-glass masterpiece that fits into the ceiling of the lobby. The lobby also features a mosaic tile floor, marble walls, and a grand marble staircase. He commented that because of its size and age, maintaining a hotel like the The Capital is difficult and costly, but that he concentrates on finding and fixing any problems before a patron notices them. His experience with other hotels is that a lot of "red tape" is involved in getting projects approved, but this is not the case at The Capital Hotel. Owners of The Capital Hotel realize the significance of the role that the hotel has played in Arkansas history and recognize its importance to the growth and development of downtown Little Rock. Providing guests with luxurious accommodations that are equivalent or superior to those found in the best hotels in the world is the goal of The Capital Hotel. To that end, income from the hotel is routinely reinvested to maintain a standard that is fitting of The Capital's historic heritage. The fact The Capital Hotel has been named a AAA Four-Diamond hotel for the past 15 years is testimony to the achievement of this goal.

The Capital Hotel today has all of the luxuries it boasted in the 1800s plus modern conveniences, such as two phone lines in each guest room and a desk equipped with facsimile and computer capabilities. (When former Gov. Bill Clinton was elected President in 1992 and re-elected in 1996, and often during his two-term tenure, hoards of widely traveled reporters from throughout the world descended on Little Rock to cover events. Many of them insisted on staying at The Capital Hotel, which speaks volumes about its accommodations and service.)

The suites offer a bedroom and a living room that holds a conference table. Rantisi pointed out that when a family checks in, one parent and the children can relax in one room while the other parent is in the second holding a meeting. All of the hotel rooms are decorated with period furniture. Occasionally, Rantisi said, he receives calls from patrons who want to know where they can purchase a bed like the one in which they slept at The Capital Hotel!

Fine dining is a long-standing tradition at The Capital Hotel that is upheld by its award-winning restaurant, Ashley's At The Capital. Recipient of the AAA Four-Diamond Award for 10 years, Ashley's is renowned in Arkansas for its large wine selection. Connoisseurs who are familiar with wine dates and labels come to Ashley's because they know they will be pleased with the selection, Rantisi said, adding that the restaurant staff makes it a point to know the histories of the wines, too.

The restaurant has chefs who can "turn any dish into a beautiful creation," he continued, and the staff is trained to provide flawless service befitting Ashley's use of fine china and thick white tablecloths. "It's a show," Rantisi said, beaming. "You can get food anywhere, but if you want a dining experience, then come to Ashley's."

Ashley's also is legendary for its desserts. Restaurant staff members wheel a dessert cart to the diners' tables that is loaded with an array of treats, but Rantisi said the signature dessert is the baklava cheesecake, an international favorite. All of the desserts are prepared "from scratch" at the restaurant. The hotel will be opening its own bakery soon, the manager said, so that the restaurant will be able to offer homemade breads and rolls as well.

A key part of his job as manager, Rantisi explained, is to notice and be receptive to the needs of hotel patrons. For example, he observed that many hotel guests were leaving for the day without eating breakfast. When he asked why they were not taking advantage of Ashley's breakfast menu, they responded they did not have time to wait. This led to the creation of a breakfast bar where guests can serve themselves, he said.

The hotel business, Rantisi said, is something that "you love or you leave it." He and his staff love what they do, and it shows.

As in the 1870s and 1880s when Little Rock was bustling with excitement and growth, many exciting developments and events are taking place downtown, and The Capital Hotel is right in the middle of them. Rantisi said the hotel enjoys serving the large crowds attending events at the expanded State House Convention Center across the street, that the River Market two blocks east is attracting, and it is looking forward to providing the lodging and meals for many who will be going to events at the new Alltel Arena across the Arkansas River in North Little Rock. It's a great time to be in Little Rock, he said.

Central Arkansas Library System
Meeting The Needs Of The New Century

Established through the initiative of progressive-minded citizens in the early 20th century, the public library of Little Rock has evolved from a solitary public resource into 10 libraries comprising the most valuable and enduring cultural institution in the area.

A group of Little Rock citizens applied for and received a donation from the Carnegie Corporation to build the city's first municipal library in 1910, and about 500 people applied for a library card when the building opened. Nearly 90 years and 9 branches later, the Central Arkansas Library System has 113,000 cardholders, circulates more than 1.2 million volumes, and provides thousands with reference materials and computer access in Perry and Pulaski counties.

The city's first public library was a 23,000 square foot building located at 7th and Louisiana streets and initially housed a collection of 2,150 books. In 1917, the library established its first branch with a library for the African-American population of the city. The library was named for Helen Booker Ivey, a former principal at Capitol Hill Grammar School. The Ivey Library was closed in 1972 as the role of the bookmobile, a vehicle that brings books to inner city neighborhoods, increased.

The Pulaski County Library was established in 1933 and utilized bookmobiles to serve residents living outside of Little Rock. The library was headquartered in the Little Rock Public Library and merged with the Perry County Library to become the Pulaski-Perry Regional Library in 1961.

The Little Rock Public Library's next branch was the

John Gould Fletcher Library, established in 1974 to serve the populous western area of Little Rock. The library was named for the Pulitzer Prize-winning poet from Arkansas.

The Little Rock Public Library and its Fletcher branch, and the Pulaski-Perry County Library and its Sherwood and Jacksonville branches merged in 1975 to form the Central Arkansas Library System. The board of trustees for both libraries voted for the merger to provide more effective library service in the coverage area of the system.

A sixth branch was added to the system in 1976 with the establishment of the Southwest Library in southwest Little Rock. Southwest was initially a storefront library in the Southwest City Mall, but a capital improvement bond election in Little Rock provided funds for construction of the present building in 1979.

The other four branches of the system were established in the 1990s, beginning with the Adolphine Fletcher Terry Library in the northwest portion of Little Rock. The Maumelle Library, the Aerospace Education Center Library, and the Sue Cowan Williams Library followed.

The Sherwood Library was renamed the Sanders Library in 1988 in honor of Amy Sanders, a retired Sherwood city clerk; the Jacksonville Library was renamed the Nixon Library in 1992 for longtime librarian Esther Nixon; and the Perry County Library was renamed the Milam Library in 1993 for Max Milam, a Perry County native who was director of Finance and Administration for Arkansas governors Winthrop Rockefeller and Dale Bumpers.

The growth of the system is evident not only in the establishment of additional branches but also in renovation of existing libraries and an overall increased use of the libraries. The Main Library moved in 1997 to the former Fones Building in the River Market District, and

For more information:
Central Arkansas Library System
100 Rock Street
Little Rock, Arkansas 72201
501-918-3000

The Main Library of the Central Arkansas Library System.

plans are pending for a new Southwest Library. A new John Gould Fletcher Library was built in May 1996, and the addition of an art gallery, coffee shop, and used bookstore is planned in the 93-year-old Cox Building across the parking lot from the Main Library. Renovation of the building should be complete by fall 2000.

The system has also experienced a remarkable increase in usage in the last 10 years. In June 1999, CALS achieved record circulation for a one-month period. Five years ago, annual check out of materials was about 865,135. The figure for 1999 is projected to be about 1.25 million.

CALS has expanded its role as the primary public information outlet by providing access to technology with an online catalog and CD-ROMs. All 10 libraries now provide free access to the Internet.

The system also features the largest membership of any library alliance group in the nation for the size of its budget. The 1,300 members who comprise the Friends of Central Arkansas Libraries volunteer and work actively to promote all 10 libraries, and the organization funds and sponsors projects such as Read to Me and Reading is Fundamental, which encourage reading among young people.

"Trustees and library staff members have historically played major roles in local and statewide library development," said CALS Associate Director Bob Razer. "Involvement of employees in local and statewide library efforts is encouraged and supported. Strong libraries make Little Rock and Arkansas better places to live."

The continued expansion and improvements of the system can be largely attributed to voters' approval of a millage increase in 1993, and the approval of an initiative to allow the issue of bonds in 1998. These votes of confidence will allow the library to update library technology to meet the needs of the new century.

Comcast

19-Year-Old Firm Continues To Seek Ways To Stay Ahead Of Competition

When cable television first appeared in Little Rock, the plan was simply to provide a much clearer picture to viewers of the few over-the-air broadcast stations in the area.

Nearly two decades later, Comcast Cablevision of Arkansas is providing not just all sorts of television and CD quality digital radio imaginable, but it's on the verge of offering access to the Internet, all through 560 miles of fiber-optic lines throughout the area. Comcast's reach extends from Bryant to Jacksonville, serving 86,000 customers.

"It's been a real exciting time to see the industry grow," says Mike Wilson, who came to Little Rock as general manager for what was then Storer Cable in 1986, when cable development was taking off with satellite "superstations" and specialty channels. "I'm convinced there is so much more growth out there, and we are extremely excited about the future."

Comcast in early 1999 launched a 134-channel digital television service. But the company's biggest area of growth is through fiber optics, and Comcast is in the middle of a $45 million upgrade of its Central Arkansas cable system by moving to fiber-optic lines. Wilson happily reports that the project is ahead of schedule. The target date for completion was July 2002, but Wilson says that "with the rate we're going, it will be much sooner than that. We'll have high-speed Internet access in some areas by midyear [2000]."

Where fiber optics will improve Comcast's offerings is with access to more basic channels, digital channels and an Internet connection that will be "hundreds of times" as fast as what web surfers now enjoy, Wilson said. The transmission speed will be approximately 75 times faster than an ISDN line. Access to Comcast @Home will be available at all times from a home computer. E-mail, chat rooms and round-the-clock support service will be available.

"If you ask people what their No. 1 problem with the Internet is, it's the speed," he says. "With cable modems, that's not an issue anymore."

All the improvements go hand-in-hand with Comcast being ready for the 21st century, Wilson notes.

"The industries are converging," he says. "People will be able to work on their TV or watch TV on their computers. The high speed will make a huge difference."

And, though television has big ideas but nothing very definite on high-definition TV for the next decade, the cable industry is readying, Wilson says. "As we look to the industry, we will need to deliver to the home what the consumer wants."

Comcast of Arkansas began in 1980 as Riverside Cable TV Inc., an affiliate of national company Storer Cable. Stephens Inc. was one of the original investors. Riverside received the first cable franchise for Little Rock and set up shop in the old Boys Club building at Eighth and Scott streets.

In 1985, Storer acquired the cable system covering North Little Rock and Sherwood from Times-Mirror. Three years later, publicly traded Comcast Corp. of Philadelphia purchased a 50 percent ownership in Storer and in 1992, the local name was changed to Comcast.

In the 1990s, the industry competition has taken a steep upward swing: home satellite dishes have been Comcast's biggest concern, but also competing cable companies with wireless or microwave-type signal tech-

For more information:
Comcast
801 South Scott
Little Rock, Arkansas 72201
501-375-5755

nology are showing up in apartment complexes in the market.

"People lose sight of it being a competitive industry," Wilson says. "We were strictly competing with the home antenna when this began. People were receiving only five or six channels when cable started. Now, there are nine over-the-air broadcasting stations alone. We know we have to be competitive in every aspect."

To compete against satellite offerings, Comcast pushes its digital product as a strong selling point to potential "dish" users, Wilson says. "With us, you don't buy the equipment. The risk and the investment are ours."

When the fiber optics are up and running, "that will automatically improve the picture," Wilson says. "It means more channels and more reliability. You have a lot less points where there can be failure; the signal doesn't pass through five or six amplifiers, it's just light traveling through glass, and the picture you put on the glass at one end is what you see on the other."

Comcast's current, new digital option allows for 89 video channels (including 29 premium channels and a channel guide) and 45 CD-quality audio channels.

Comcast's commitment locally was further spelled out recently when Wilson was named vice president and general manager of a Comcast area that includes parts of Tennessee, Kentucky, Illinois and Indiana, as well as Arkansas, making Central Arkansas a hub of the company's middle America operations.

Wilson says Comcast is determined to stay competitive with its rates "and we need to. We are very competitive with the various levels of service we do offer."

But, he adds, as Comcast grows with next-century technology, it's not losing sight of the customer who just likes it the way it was in the 1980s.

"We are all very excited about the future, but we try not to — and I insist on this — that we not lose sight of the people who are interested in just plain vanilla cable," Wilson says. "In the old days cable was just a way to pick up stations and make them clearer. Our plans are to have basic service as well as the top premium service."

Comcast's new state-of-the-art headend facility is nearing construction on Gill Street, where 10 satellite dishes are being installed overlooking downtown Little Rock.

Customers can choose from a 12-channel basic package for $8 a month to the 134-channel digital package that runs $69.95 a month.

Comcast is one of the few cable systems in the country to offer a separate black access channel (Channel 14). Evangeline Parker directs the channel as Comcast's public affairs coordinator. The channel produced 790 30-minute public affairs programs last year.

Comcast is committed to local education, having installed cable in all area schools. It also provides Cable in the Classroom–540 hours of commercial-free programming monthly. Comcast carries UALR basketball games and replays of high school football games and is involved in Partners in Education.

When those children are grown, there's no telling what the face of cable will look like, but Wilson assures that Comcast will be in the middle of it.

Cuzins Sports Cafe
Favorite Sports Bar Is Home Owned

Schmoozing with the owner is an everyday thing at Cuzins Sports Café.

Darrell Rhodes and Todd Taylor make a point of being in their sports hot spot every day.

"If you have a problem, we're right here," Darrell says.

Since opening at 9700 Rodney Parham Road in December, 1997, Cuzin's has rocketed to the top of the local sports bar scene. *Arkansas Times* readers voted Darrell and Todd's place the state's best sports bar in 1999.

Darrell and Todd really are cousins, sons of twin sisters. Cuzins was born when Darrell, a former professional baseball player in the Toronto Blue Jays organization, his brother Gary, and Todd, a 17-year veteran in the restaurant business, decided that Little Rock needed a Las Vegas-style sports bar, with enough big screen TVs to show, literally, every sport being broadcast on satellite.

With 11 TVs, including 80", 64" and 48" models, hooked to ten satellites, Cuzins is the only place in town where every single National Football League game is available every weekend.

"Whatever your team is, you can see them play here," Darrell says. Though the Cowboys, Steelers, Packers and Vikings have developed regular, large contingents, an Eagles or Bears fan can make himself at home, eat and root for his favorites as well.

In keeping with the athletic theme, Cuzins features six pool tables, foosball, dart boards, pinball and a basketball hoop machine.

Razorback games really blow the lid off Cuzins. Six former members of the Razorback marching band help to raise the volume, making the atmosphere just like attending a game, Darrell says.

Familiar faces make Cuzins a welcoming place for regulars. Along with Darrell and Todd, most of the "core crew" who started Cuzins is still in place.

"When you walk in, they can set a beer out there and know what you drink," Darrell says. "That's a plus."

More than the city's top sports bar, Cuzins offers live entertainment five nights a week, with no cover charge. Friday night is Karaoke Night, when "It's standing room only from 9:30 to closing," Darrell says.

Cuzins serves lunch and dinner, offering, along with the mandatory appetizers and burgers, Italian grilled chicken, catfish, Philly steak sandwiches, and numerous other dishes. A plate lunch special is available Monday through Friday from 11 a.m. to 2 p.m.

Cuzins is open from 11 a.m. to 2 a.m. seven days a week.

For more information:
Cuzins Sports Cafe
9700 North Rodney Parham Road
Little Rock, Arkansas 72227
501-228-7880

Todd Taylor and Darrell Rhodes, the cousins who own Cuzins.

Democrat Printing And Lithographing, Co.
A Family Business Of Generations

Frank Parke is a fourth-generation printer.

His family's been printing in this state for nearly a century, more than 60 years of that with Little Rock's venerable Democrat Printing and Lithographing Co., according to Parke, who is executive vice president of the privately held company.

"My great grandfather, A.W. Parke, was really a newspaper writer," he says. "He got into the statewide news service with Cleo Harper. Harper's grandson, Lawrence Harper, is currently a DP&L sales representative."

Parke's grandfather, Frank H. Parke, began working in the business in the early 1920s and was active until the last three or four years of his life. The Parke family bought into Democrat Printing and Lithographing in 1936, and his son Bert Parke went to work for the company in 1943.

"My farther, Bert—really Frank H. Parke Jr.—continues to serve as chairman of the board," Parke said. Bert Parke's other son, John Parke is a salesman with the company.

"You very seldom see that kind of continuity," says Parke, who off hand could think only of a handful of other Little Rock family traditions equally long—the Colemans, the Worthens, the Penicks and the Riggs families among them.

The Democrat Printing Company was founded in 1871 at 210 E. Markham, where it published a newspaper and did commercial printing. For some long-forgotten reason, the two ventures parted ways in 1906, with

the paper becoming known as the *Arkansas Democrat* and the printing portion becoming Democrat Printing and Lithographing, or DP&L.

"I mainly do management, sales, customer service—a little bit of everything," says Parke.

He remembers running loose all over the building as a kid with its massive presses and tons of stored paper.

"I don't imagine OSHA would put up with that now," he says.

"I worked here all my life, but started full time in 1980 after I graduated from Hendrix College. [The family business] was never forced on me by any means," he says, but he knew his future was with the company. In college he worked on getting a well-rounded education, graduating with a degree in American history.

Despite the country's headlong rush into the computer age, Parke, who just turned 42, says "I can't imagine a time when you wouldn't want to pick up a newspaper or magazine. We'll always have printed material. Look how many computer magazines there are on the grocery store racks," he points out.

While print media is here to stay, Parke points out several changes in the industry and at his plant over the years. For instance, although much of the composing today is done on computer, DP&L receives jobs electronically, on page negatives and even pasted up pages to be shot. Gone, however, are the hot lead Linotype machines the company occasionally used as recently as a few years ago.

One went to a museum at Arkansas Post, one to Arkansas State, which has a printing program, two went to private collectors and two are in storage until they can be appropriately displayed at the company headquarters.

While DP&L—which can run jobs on five big web presses at once—is huge by Arkansas printing standards, it's fairly modest in this day of consolidation,

---

For more information:
Democrat Printing And Lithographing, Co.
6401 Lindsey Road
Little Rock, Arkansas 72206
501-374-0271

The original home of Democrat Printing and Lithographing Co.

Parke says.

DP&L is capable of running more than 5,000 pieces a day and uses more than a thousand tons of paper a month, most of it coated magazine stock.

"We print for probably 100 publishers, some of them with multiple titles and monthly issues," says Parke.

DP&I billed $23 million last year, an increase over the $19 million and $20 million it had billed in recent years.

The company's also looking at available technology that would allow the metal printing plates to be burned directly from computer generated digital information, instead of from page negatives.

DP&L also is investing in some new binding equipment for its magazines and other publications.

Among the titles the company prints is "Surgical Practice News," "Pharmaceutical News," and "Family Practice News." It also publishes school supply catalogs, an outgrowth of the time when DP&L actually sold business and school supplies.

The print runs on DP&L jobs typically runs between 50,000 and 75,000 copies.

"Virtually all of it mails out of our plant," Parke says. Labels are applied, magazines sorted , loaded into trailers and the paperwork done.

"Technically, we're a branch post office," he says.

The Democrat Printing Company was founded at 210 E. Markham. It expanded in 1922 to the building at 114 E. Second Street, a building designed with reinforced floors and other unique structural details to support the weight of the massive printing presses.

That building has been sold and is being renovated into loft apartments, Parke says.

The presses now are at 6401 Lindsey Rood at the River port, as they have been since 1973.

Parke is not the only one with a lot of history at the company.

The president of the firm is Haynes Whitney, whose father joined DP&L in the late 1960s. Haynes joined in the mid 1970s and has been there ever since.

Another important cog in the wheel is L.H. Elmore, the press foreman, who has been with the company more than 40 years.

"I've known L.H. all my life," says Parke. "It's pretty typical, he joined us straight out of school. He's been very loyal, and a good friend and we enjoy working with him."

Bindery superintendent Otis Price is the same way. Larry Brown has been plant manager for probably 14 or 15 years. These are the kinds of relationships that can endure in a family business, but which are less common in the bottom-line corporate world.

Chances of a fifth generation of printers in the Parke family are modest, Frank Parke says. His two girls, 11 and 13 years old have not expressed an interest and "I don't push them."

His goal for the future? "For the company to continue to grow and to be a good [corporate] citizen for Arkansas and to try to be a good place to work, providing jobs for people in Central Arkansas."

Hadidi Oriental Rug Company, Inc.

Lasting Customer Satisfaction Is Our Goal

When someone telephones to say he has found an old rug that is still is good condition but he doesn't really know what he has on his hands and wants an expert to examine it, Davoud (David) Hadidi feels a surge of anticipation.

"You just never know what's going to come [through the door], and if it turns out to be a 100-year-old piece, it's like seeing a piece of art...it's exciting," Hadidi said. Incidents like this, the challenge of finding what a customer wants, and the fact the rug industry is changing keeps David Hadidi at the top of his form in the Oriental rug business he and his older brother, Yossef, established in Little Rock in the late 1970s.

The Hadidi brothers were frequent visitors to the bazaars and markets in their native Iran and literally grew up watching the master craftsmen of Tabriz weave the high-quality, intricately designed carpets for which the area is renowned. They watched and they learned about the process, giving them a solid foundation on which to build when they opened their business.

"When I was a child, about 10 or 12 years old, my father, my uncle and I would go to the bazaar for lunch. Then we would visit the rug weaving center because the family always had a rug for our house being made on special order. We would go check on the progress...;it was a very slow process. I was amazed at the time spent on these rugs," David Hadidi recalled. "They're all handmade, so sometimes it took two years to weave just one rug." Hadidi noted his family had a say in different aspects of the rugs' production, including specific use of colors and designs. "All that is what got me interested in

For more information:
Hadidi Oriental Rug Company, Inc.
8116 Cantrell Road
Little Rock, Arkansas 72227
501-225-8999

Oriental rugs. I grew up with them," he explained.

A family friend recommended the Hadidi brothers attend college in the United States— specifically in Arkansas, where he had contacts. Yossef arrived in 1970 and earned a master's degree in electrical engineering from the University of Arkansas at Fayetteville. Brother David followed four years later and earned bachelor's degrees in math and business administration from the College (now University) of the Ozarks at Clarksville followed by a masters of business administration (finance) from the University of New Mexico.

Though their interest in Oriental rugs is long-standing, the Hadidi brothers did not start out in this business. "In the beginning," David said, "we were in the real estate business, but because of our background growing up in Tabriz, we were always interested in Oriental rugs and people that we met through our business soon were consulting with us before they bought a rug." Interest was so intense, in fact, that the Hadidis began displaying a few rugs in their real estate office. "People were always recommending that we go into the rug business, so we began to ask ourselves why we didn't open our own store," he recalled, adding, You might say that the people of Arkansas made the suggestion, and we followed it. We've never been one of those aggressive dealers."

Hadidi described the Oriental rug business as "very tricky" because "You can read books on the subject, but experience is the key. You have to see, feel and study each rug. You 'get to know' the rug, what goes into it, the quality, everything. All this experience and knowledge goes to help educate the customer, too—to let them know the differences in these individually handmade rugs and those that are machine made."

Hadidi Oriental Rug Company, Inc., opened originally in west Little Rock but moved in 1984 to its present

David Hadidi with his fine selection of oriental rugs.

ness directly imports some of its pieces. Eight years ago, Yossef moved to California to enter the real estate business. Within two years, however, he was back in the rug business, opening a California office of the Little Rock-based firm in an upscale Los Angeles neighborhood. "This helped us," David Hadidi said, explaining that having a California store "gives us access to sources on the West Coast for our customers." Hadidi already had numerous solid sources on the East Coast, "but we like our customers to have the same access [to products] in Little Rock that they would have in New York" or any other city in the United States, David said. "The more sources you have, the more options you can offer customers...it's a great service for the state."

The rug business continues to change rapidly today as it has for at least the last decade, and David Hadidi attends trade shows in Atlanta and in High Point, N.C., several times a year to stay abreast of trends. He also works closely with local decorators and furniture stores.

As with clothing and furniture, "fashion" colors now tend to change almost annually. Oriental rugs traditionally are navy, red, and burgundy; tradition continues, of course, but now the trend is toward "more decorative" pieces—high-quality rugs in more fashionable colors as well, including black and golds. "And brown and beige are coming back," he noted.

Customers range from cost-conscious couples who are furnishing their first home to those interested in top-of-the-line antique rugs. Interior designers in search of the perfect rug to enhance a room or rooms make up the third category of Hadidi's customers. Lasting customer satisfaction is Hadidi's goal, David said. This includes working one-on-one with customers to understand their decorating needs. If the store doesn't have a rug in stock, Hadidi will contact sources throughout the country or the world until a rug is located. "We want people to be happy. These rugs are going to last a lifetime; they are like artwork in that you can walk on them and have them for years and years and yet they hold their value."

Hadidi also specializes in rug cleaning, restoration, padding, and appraisals. Business in all aspects has been so good that David recognizes "We need more space!" He is pondering whether to expand Hadidi's existing location or open another store in the burgeoning western part of the city.

location in an attractive rock-and-cedar building across Cantrell Road from the entrance to Pavilion-in-the-Park. The clientele has grown steadily, and the store's inventory has expanded from a focus on hand-woven Persian rugs to pieces from throughout the world. "We have the largest selection in the state," Hadidi pointed out, and people from across Arkansas and from surrounding states visit the company's showroom featuring displays of rugs made in India, Pakistan, Turkey, China and Romania.

The inventory ranges today from one-of-a-kind antiques and antique reproductions to contemporary chainstitches and needlepoints. Hadidi holds the exclusive Arkansas franchise for three top lines, and the busi-

Heifer Project International

Helping People Have A Better Relationship With The World

There's a new baby panda in China, and its name is "Heifer." The incongruity remains but the mystery vanishes when Heifer Project International's Communications Director, Anna Bedford, explains that the fragile newborn was named as part of the celebration for the one millionth animal that Chinese families have received through the Little Rock-based organization, headed by president and CEO Jo Luck.

Pandas have been dwindling at an alarming rate, primarily because a minority group in China's interior has been destroying the animal's exclusive food source, bamboo, in order to grow crops for their hungry members. The situation cried out for an alternative, and Heifer Project International came up with one by providing the people with goats, which also happen to supply milk for the baby pandas, and with training in planting and growing fodder trees.

With the addition of the panda and of the silkworm earlier, HPI now uses 22 different kinds of animals to help people around the globe learn to feed and clothe themselves.

Goats to China is but one example of how Indiana farmer and church educator Dan West's vow to sacrifice as much for peace as a soldier does for war has spread throughout the world in 55 years. The dream is growing so rapidly today that Heifer Project International must start a capital fundraising campaign in the spring to build a new and larger headquarters in downtown Little Rock.

West's vow to be a peacekeeper was transformed into action when he went to Spain to help the American Friends Service Committee with Civil War relief efforts. Part of his job was to help distribute limited powdered milk supplies to orphans. There was never enough for all, so he and others were compelled to decide which babies had the best survival chances. Amid these tragic circumstances, West had an idea: why not send cows to Spain so that the people could have a continuing source of milk?

On his return to Indiana, West's idea quickly took root with his friends and neighbors who agreed to raise and donate dairy heifers for shipment and formed a "Heifers for Relief" committee in 1939. When the heifers were mature enough to be shipped, however, World War II had begun and it was impossible to send the animals to Spain. The committee did not give up, and in June 1944, it loaded 17 heifers on the liberty ship William D. Bloxham bound for Castaner, Puerto Rico. One heifer named "Faith" went to a family with 12 children who had never tasted cow's milk.

This was only the beginning. World War II caused such poverty and devastation in Europe that the United Nations Relief and Rehabilitation Administration (UNRRA) immediately arranged to transport more "relief heifers" and developed its own livestock program. The Maryland District of West's Church of the Brethren, having adopted Heifer Project as an official program, recruited more than 7,000 ministers, teachers, farmers and laborers who became "seagoing cowboys" attending the animals on shipments to France, Germany, Greece, Poland and other war-ravaged countries.

In the 1950s, HPI shifted its focus to training, establishing long-term relationships through on-site advisers, and developing partnerships with individuals, gov-

---

For more information:
Jo Luck, President and CEO
Heifer Project International
1015 Lousiana Street
Little Rock, Arkansas 72202
1-800-698-2511   Fax:501-907-2903
E-mail: info@heifer.org   www.heifer.org

In Tanzania, Loti Sandilen (right) and his wife, Lightness, show a neighbor how they carry fodder to their Heifer Project cows instead of allowing them to roam. HPI partners learn to conserve water and improve the soil by contour planting special fodder trees and grasses. The Sandilens have passed on their knowledge and several pregnant heifers to other families.

ernment and private agencies in the countries. Working with partners in receiving nations is still its approach. The 1950s also saw landmark heifer shipments to Korea, Japan, and the former Soviet Union, making Heifer Project's reach truly global. HPI sent dairy cows to the Dominican Republic during that country's civil war, and there are reports a cease-fire was observed daily to allow milk trucks to travel through the front lines to a children's hospital.

In addition to helping Korea and Japan establish poultry and dairy industries, HPI animals played a key role in India's "White Revolution" when bulls the organization provided were crossbred with local stock, leading to hundreds of thousands of improved cattle, increased milk production, and the establishment of modern dairies. President John F. Kennedy's Peace Corps became a source of new volunteers for education and technical assistance in the 1960s, and HPI began a practice in that decade it continues today of purchasing animals in or near project countries rather than shipping them from the United States. This not only saves transportation costs but assures the animals are better suited to local conditions. Donor and recipient nations do not always have to be in proximity, however, as illustrated by the fact Bothar, a partner organization in Ireland, recently shipped cows to Uganda.

Heifer Project International does not approach conquering the poverty and hunger in the world with a "grand solution," Bedford said. Rather, it focuses on helping one person, one family, one community at a time develop their own solutions in ways that honor their cultures and preserves their dignity. HPI does have one expectation that distinguishes it from almost all other assistance groups: when an animal reproduces, its owner is expected to pass one or more offspring to another person, along with the knowledge that has been gained about how to use and care for it. The animals not only provide food, but also the milk, eggs, wool, draft power and other benefits can generate extra income for health care, education, and other necessities.

The United States suddenly was awash in surplus cattle in the 1970s when Congress changed the law so that investing in cattle as a tax shelter was no longer profitable, some of those affected wanted to give their animals to charitable organizations. One group offered a large donation of black Angus beef cattle was given to Heifer Project, Inc., which then had a staff of six based in St. Louis. Heifer Project wanted the Angus but obviously had no place to hold them until its executives, Thurl Metzer and Jerry Bedford, found and arranged the purchase of the 1,200-acre Fourche River Ranch in Perryville (Perry County). Little Rock, particularly the group of business leaders known as Fifty for the Future, welcomed the organization to the capital city. This paved the way for a name change to Heifer Project International and a move of the headquarters to Little Rock.

Fourche River Ranch has become an International Learning and Livestock Center that attracts 30,000 visitors annually, ranging from senior citizens who arrive in their RVs to spend a month working or learning as participants in the popular Elderhostel to school children and youths who have a simulated international learning experience when they draw for lots to determine where they will sleep—perhaps in an "African hut" or a "Brazilian shantytown" called a favela. The youth also draw lots to see who gets access to water and who gets a rice ration or perhaps a live rabbit, all for the purpose of teaching them how to work together and share their resources as those in numerous other countries must learn to do to survive.

The Perry County ranch is one of three learning centers HPI operates at which sustainable agriculture is emphasized is keeping with the organization's concern about making the environment more hospitable. Among other activities, HPI's Overlook Farm in Massachusetts is now assembling goats, donkeys, and sheep to ship to Honduras. Ceres Center in California is the third facility.

With the recent additions of Myanmar (Burma) and Lithuania, HPI now has projects and partners in 42 nations. Central and Eastern Europe became open to HPI after the collapse of the Soviet Union, Anna Bedford said, and the organization is there with the goal of helping the people help themselves and building democracies. The people were adrift, actually and psychologically, when the collective farms closed because they had grown so accustomed to having many needs supplied that they had lost the concept of sharing, she explained.

Russia, the Ukraine, Poland and Romania are the former Soviet bloc countries in which HPI has projects and partners. It had just started working in Albania when the United Nations began bombing neighboring Kosovo last spring to stop the "ethnic cleansing" there by the Serbs. Refugees streamed across the border from Kosovo, many to join family members still living in Albania. Forty refugees descended on one of HPI's partners, but

he did not turn them away; instead, HPI helped him add to his resources. Because of various recent wars in and around Albania, the country is bristling with guns, and HPI is developing a program with the government under which citizens will be encouraged to exchange weapons for a cow.

HPI has long-standing relationships with Tanzania and Kenya in Africa and recently added Ghana and South Africa. Its partners in the latter nation are moving toward autonomy, which means they even will be doing their own fundraising and organizing their own policy-making boards.

Some may think HPI neglects the United States, but they are wrong. In addition to 50 rural projects, young persons in Chicago and Milwaukee inner-city neighborhoods are raising earthworms that make humus, the enriched soil for which apartment dwellers and suburbanites will pay $10 a bag to put in their window flowerboxes or gardens. Also, HPI is generating hope in inner city Chicago youths living in high-rise housing projects by teaching them how to grow fish in tanks and then sell the results to restaurants!

In 1991, HPI took "a huge step forward" by establishing a foundation to assure long-term sustainability of both HPI and it country programs. According to Jerry Bedford, executive vice president of the foundation, the aim is for each country eventually to raise money from local and international donors to maintain and expand its programs.

Asked why Heifer Project International has been experiencing such rapid growth in the 1990s, Anna Bedford said she believes it is because of the unprecedented genuine concern Americans have about their environment and their expanding knowledge of the disparities that exist between their lifestyle and those others in the world are having to endure. "People want a better relationship with the world around them and the planet, and they are excited when they find a positive program like Heifer Project International that helps them do this," she continued.

Bedford attributed much of this to the "new marvelous communications we have" that are bringing the world together as never before. Part of the new communications is the Internet, and Heifer Project International can be found on it, of course, at www.heifer.org.

Jack, Lyon & Jones, P. A.

Practicing Law In A Family Atmosphere

When law is practiced well, it can be a curious blend of science and art.

Sometimes it's like that at Jack, Lyon & Jones, where the founding philosophy of big-firm experience in a small-firm environment is increasingly confronted by the growth and success it has engendered.

In fact, since founded in 1986 by Donald T. Jack Jr., Philip K. Lyon and Stephen W. Jones, the firm has grown to include 19 lawyers with offices not only on the 34th floor of the TCBY Tower in downtown Little Rock, but on Music Row in Nashville and, since late spring, in a new Conway financial district.

Jack says that with the growth, the partners have had to work harder at maintaining the family atmosphere that was once the natural outgrowth of three young friends setting off on a business adventure.

Jack, Lyon & Jones practices a wide variety of general corporate law, including real estate, finance and securities, banking, employment, civil rights, health care, labor and entertainment law.

It's probably the intersection of labor and entertainment law — particularly in Nashville — that has given the firm it's most distinctive niche.

In the Little Rock area, however, the firm's well-known for able and long-standing representation of the North Little Rock School District and St. Vincent Infirmary Medical Center, which it serves as general counsel.

Jack, Lyon & Jones has represented the school district since 1984 and helped win a reversal of a county-wide consolidation of the three districts in the ongoing school desegregation case.

In order for a small firm to have big-firm know how, each attorney must be not only a generalist, but stay current in at least two areas of concentration. "Lawyers having multiple areas of concentration is critical to our growth," says Jones, the managing partner. "However, knowing the law is not enough. Clients not only need to trust their lawyer's advice, they need to know the lawyer will respond when they're needed. Without our commitment to service and modern technology, we would not be able to expand the way we have."

"It's always been our desire, and it's been picked up by the people we've hired, to have more of a family atmosphere," according to Jack. "We have an obligation to support one-another professionally and as human beings. I think that extends to our clients."

"We're small. We know each other's family," says partner Joseph W. Gregory.

Speaking of family, when Gregory's wife, Gena Gregory, joined the firm in April 1998 from the Little Rock firm Laser, Wilson, Bufford & Watts, P.A., she brought a wealth of additional litigation expertise, according to John W. "Jack" Fink, a senior partner.

Among other recent hires is Jeff Look, who clerked at the firm, and has returned, bringing with him additional knowledge in intellectual property rights and trademark law, according to Fink. Intellectual property

---

For more information:
Jack, Lyon & Jones, P.A.
- *3400 TCBY Tower, 425 West Capitol Avenue, Little Rock, Arkansas 72201   501-375-1122*
- *Park Place Office Complex, 400 Salem Road, Suite 3, Conway, Arkansas 72032   501-329-1133*
- *#11 Music Circle South, Suite 202, Nashville, Tennessee 37203   615-259-4664*
www.jlj.com

(Left to right) Don Jack, Jr., Stephen W. Jones, Philip K. Lyon.

rights law, including copyrights and trademarks, is important not only to a firm that represents country music artists and management, but also in an economy where, increasingly, production involves information — digits instead of widgets.

Another thing Joe Gregory likes about the firm — "We return phone calls," a practice he says is not always common in the profession.

Another strength of the firm, he says, is working out tough business situations, particularly those involving the shareholders of closely held companies.

The firm's Nashville connection grew out of Lyon's long interest in country music and a law school friendship with Bill Carter, who later managed several country heavyweights.

While Jack, Lyon & Jones originally represented country artists like Hank Thompson, David Allan Coe and Confederate Railroad, Lyon says the practice has matured. It now frequently represents management, particularly in labor matters, including the management of Crook & Chase, High Five Productions, Curb Records and the Country Music Association. It also represents Bill and Gloria Gaither, Gospel artists who have an extensive production company.

"The Gaithers have more businesses than Carter has little pills," Lyon says.

The new office in Conway evolved because partner Gary D. Jiles lives there and because the firm became general counsel for Conway Regional Medical Center and First Community Bank, according to Joseph Gregory, also a partner. "We've had clients there for years," said Gregory. "It's a growing market and a natural place for us to locate a new office."

Both the Little Rock and Nashville offices have been recognized in the Martindale-Hubbell Law Directory with ratings of A and V, the best ratings given in the categories they measure. The A rating pertains to the quality and ability of a firm's legal staff, while the V rating is given to firms that uphold the highest standards of ethics and integrity.

Jack and Lyon have also been consistently named among "The Best Lawyers in America," with Jack recognized in the areas of health care and corporate and Lyon in the labor law/employment area.

Jack, Lyon & Jones formed in August 1986, after leaving the large and prominent Little Rock firm of House, Holmes & Jewell, P.A. Although philosophical differences over management led to the trio's departure, Jack says the experience they gained there was invaluable.

"We would not have enjoyed the success that we have, had we not had the opportunity to have associated with the many fine lawyers at the firm," Jack says. He singles out Horace Jewell as a mentor to him and Lyon.

"I really enjoy coming to work every day," says Jack. "I look forward to what I do. The common denominator is that everybody here likes being a lawyer and does it well."

Jones Productions
High-Profile Past, High-Definition Future

In 1974, Gary Jones was 28-years-old and already a veteran film maker. At the time he was supervising 135 employees at a new Canadian film studio and television facility, while producing and directing network concert specials. Twenty-five years later, Jones' company in Little Rock provides motion picture and video facilities and services to clients which include Mid-America's leading advertising agencies, corporate video users and television program producers. Jones Productions has also created original programming for the low-budget theatrical, television, home video publishing and syndicated commercial markets. As Arkansas' only resident accredited IMAX® cinematographer, Gary is at the forefront of the world transition to high-definition television.

"With the advent of digital television (DTV) and—more importantly—high-definition television (HDTV), the quality of production will become more important than ever. The type of 65mm, 35mm and Super 16mm shooting that we pioneered in Arkansas will become a requirement for advertisers wanting top-quality images for their commercials and programs," Jones predicts. "And with producers and post-production artists like Rich Ross, Tim Schick, Les Galusha and Mitchell Gates, we offer the best high-def editorial and animation, too."

Gary Jones started Jones Television Productions February 1, 1981. However, the story of Jones Productions begins much earlier, with the purchase of a still camera in England at the end of World War II by Glenn Jones, a young Arkansas aviator who later died serving

For more information:
Jones Productions
517 Chester Street
Little Rock, Arkansas 72201
501-372-1981

his country in the Korean War. Glenn liked to take pictures with the fancy camera, and he passed on to his three sons the same affinity for photography. Gary, his oldest child, was experimenting with photographic special effects and 8mm film making while he was still in grade school in Jonesboro, AR. He became photographer for the school newspaper and was one of the first employees of KAIT-TV when it went on the air July 1, 1963. By the time Gary graduated from Jonesboro High School in 1964, he was already directing local programs and had purchased his first 16mm camera.

After graduate school at the University of Illinois and stints with WFAA in Dallas and ITV in Edmonton, Gary repatriated to Arkansas in 1976 to work for Faulkner & Associates. In the fall of 1981, Jones Productions moved into the building at 517 Chester and became the first independent, professional full-service, film & video production facility in Arkansas. Other Arkansas "firsts" for Jones were the state's first 35mm sound camera package (1984), first Panther dolly in the U.S. (1985), first D2 edit

Father's WWII-era camera inspired Jones Productions' founder.

173

(Left to Right) Alex, Gary & Ryan Jones with some tools of the film trade.

suite (1989), first AVID non-linear editing system (1992), first high-speed 35mm camera system, first production internet web site <http://www.jonesinc.com> and first 100% uncompressed digital edit suite with D5 format (1995), first Master Series Steadicam (1997), first Javelin crane and first digital Super Panther III dolly (1999).

During the summer of 1987, JPI produced its first low-budget theatrical film, "Stay Tuned for Murder" which was distributed world-wide by Imperial Entertainment. JPI produced its second film "Too Scared to Laugh" in January of 1989.

Also in August, 1989, JPI acquired both the former KATV mobile production unit and the services of former KATV mobile operations manager Bob Derryberry. In 1993, Derryberry and Marlene Lamar started Jones Mobile Television.

In 1991, Jones Productions expanded its computer graphics suite. To celebrate its 11th Anniversary in February 1992, Jones Productions upgraded and tripled the size of its second digital editing suite in order to provide the most professional editing facility between Dallas and Atlanta.

In 1995, Gary photographed the first 65mm IMAX® project to be shot in Arkansas. That same year, he and Mitchell Gates, introduced Electric Ink and high-end 3D computer animation to Arkansas.

In 1997, Gary filmed Michael Jordan in IMAX®. In 1998 he traveled to France to film World Cup soccer in IMAX® and in 1999 helped film in IMAX® the final game of hockey great Wayne Gretzky from Madison Square Garden in New York.

After 36 years in the film business, the "godfather" and grand "old man" of Arkansas production shows no sign of slowing down. "My bankers won't let me," Jones claims. He looks forward to working with new generations of eager film makers, including sons Zachary Alex, a junior at Catholic High, and Geoffrey Ryan, a 1999 graduate of Hendrix College.

Gary was the 1989 AAF Advertising Person of the Year and a recipient of an Distinguished Alumnus Award from Arkansas State University in 1991. He is the author of eight screenplays and numerous trade magazine articles.

"Over the next 25 years, the communications business will provides more creative challenges and rewards than ever," Jones concludes. "The trend is toward small, efficient production organizations and strategic alliances with experts in other fields. We will continue our community involvement, technical leadership and creative innovations."

Landers

Honesty *Is* The Best Policy

Landers has become a household name throughout Arkansas, one synonymous with "a good deal" on a car, truck, or sport utility vehicle.

Of course, Landers wasn't always the state's largest or best known automotive dealer. In fact, its beginnings in Benton were rather humble, to say the least, and what Landers has become is a monument to the hard work, determination, and old-fashioned honesty of the Landers family.

Steve Landers realized he had an interest in cars that could not be denied when he was in his late teens and was "hanging out" at a car dealership on University Avenue in Little Rock. "My mother thought I was attending school at UALR (the University of Arkansas at Little Rock) and going to be a chiropractor, but I would walk from the school to the Ford place," Landers recalled.

Soon he was able to talk the dealership's owner into hiring him as the youngest sales man at the business. Steve quickly realized he had found his life's work, though he did not remain there long before moving on to another new car dealership.

When that dealership would not pay him a commission, Steve Landers knew the next step for him and his father, Bob, was to start their own business. They had to find a location and figure out how to buy the cars they needed on what Steve described as a very small budget.

Their first location was a 10-by-40-foot trailer located on a small lot on Military Road. The smallness of the trailer and lot were the least of their worries, however. The trailer also was near some woods, and the mosquitoes were always in an attack mode, Steve said. "The mosquitoes were so bad that we had to start a fire to get rid of them," but it did the job, he said.

The elder Landers and his son had decided to sell used cars. From the outset, they dedicated themselves to customer service, which meant Steve would deliver many of the autos to customers himself. Many times people would see him hitchhiking back to the lot or to his home after delivering the cars.

They also found that their first business decision was shaky. The Landerses had bought used cars—large used cars, and the nation suddenly found itself in an energy crisis when the Arab oil-producing countries invoked an embargo in order to drive up crude prices. Having large used cars on hand was not the best situation to make sales, Steve Landers mused.

But true to what would become their reputation, the Landerses did not give up, and by 1978, the family owned a one-acre lot on which 60 to 70 used cars were displayed. In addition, the family stuck to its belief that an agreement with a handshake was as good as any law.

"If the customer had a problem, then we made it right," Steve Landers said. Soon word spread that a good, fair deal could always be found at Landers. During this time, Bob's nephew, John Landers, joined the team and began contributing what Steve called "a great deal" to the success of the business.

The fruits of the family's labor showed in a new 10,000 sq. ft building. Steve said it was a used car operation that was presented to the public in a style much like one for new cars.

For more information:
Landers Oldsmobile-GMC, I-30, Exit 118, Benton, Arkansas 72015   1-800-264-6365
Landers North, 6055 Landers, Road, North Little Rock, Arkansas 72117   1-888-945-5885
Landers Jeep-Eagle-Chrysler-Plymouth-Dodge, I-30, Exit 121, Benton, Arkansas   1-800-582-2869

Landers first location, complete with a 10x40' trailer and neighboring mosquitoes.

Landers Buick Pontiac GMC, an award winner and the regions largest.

In 1989 Landers purchase a GMC/Olds franchise and was awarded a new Jeep point on Military Road. As a Jeep franchise, Landers was required to sell at least 69 automobiles a year, but the company was doing much more than that, selling over 70 vehicles a month.

Steve Landers said Dwight Everett was an influential member of the Jeep operation, and credits him with helping lead the dealership to its success. The dealership was selling so many Jeeps that it soon found itself with over 200 to sell. "I didn't have a place for all of those Jeeps....The whole city was in a buzz over Jeeps," Steve Landers recounted. Everett has risen from managing the Jeep part of Landers to the president over all operations.

Conditions began to look even better for Landers in 1991 when the dealership was awarded a Chrysler-Dodge franchise, bringing with it 1,053 new cars. By now Landers had over 1,000 new cars and over 400 used cars on a 30-acre lot and a newly purchased dealership building.

The company was raking in awards, too, being named the number one Chrysler dealership in Arkansas, the number one GMC Pontiac dealership in the state and the same for Ford. It also was tops in truck sales in the state, receiving an award as the number one GMC truck dealership in Arkansas. And the readers of Arkansas Times chose Landers as the number one place to buy a car in Arkansas.

Steve Landers said the company constantly receives top customer satisfaction ratings. Arkansans have grown accustomed to seeing the Landers stamp on the bumpers of vehicles, because people from all over the state now travel to Benton to buy new cars, trucks, and SUVs. "They know they'll get good deal and that they'll be dealing with honest folks," Landers said.

Steve Landers credits his wife, Sandy, with much of the dealership's success. He said she has always supported his endeavors and has been a strong influence in his life.

The ability to adapt to changing times while keeping customers foremost in its operations is a major reason Landers has thrived. The Landers of today still has good deals and honesty but a sophisticated edge has been added to get the word out for the 21st Century.

Landers now uses computers to process paperwork and to handle some of the vehicle purchases. Landers once wrote out contracts by hand, but now they are completed on a computer system.

In addition, Landers has a site on the Internet that gives potential customers informa tion on the availability of vehicles, their prices, and an idea of the style and philosophy of the business. Landers' World Wide Web home page contains its motto, "Where character and reputation do make a difference." This is Landers' philosophy in a nut shell, and people throughout the world can read about it while surfing the "Net."

Landers also is gearing up to offer Internet specials. Potential customers will be able to find good deals just by clicking onto the Web site, and they will be able to learn more about the people who make the dealership what it is through pictures and information on the

Landers Chrysler Plymouth Dodge Jeep, the world's largest Chrysler Dealer, located at Alcoa Exit 121.

Landers Ford (Arkansas' Largest), located on University Avenue.

employees.

Since the late 1980s, Landers has become a household name with the help of a friendly, wholesome girl-next-door spokesperson, Leslie Basham. She has taken to the airwaves, inviting Arkansans to Landers for a selection of motor vehicles and deals they cannot find anywhere else. Indeed, people most often connect Landers with the friendly face of Leslie Basham.

Landers is not shy about using television and radio to tell the public about its deals. The dealership's leaders believe communications are important and give them priority.

Steve Landers said he could not do what he does without his staff that now numbers about 700. These individuals love what they do and they like to serve people, he said, but the most notable common denominator among the sales staff is their desire to be above average in their work.

"If you want to be above average, you have to put forth effort. Our people put in 70 to 80 hours a week," he explained, adding in a tone of determination, "They like to win; they like to be on top."

Landers emphasized that a critical part of having a competitive spirit is finding a customer the best deal possible. This means being straightforward, a practice that produces a future pool of customers. "When people know they can get a good deal at Landers, they will keep coming back for good deals in the future," he pointed out, adding that people like familiarity. "Arkansans like to know the businesses they deal with."

Conway resident Jack Spurr III is among those who has been won over by the employees at Landers. "We weren't planning on buying a car, but we went down there and looked, and we test drove a Jeep. We liked how it drove and the deal we were getting, so we ended up buying it," Spurr recounted. "The lady we dealt with was very friendly and sold us on the car," he added.

Steve Landers said he values his employees and credited them with the company's success. He said he knows he has a strong team, and he is not afraid to tell anyone who will listen about it as he mentions people by name and by the divisions in which they work. He demonstrates that the employees are not just faces to him; he knows them, and he's proud of the work they do.

Landers does not just "talk the talk"; he makes every effort to show the employees that they are appreciated, too. The Landers hosts picnics to which staff members are encouraged to bring their families. This year more than 600 employees and their families enjoyed a picnic and a day at Wild River Country.

The dealership also has a service department where cars and trucks are repaired and serviced with parts that are kept in inventory. Spurr said the service department impresses him. "I have had my vehicle fixed there a few times and they have been able to diagnose the problem and they got it fixed," he said.

Spurr described the dealership as "very accommodating." On one occasion, he recalled, "I took my car in to get it fixed and they shuttled me to work." According to Steve Landers, treating the customer as if he or she is the number-one priority is what keeps people coming back.

The Landers team believes to whom much is given, much is expected in return, and this drives the family's record of community service. Donations have been made to the Susan B. Komen Race for the Cure [of breast cancer], the Juvenile Diabetes Walk, the Arkansas Heart Walk, Arkansas Children's Hospital, CASA of Saline County, Inc., and UALR. The list of community service done by those who work at Landers is far too extensive to publish.

Customers are not the only ones who benefit from Landers. The entire Central Arkansas area does, too, through its impact on the economy—particularly on the unemployment rate which continues to go down.

Employees at Landers seem to be approaching the new century with great excitement as they anticipate changes—expanding and diversifying. With this growth will come more jobs for Saline and Pulaski County residents.

To ensure that Landers keeps the service for what it has become renowned, many younger members of the family have entered the business, and they have a stake in keeping the firm's reputation unblemished.

In 1995, the Landers family sold 80 percent of its stock in the dealership to the publicly traded United Auto Group, and Steve Landers has become president of its South Central Region. Roger Penske bought control-ling interest of the Auto Group earlier this year.

Steve Landers was able to think about all of those Arkansas side roads on which he hitchhiked in the early days as he stood on New York City's Wall Street and watched the company's symbol run across the trading board after the sale to United Auto Group.

History has been both harsh and kind to Landers, and the company has met every challenge along the way. From a start on a small mosquito-infested lot filled with big cars in the midst of an "energy crisis," Landers has become Arkansas' largest dealership with the best deals and with a philosophy that the customer is number one. "They are so big that they are able to offer a lot of the extras," Conway customer Spurr said, awe in his voice.

Asked how his company came from a beginning in a trailer to being one of the biggest and best dealerships in the nation, Steve Landers paused and then replied reflectively, "We've been awfully blessed. We've given a lot and received a lot. And we've got some really good people here, and we have good deals."

Determination and customer satisfaction achieved through the old-fashioned value of a handshake coupled with working hard and giving the customer the best deal possible are the principles the Landers family has had from the beginning. By consistently applying these principles, Steve Landers and his family hitched a ride to success.

Little Rock Convention And Visitors Bureau
We're Big On Little Rock

A $23 million, 117,000-square-foot expansion of the Statehouse Convention Center opened in July, marking yet another milestone in Little Rock's inexorable journey to becoming a major player in the nation's lodging and travel industry.

Barry Travis, executive director of the Little Rock Convention and Visitors Bureau (LRCVB), confessed that "it's sometimes difficult to look back" to see where you've been when your attention and energy have been riveted for years on completing an expansion to meet the present and future needs of a city and state that are becoming increasingly attractive as destinations for national and international travelers.

With continuing post-World War II prosperity and the broadening of the nation's infrastructure through super highways and airports, it had become obvious by the late 1960s that tourism, conventions, and business travel would be a major growth industry for decades. Arkansas and its capital city were determined to be a part of that, which is why Little Rock established an Advertising and Promotion Commission to oversee a Convention and Visitors Bureau in 1970.

"We basically began with a single building," Travis recalled, referring to the Robinson Memorial Auditorium, which was built in the late 1930s on the northeast corner of Markham Street and Broadway and named in memory of former Congressman, Governor, and U.S. Senator Joseph T. Robinson.

"Little Rock just didn't have what it needed to

Robinson Memorial Auditorium, now known as the Robinson Center, is home to the Arkansas Symphony Orchestra and many other productions that provide outstanding entertainment for citizens of our city and state.

compete," said Wally Allen, the Commission's current chairman. "The age of the building we had [Robinson Auditorium] and the lack of necessary meeting space would not even permit many groups and conventions to consider coming to Little Rock." Travis agreed, saying, "We saw the need for additional facilities" if Little Rock was going to achieve its goal.

The Commission put the Bureau is charge of seeing that changes were made. Phase 1 of the city's convention strategy was achieved in 1973 when the Camelot Inn (now the Doubletree Hotel) opened adjacent to Robinson Auditorium, which was undergoing a major renovation and whose name had been changed to the Little Rock Convention Center. Now the city had a true convention and meeting facility that included the necessary items to lure groups: an exhibition hall, meeting rooms, and a connecting hotel. "Looking back, I think, 'How did we

For more information:
Little Rock Convention And Visitors Bureau
P. O. Box 3232
Little Rock, Arkansas 72203
501-370-3290
E-mail: lrcvbpr@littlerock.com

make do with just Robinson and the Camelot?' But at the time, that was all we had. Our staff did a great job and made it necessary to expand," Travis said.

Phase 2 of the city's strategy began in 1980 when two of Arkansas' oldest hotels, the closed Marion and Manning Hotels overlooking the Arkansas River, were razed to make way in two years for the Statehouse Convention Center and the Excelsior Hotel. At last, Little Rock had what truly could be called a convention facility.

Retired banker B. Finley Vinson, then chairman of the A&P Commission, spearheaded the effort to name the new convention center. "Statehouse" was chosen to reflect the significance of the center's location next door to The Old State House, which was Arkansas' first capitol when it became a state in 1836. The names of the individual meeting rooms within the convention center also reflect Arkansas' heritage.

"Again, at that time, we were where we needed to be" in terms of facilities, Travis said. "We had some huge meetings and conventions in the original Statehouse [Convention Center], including visits by President Reagan and President Clinton that drew thousands of people to downtown Little Rock."

"It takes more than just facilities to lure people to Little Rock. We know that," Allen said. "What we try to do is build on and publicize all of the great things that Little Rock has to offer as a city. The grandest building in the world would be empty if there were not other things to do and see around it. We knew that what we were doing was working, however, because after 13 years, the Statehouse was not big enough. Larger groups wanted to come or continue to come to Little Rock, so it was imperative that we enlarge our facilities to accommodate them." Little Rock was host to 759 conventions in 1994, and many other groups expressed an interest in coming to the city but could not because the 113,000 square feet of space was either booked completely or was too small. In addition, the Bureau had to pass on trying to attract more than 800 possible conventions to the city because the facilities were too small to hold the groups.

Pulaski County voters approved a one-year, 1-cent local sales tax increase in August 1996 to finance an expansion to the Statehouse Convention Center and to build a multi-purpose arena across the Arkansas River in North Little Rock. The convention center expansion features a new street-level lobby, a registration area, a new exhibition hall (the fourth), and a 20,000-square-foot ballroom. The Statehouse Convention Center now boasts a total of 230,000 square feet.

"Even before our opening in July, we knew the potential benefits of the expanded Statehouse Convention Center, and we were booking meetings and conventions based on that potential," Allen said, adding, "It's already paying high dividends. We can list many examples of conventions booked because of the added space that would have gone elsewhere if Little Rock hadn't met their convention size requirements. Little Rock had to do this. We did it, and it will pay off in a big way for our city and state." The Convention & Visitors Bureau also has initiated many programs designed to encourage local residents and all Arkansans to live, work and play in downtown Little Rock. For example, the "Big on Little Rock" program is a self-promotion initiative for the city designed to increase awareness of Little Rock's benefits, thereby heightening pride. "Big on Little Rock" events have included Alltel's "Big Downtown Thursdays," the "Big Jingle Jubilee," and "The Big Dine Out."

Members of Travis' staff are in the throes of moving into new offices in the expanded portion of the convention center where they will continue to work to increase the number of "person-trips" made to Arkansas' capital city. "Person-trips" are defined as individuals who travel at least 100 miles to reach Pulaski County and who stay at least one night. According to the state Parks and Tourism Department, Pulaski County had more than four million "person-trips" in 1998, and this does not include such individuals as college students and those who work in transportation industries such as airline pilots and flight attendants.

"We sincerely hope that in time we'll need to expand our facilities again," Travis said. "Growth is a great problem to have; in fact, we're trying to create that kind of problem every day."

Little Rock National Airport
A Proud Past...A Bright Future

It started small — way back in 1917. Since that time, Little Rock National Airport has grown into the 76th largest airport in the nation.

Commercial air service was launched in June 1931 by American Airways, now American Airlines, which still serves Little Rock almost 70 years later. From the Jenny to jets, Little Rock National has continued to grow and evolve in order to fulfill its role as the major link in the air transportation system for a vast majority of the state.

Twenty five years ago, Little Rock National handled a total of about 850,000 passengers, compared to more than 2.6 million passengers in 1998.

Quality facilities and quality air service go hand-in-hand. During the decade of the 1990s, about $170 million has been invested in the facility in order for Little Rock National to continue to well serve the traveling public into the new century.

Nine airlines serve Little Rock, with non-stop service to eight national/international gateways, making Little Rock truly one stop away from the world. The level of air service at Little Rock meets and exceeds that of many cities its size. In fact, Darryl Jenkins, director of the Aviation Institute at George Washington University, said that, for its size, Little Rock may well have the best air service in the nation!

The airport operates for today, but plans and builds for tomorrow. If growth is to continue, facilities must be in place to accommodate that growth. The philosophy

For more information:
Little Rock National Airport
One Airport Road
Little Rock, Arkansas 72202
501-372-3439
http://lrairport.dina.org

is a simple one -- standing still is not an option at Little Rock National. The list of improvements is testimony to an adherence to that philosophy :

• A new terminal was opened in 1972

• Runway 4-Right/22-Left was opened in 1991, giving the airport two commercial service runways, along with one used primarily by general aviation aircraft

• Runway 4-Left/22-right was extended by 1,100 feet and overlaid with 15 inches of concrete. All three runways at the airport now boast stronger, more durable concrete surfacing

• A new Air Traffic Control Tower has been constructed

• New state-of-the-art navigation instruments have been installed

• Food/beverage and merchandise concessions are being expanded

• A new multi-story parking deck is being built

• Architectural modifications will soon be made to the front façade of the terminal — the first major facelift since the building was opened more than 25 years ago

• It was announced in September that The Arkansas Gallery, a showcase for Arkansas art as well as other cultural and educational opportunities, will be built at the airport

• At the same time the airport's physical plant has undergone tremendous changes, air service has improved as well. The nine airlines serving Little Rock offer frequent service to many destinations and all at competitive fares.

The Regional Jet, the newest addition to the commercial aircraft fleet, is now serving Little Rock. Comair, with service to Cincinnati and USAirways Express with service to Charlotte, both fly the 50-seat Canadair RJ to Little Rock National. The Regional Jet gives airline schedulers more flexibility both in terms of flight

From its beginnings in 1917, Little Rock National Airpoirt has expanded with the times. Now nine airlines serve Little Rock, with non-stop service to eight national/international gateways, making Little Rock truly one step away from the world.

frequency and markets served. Regional Jets, which fly as high, far and fast as their larger cousins, are expected to take the place of many turbo-prop aircraft in the near future.

In today's competitive atmosphere, you can never take the air service you have for granted, or it could quickly become the air service you had. In recognition of that fact, Little Rock National launched a major Air Service Development Program in 1996. The purpose is simple: to seek enhanced air service from incumbent airlines and work to attract potential new carriers to serve Little Rock.

The strong local market makes Little Rock attractive to airlines, coupled with the fact that the airport makes every effort to ensure that our airline partners operate in a business friendly environment. The airport, for example, charges no Remain-Overnight (RON) free making this airport a good place to park aircraft for the night, resulting in a very heavy early morning flight bank for our customers. All of the improvements at the airport have been made in a fiscally prudent fashion. Despite the significant enhancements to the airport physical plant, the cost-per-enplaned passenger (representing the cost of doing business for airlines) at Little Rock is

$2.34, compared to an average of $5.10 for airports our size.

Not only does the airport periodically make face-to-face visits with carriers, but we are in regular communication with them in-between those visits — outlining air service requests, and ensuring they are aware of positive economic developments in our city and state, developments that could well translate into new air service.

The airport is also home to a number of businesses and industries that make substantial contributions to the economy. The list is impressive and includes: Dassault-Falcon Jet, Raytheon Aircraft, the Southwest Airlines Reservation Center, United Parcel Service, Timex and our three Fixed Based Operators — Central Flying Service, Midcoast-Little Rock and Omni Air. Counting the businesses and industries located on or adjacent to the airport and those who are employed by the airlines, rental car companies, concessionaires and others, a total of about 4,000 people work at the airport, representing an annual payroll of about $40 million and direct economic benefits exceeding $260 million.

Little Rock National Airport has a proud past and can look forward to a bright future.

The Lloyd Schuh Co.

Experience And Honesty The Basis For Long-Term Client Partnerships

For over half a century, The Lloyd Schuh Company has focused on improving its own true strengths and abilities as well as changing to provide customers with the services they need. In the early years, in addition to being a direct mail house, the company offered a variety of ad agency and association management services. But during the past 25 years, its focus has moved completely to direct mail production and promotional products sales. The Lloyd Schuh Company hasn't looked back since.

Says owner Scott Schuh, "While we are commited to using the latest mailing technology as well as providing the highest quality products, that's not what has gotten us where we are today."

"Our customers know that our experience makes the difference," he says. "Nobody in the state has been in our specialty areas of business longer."

The company has maintained relationships with several clients since its 1948 inception by knowing its business and being "painfully honest," Schuh says.

He recalls temporarily losing a large account by refusing to promise a delivery time he knew he couldn't make. The client called a competitor, who sent a van to pick up the ad materials and promised to make the desired delivery time of noon the next day. The following day, Schuh recalls, he saw the competitor delivering the job to the post office late in the afternoon, at about the time Schuh had promised. "They just kept their mouth shut" instead of being honest about the delivery time, Schuh said.

For more information:
The Lloyd Schuh Co.
2207 Cantrell Road
Little Rock, Arkansas 72202
501-374-2332
www.lscmarketing.com

The management team at The Lloyd Schuh Co. has over 100 years of experience in their business. From left: Brian Gould, Pat White, Lloyd Schuh Sr., C. Scott Schuh, Valerie Cox and Greg McMahon.

J.A. Riggs Tractor Co., a client since the early 1950s, keeps coming back because of service, experience and a commitment to making the customer happy.

"How you take care of mistakes when they happen provides a key test of a firm's desire to satisfy clients," Schuh says.

It's been that way since Scott's father, Lloyd Schuh, started the Art Lloyd Co. with fellow Royal typewriter salesman Art Schnipper Jr. Schnipper convinced his partner, who had been one of the top five Royal salesmen in the U.S., that direct mail was the way to go, and the business was born.

Schuh soon bought Schnipper's part of the business, and, for the next 12 years, served as principal and partner in the Little Rock ad agency. In 1962, he went solo with Lloyd Schuh Advertising. In addition, Schuh was executive director of the Sales & Marketing Executives Association in Little Rock and held the same position in the Arkansas Ready-Mixed Concrete Association.

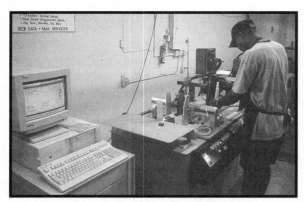

The latest in computerized, high-speed technology enables The Lloyd Schuh Co. to meet the differing needs of all their clients.

Many years ago the business was much more labor-intensive, with all envelope stuffing and addressing being done by hand. Some mailing lists were literally compiled by canvassing neighborhoods on foot. Address labels were hand-typed onto gummed-back sheets and cut into strips.

In 1996, the business moved from its long-time location at 1007 West Seventh St. to the Capital Park business complex, off Cantrell Road. With the move came the name change to the Lloyd Schuh Company.

Today the company is computerized from the receiving dock to the delivery van. In addition to producing millions of mailing labels per year, the company uses ink-jet technology to print addresses directly onto mail; as many as 30,000 pieces can be addressed per hour.

Another machine can insert multiple pieces in an envelope, address and seal the mail at a rate of up to 8,000 envelopes per hour.

The company also offers promotional products, such as caps, t-shirts, golf shirts, totes and mugs sporting a client's logo. Using special software, the company searches for the best available promotional items, taking into account not only price, but quality and shipping costs as well.

Electronic transfer of ad art represents the biggest change since the mid-1980s, says vice president Brian Gould.

"We used to read ad copy line-by-line to our supplier over the phone," Gould says. "If I did that now, they would laugh my ear off." Telephone descriptions gave way to overnight mailing years ago; in turn, overnighting gave way to e-mail, Gould says.

The Lloyd Schuh Co. literally sends out truckloads of mail every day.

"We're manufacturers of mail," Scott Schuh says. So much of it, in fact, that the post office comes to them. A U.S. Post Office representative provides daily in-plant acceptance of the firms many bulk mailings. Any possible problems are found and fixed before the mail ever leaves the building.

Though the name and much of the equipment is new, the firm's commitment to clients remains the same, Scott Schuh says, pointing to the veteran management staff.

Thirty-eight people, with hundreds of years cumulative experience, run the show at the Lloyd Schuh Co. Lloyd Schuh serves as chairman of the board, while Scott, who came on board in 1976, occupies the president's chair and is now majority owner. Four vice presidents help the Schuhs: Gould, with the company since 1984; Pat White, since 1977; Greg McMahon, since 1988 and Valerie Cox, since 1982.

The Schuhs haven't been part of the Little Rock community for 51 years without pulling their weight. The company was recognized in 1995 by the Governor's Office of Volunteerism as the outstanding company in the state (with fewer than 100 employees) for its work with almost 40 different non-profit groups, including Easter Seals and Children's Hospital.

Whether in client or community relationships, the Lloyd Schuh Co. has 51 years of trust to fall back on.

As Scott Schuh says, "We strive to establish a partnership with our clients. And with many we've developed true friendships, and that's the best of both worlds."

North Little Rock Funeral Home
Family And Tradition For Four And A Half Decades

Just ask anyone associated with the North Little Rock Funeral Home what their business is about, and they'll tell you without hesitation it's about family and tradition.

Clifford L. Smith, the funeral home's founder, loved people and wanted to spend his life working in a business that valued them. "He had no previous experience" in the funeral home industry, but "picked it because it was a people business," according to his daughter, Anne Powell-Black.

In February, 1955, Smith bought property at 20th and Main Streets from Dr. Shelby Atkinson. Smith chose the property because it was centrally located in North Little Rock and was close to the Main Street Bridge connecting the city to Little Rock.

The location proved to be ideal—giving the business a "high profile" to the thousands of motorists who use Main Street everyday.

After the remodeling was completed, Smith, his wife, and their two children moved upstairs, making it a home as well as a funeral home. An intimate connection developed between the children and the funeral home, one that served them well years later when they took over the family business.

"We lived in the house until we went off to college," recalled John S. Smith, who is now president of North Little Rock Funeral Home. Smith and his sister, Anne Powell-Black, were able to study their father's approach to the business—that he put people first. John and his wife, Kay, carry on this tradition at the home today, and

From left: Anne Black, John Smith and Kay Smith.

Powell-Black does likewise in the insurance division, American Home Life Insurance Company.

As people are guided through the funeral home, one notices the warm, peaceful atmosphere. There are flowers, fountains, and a chapel where mourning family members can meditate.

There also is an area where family members can meet before a funeral to relax and to prepare themselves for the service ahead. The North Little Rock Funeral Home, Kay Smith said, has been designed "with the family in mind."

In 1960, Clifford Smith expanded his business interests by applying for and receiving an insurance charter, but it allowed coverage only for products and services up to $500 a person. State law was changed six years later when Gov. Winthrop Rockefeller was in office, and Smith was allowed to issue cash policies. These were the beginnings of American Home Life Insurance Company. Clifford Smith retired in 1972 leaving his

For more information:
North Little Rock Funeral Home
1921 North Main
North Little Rock, Arkansas 72114
501-758-1170

children to operate the family businesses. Anne Powell-Black is president of American Home Life while John and Kay operate the funeral home.

American Home Life has grown to what it is today under Powell-Black's leadership. She returned to Arkansas after living several years in other states and enrolled in a class on insurance at the University of Arkansas at Little Rock (UALR) and began learning state laws and methods to improve the company.

American Home Life now has seven employees in addition to a sales force of 10 and has $10 million in reserve to pay policyholders' claims. The company is located across the street from the funeral home.

Why have these businesses done so well? John Smith said there's no mystery involved. People are his family's number one concern. Speaking of the business he operates, Smith explained, "One thing that makes us unique is that we are one of the leading independent funeral homes in the Central Arkansas market. We think that in a family-oriented business, this makes a difference."

Many funeral homes are now owned and operated by large corporations. North Little Rock Funeral Home continues to be family owned and operated. John Smith believes it is important for people to be surrounded by a family they know and trust during times of bereavement.

Clifford Smith's son, who grew up around people saying goodbye to their loved ones, said people choose funeral homes differently from the way they choose other services. Choosing a funeral home, he said, is much like choosing a doctor. People often select a physician based on what friends have told them and from community reputation, and this is how he said they choose a funeral home. Choosing a funeral home is one of the most important decisions a family can make in terms of its emotional well-being, he added.

The people at North Little Rock Funeral Home and American Home Life are involved in their community and state. Kay Smith is on the Board of Directors and active in the North Little Rock Chamber of Commerce. John Smith is a member of the North Little Rock Rotary Club and Secretary-Treasurer of the Arkansas Funeral Directors Association and will become president of the organization in two years.

This community involvement has brought families to the funeral home for its services. John Smith said the business has grown "a great deal" over the years and now has 19 employees, including those working part-time. The home conducts an average of 450 services a year, making it the second largest in the area.

Powell-Black is a past president of both the Arkansas State Life Underwriters and the General Agents and Manager. She also has been president of the Arkansas CLU and the ChFC Chapter.

Many persons don't seem to understand, that both the funeral home and the insurance company serve all of Pulaski County, not just North Little Rock. In fact, John Smith pointed out, 25 percent of the home's customers are from Little Rock.

Family and tradition have kept these North Little Rock businesses going for four and a half decades and neither has any interest in doing anything other than continuing to serve people. That's Clifford Smith's legacy.

PC Hardware
Fifty Years And Three Generations

If you really like hardware, this has always been the place to be. Since P.C. and Betty Prousnitzer started PC Hardware and Machinery in 1949 on 4th Street in Little Rock, two things have remained constant: quality hardware and a Prousnitzer in charge.

Today, P.C.'s son Chuck is grooming one or all of his three sons to take over the store's 25,000 square-foot location on West Markham. PC Hardware no longer carries toys and cookware like in the old days, but it does include an entire store, Light Innovations, devoted to lighting and fixtures.

P.C. Prousnitzer was a top salesman for Porter-Cable and Stanley Power Tools up until the companies stopped using factory representatives. With a family and new baby (Chuck's sister) arriving, the time seemed right for P.C. to settle down. In 1949 he started his own store. Both Porter-Cable and Stanley remain in business, and both are available at PC Hardware.

"I grew up in the business." Chuck Prousnitzer says, "I've been coming to the store as far back as I can remember. I literally was raised in the back room playing and doing odd jobs."

Chuck was born in 1958, six years after the store moved to 313 W. Capitol before relocating to its home for the next 33 years, 1021 High Street (now Martin Luther King Drive).

On May 2, 1964, the High Street location of PC Hardware opened with a bang, offering $500 in door prizes, Thor shop bench grinders for $15.95 and one-third off of all grass clippers, hedge shears and pruning

Chuck Prousnitzer pictured in the store's current location in 1999.

shears. Vendor-supplied "gifts and souvenirs" beckoned to potential customers.

Along the way, the merchandise mix moved toward decorative and commercial hardware.

Chuck Prousnitzer joined the business full-time in 1981, upon his graduation from Louisiana State University with a degree in business administration. Two years later, after conducting a brief apprenticeship for his son, P.C. Prousnitzer died suddenly, leaving Chuck in charge.

In 1987, while trying to remodel his house, Chuck had the idea that became Light Innovations. After getting poor service at a lighting retailer, he told his wife Charlene, "We've got to open a lighting store."

In 1997, Chuck and his crew moved to their current

For more information:
PC Hardware
9101 West Markham Street
Little Rock, Arkansas 72205
501-224-1724

P.C. Prousnitzer, Jr. photographed in 1951 amongst the tools he knew and loved.

location, 9101 West Markham. Betty Prousnitzer gave the old building to the Arkansas Children's Hospital.

Light Innovations is dense with light fixtures of every kind, while the hardware showroom stretches open and roomy, containing everything from circular saws to golden swan lavatory faucets.

The move west, to the building formerly occupied by a Weingarten's supermarket and an Ike's discount drug store, has accompanied a dramatic increase in sales, Prousnitzer says. He plans to stay put. "I've made my big move for awhile," he says.

According to Prousnitzer, business has been impacted only slightly by the opening of big home supercenters. "It takes you ten minutes just to get in from the parking lot," he says.

PC Hardware, Chuck says, has lost only one type of customer to the superstores: The 30- to 50-year-old man who's watched home shows on television and thinks he knows it all. But, he says, the store has gained back the wives of those customers, trying to straighten up the mess their husbands made.

"The main thing I offer is service and help with what they're trying to do," he says.

Many of his customers are West Little Rock homebuilders, he says, but not all are new to PC Hardware. "We get a lot of second- and third-generation customers," he says. "The father bought from my father and the son buys from me."

Though the store doesn't sell toys anymore, kids can still find some diversion in the activity area outside the office at the back of the store. Meanwhile, big kids will find their kind of toys everywhere. Tools for the men, beautiful fixtures for the women, or vice versa.

Chuck manages the store with help from Betty, Charlene and 30 employees. Another 20 people man a store in Fort Smith, and the firm's door and frame shop on E. 15th Street in Little Rock employs another 10 people.

For Chuck Prousnitzer, the key is pride and continuity. "My grandfather sold machinery. My father sold machinery. I'm here, and I have three sons who are interested in the business," even though "one day they're going to be race car drivers, and the next day they're going to work at PC Hardware."

He offers skeptical customers the best guarantee he knows. "This is my business," he says. "My office is right over there. I've got three sons I want to be able to walk into this business."

Pro Travel

All Types Of Travel - Corporate, Leisure, Cruises

Pro Travel has only been in business six years, but it's built a following of loyal and satisfied customers. Manager Dana Burnett says this is the only way a small, independent agency can hold its own against the big chains that dominate the travel business today.

It has been the strategy at Pro Travel since the beginning. The president and founder of Pro Travel is Dr. John McCracken, a retired surgeon. When he gave up his medical practice, after 30 years in the Little Rock area, he started Pro Travel to provide jobs for two people who'd worked for him in the medical practice — Burnett and Diane Fulbright. Fulbright has since left the travel agency and moved from Little Rock.

"When we started, we had one fulltime person [Burnett] and one parttime person [Fulbright]," Burnett said. "We now have two fulltime, including me, and two parttime."

The agency opened on Merrill Drive in west Little Rock. About three years ago, it moved to Saddle Creek Center at the Johnson Ranch on Highway 10.

"When we first opened up, we relied a lot on Dr. McCracken's doctor friends from his days at Baptist Medical Center, and his friends from the country club," Burnett said. "We'd worked for Dr. McCracken and we knew how persnickety he was about his travel arrangements, because a doctor's time is so precious. So we could call other doctors and say, 'We know how you want to travel.'

"We do all types of travel — corporate, leisure, cruises. We just do everything. We love large groups."

For more information:
Pro Travel
8201 Ranch Boulevard
Little Rock, Arkansas 72223
501-868-9959

Pro Travel—(Left to right) Dr. John McCracken, owner; Dana Burnett, manager; Shasta Bumgardner and Wendy Crain.

The Caribbean, including Cancun, Mexico, seems to be the primary hot spot for travel at the moment, Burnett said. But some tourists are choosing Hawaii over the Caribbean, because the problems of the Japanese dollar have meant fewer tourists for Hawaii — and better prices for those who come. "So it's a good deal for the money."

"We just sent a group from Pleasant Valley Country

Club to Scotland for a golf package. They had quite a time over there. Another doctor had us book the same kind of golf trip for him, so he could play St. Andrew's and some other golf courses. Another physician and his wife went to Maui to the Four Seasons resort. That's a first-class trip."

"We plan to try and take a group next fall on a European cruise," Burnett said. How many people does it take to make a group? "You can have six or 60. I'm going with one in May that has 60 people. They're going to the eastern Caribbean. We always escort the large groups."

That eastern Caribbean trip will be on what the brochure calls "The very first smoke-free ship! Carnival's new Paradise is a masterpiece of modern technology and a tribute to the past."

A March casino cruise will leave from New Orleans on the Commodore Line's Enchanted Capri. "This ship features the famous Isle of Capri Casino, with tons of slot machines, Caribbean stud poker, blackjack and a craps table. There is something for everyone. Not only does this ship offer exciting gaming activities it also has spectacular shows and a night life that is out of this world."

Burnett said she hadn't done "a lot" of traveling before she got in the business. "But Dr. McCracken had, and he's been a wealth of information for us." She has done a lot of traveling since she got in the business, of course. "To be certified by Cruise Line International of America, you have to travel on a certain number of cruise lines."

The millennium has brought opportunities for travel agents, but it has also brought the problem of rising prices, Burnett said. "The airlines are going up again right now. Because of the millennium, everything has tripled in price. Disney started their millennium celebration Oct. 1, and they're continuing through 2001.

"And the airlines are cutting commissions for travel agents again. United had another cut again today. That makes it not pleasant to be in the travel business."

But Pro Travel continues on, despite airlines cutting commissions, and despite competition from bigger and older agencies.

"We are so small, and really we're new, too," Burnett said. "We've only been around for six years. A lot of our competitors have been around 20 to 30 years. We just have to rely on the steady stream of clients that we've built up."

Pulaski Technical College

Providing Customized Job-Specific Training For Businesses And Industries

There was a time in Arkansas when a country boy could learn how to make a living by helping his father plant and harvest cotton and other crops, raise livestock, or cut timber. And a boy living in one of the few cities of any size in the state could go to his father's store or office and sweep floors and run errands, absorbing business principles by osmosis, until he was ready to run the operation or move out on his own.

This ended when the United States had to marshall its industrial might or create it when it didn't exist to defeat Japan and Nazi Germany in World War II. Arkansas lost population in droves during the 1940s, but many of the men who did return to the state after the war had experienced their first real taste of the Industrial Age and knew it would be coming to Arkansas even though the skills of most residents were ill-prepared for it.

The Little Rock School District responded to this realization by establishing the Little Rock Adult Vocational School at 601 W. Markham St. in October 1945 with a primary mission of helping World War II veterans learn the skills that would be in demand in what turned out to be a post-war economic boom. There was a nationwide housing shortage, so carpenters, roofers, plumbers, and electricians were needed. Engines were replacing the muscles of man and mule alike on the farm, and cars and trucks were beginning to fill city streets. Mechanics to keep the machines running were in short supply. And Arkansas was experiencing its first influx of industrial relocations, primarily of the "cut-and-sew"

variety in apparel and shoe manufacturing plants.

In 1969, when Republican Winthrop Rockefeller was governor, the state concluded there was a need to better prepare Arkansans for the industrial jobs that were becoming more plentiful through an ongoing effort to attract manufacturing plants. The state took over Little Rock's vocational program and made it part of a network of post-secondary schools, and its name was changed to Pulaski Vocational-Technical School. In 1976, the school moved from 14th and Scott Streets in Little Rock to a new 36,000-square-foot building at its current location at 3000 West Scenic Drive on a 40-acre tract that was part of surplus land the Veterans Administration had given to the North Little Rock School District.

Other new buildings were added in 1985 and 1987, but generally, Arkansas allowed its vocational-technical schools to languish in the 1970s and 1980s even as the state's economy diversified. Agriculture and timber were no longer the only "games in town" because about a quarter of the state's workforce was employed in manufacturing. Another large segment was working in "service" businesses, and the computer-driven Information Age was dawning.

In response to industrial plant managers and business owners who identified the need for a well-trained workforce to meet their needs, the legislature in 1991 decided that some of the vocational-technical schools would be upgraded to two-year technical colleges and placed under the state Department of Higher Education. Corporations earning $100,000 or more annually agreed to a half-percent increase in their state income tax rate to help pay for better equipment and instruction at the "new" technical colleges.

Pulaski was one of the institutions chosen for the conversion, which meant it had to and did achieve

For more information:
Pulaski Technical College
3000 West Scenic Drive
North Little Rock, Arkansas 72118
501-771-1000
www.ptc.tec.ar.us

accreditation from the North Central Association. Today Pulaski Technical College is an integral part of a network of 23 two-year technical colleges, community colleges, and branch campuses. A seven-member board of trustees appointed by the governor sets policies for Pulaski Tech within a general framework established by the Department of Higher Education and the state Higher Education Coordinating Board.

"Whether you're just starting your post-secondary education or want to improve your skills, Pulaski Tech is a modern college that is changing and expanding to meet your needs," President Ben Wyatt said. "We're also committed to meeting the needs of the industries, businesses and other aspects of our community." PTC's community includes Lonoke, Saline and Faulkner Counties as well as Pulaski.

Pulaski Tech continues to be one of the largest and fastest-growing among the state's two-year colleges. Its enrollment this fall is 4,100 students—a whopping 23 percent increase over last fall's 3,300 students. Wyatt thinks he knows why this is so. "I think it's the wide range of educational opportunities" Pulaski Tech offers, he said, pointing out that a smaller campus is attractive to many who want to stay closer to home for the first two years after high school graduation before transferring to a major university. "And we're getting a lot of first-generation college students," he added, referring to students whose parents did not attend college.

Wyatt went on to explain that Pulaski Tech students can choose from general education courses that will transfer to four-year institutions or they can pursue a program of technical/occupational education to prepare them for direct entrance into the job market after just one or two years of training or they can enroll in specific courses to improve their performance in their current jobs.

The college offers an Associate of Arts degree program and more than 40 Associate of Applied Science (AAS) degrees and certificate programs. The AAS degree is awarded to those who successfully complete one of the career programs having a minimum of 62 credit hours. Certificate programs provide short, intense concentrations on a specific technical area because they are designed for those who want to enter the workplace immediately on completion or are trying to

upgrade skills for their existing jobs. Courses in these two programs range from Internet Specialist and Networking (two years) to Paralegal Technology, Medical Transcription, and Manufacturing Technology.

The Associate of Arts degree, which also requires successful completion of at least 62 credit hours, mirrors the classwork done in the freshman and sophomore years at a four-year institution. The school has articulation agreements with the accredited four-year institutions in its service area and is the largest source of transfer students for the University of Arkansas at Little Rock (UALR). But if an individual thinks he just needs to improve his basic education levels in specific core subjects such as English, reading, or mathematics, he can do that, too, by enrolling in what are called developmental courses at Pulaski Tech.

The college charges $42 a credit hour. Wyatt said he feels the instructors make Pulaski Tech the educational center it has become because "instruct is all they do." They do not conduct or oversee research and do not have to be concerned about being published in academic journals. "We put students first. We want to see them succeed," Wyatt said.

Pulaski Technical College has developed a cadre of support services that recognize education is but one part of a person's life, and it appears determined to clear away as many obstacles as possible that stand between a student and an education. Academic advice, a library, guidance counseling, and financial aid are some of the services designed to do this. There are a variety of organizations and activities at the school that are designed to foster a community atmosphere, including a Student Government Association with representatives elected from each academic division.

The college has a Children First center that provides care and early childhood education for children of students. It also offers a Single Parent/Displaced Homemaker Career Development program at one of its off-campus sites in Little Rock. Students in this program receive assistance with career interest testing and planning, decision-making, resume preparation, job-seeking workshops, and for those who qualify, help with child care, tuition and textbooks

Individual career planning, access to large databases containing up-to-date information about occupations,

Student Success–Pulaski Tech prepares students for high-demand careers and averages a 90-95 percent graduate placement rate annually.

resume writing, job placement assistance, and honing job seeking/ interviewing skills assistance are among the work-related services Pulaski Tech provides. A computer-assisted learning laboratory where students receive individual tutoring in problem subjects is open five days a week.

The average age of Pulaski Tech's students enrolled in degree programs is 27 years, which helps explain why 80 percent of all the students hold part or full-time jobs while attending school. The college employs 100 full-time faculty and staff and has an equal number of adjunct instructors. Sixty-four percent of the faculty hold master's degrees or higher in the disciplines they are teaching.

Pulaski Tech's campus includes six modern learning facilities, featuring state-of-the art classrooms and learning laboratories. In addition to classrooms and offices, PTC's Business building contains several computer laboratories. The Automotive Technology Center features state-of-the-art automotive repair laboratories as well as classrooms, and there is an Industrial Technology Center that has laboratory and lecture rooms for machining, welding, and diesel mechanics programs.

A new four-story, 42,000-square-foot Information Technology center allows the college to provide interactive distance-learning programs as it already has done for Lonoke High School, and it has received broadcasts from the University of Arkansas at Fayetteville and UALR.

A library that also houses the college's general education division was completed on campus in 1996. It is automated, contains an online catalog and circulation system, electronic periodical indices, and full-text resources. Internet access and e-mail accounts are available to all Pulaski Tech students.

The college's division of Continuing Education and Business Outreach provides both continuing education classes and customized training services for businesses, industries, and individuals in Central Arkansas. It is one of the largest programs of its kind in the state, having served about 3,000 persons in 1998-99. Customized training was provided for employees of more than 30 area businesses and industries.

Pulaski Tech plans in November to open a 24,000-square-foot Workforce Development Center located on the Aerospace Education Center campus in Little Rock. The building will have laboratories, a distance-learning center, and a staff of six. Wyatt said the college intends to use the facility to develop and conduct training programs for employees of local companies.

"They [the employees] will become more productive and help our economy," Wyatt predicted, adding that the new center will help both the students and the community. "Our mission is to support economic development in Central Arkansas, and we will do whatever we can to provide customized job-specific training for businesses and industries" in the region as well as educations for those who want to transfer to four-year institutions to complete a baccalaureate degree or go into the workplace immediately. In the Arkansas of today with its multi-faceted economy, the new demands of global competition and the Information Age, Wyatt knows that "flexibility" has become the watchword for institutions like his.

Sissy's Log Cabin

There's Nothing Ordinary About Sissy Or Her Log Cabin

"Life's too short for ordinary jewelry."

The slogan says volumes about Sissy Jones and the business she founded in the South Arkansas pines, Sissy's Log Cabin. From a one-woman, 900 square-foot antiques store, Sissy's has grown to become the state's largest independent jewelry store, with 32 employees, including Jones' husband, son and daughter.

Sissy's Log Cabin is much more than its namesake these days, filling three buildings and 12,000 square feet. Thirty-six showcases display fine jewelry, including the store's signature slide bracelets, along with a wide selection of timepieces.

In addition, Sissy's staff designs and makes original jewelry for customers around the world. They also carry unique and exquisite gift items. And they still sell antiques, now out of a 3,000 square-foot showroom.

Sissy Jones speaks almost faster than the speed of hearing when she talks about her business. Her arms pick up the pace, gesturing as she recalls the beginning.

In 1970, Jones, then a young mother of two, noticed that an old cabin, half-hidden in the woods along Highway 79 South in Pine Bluff, was being torn down. For some reason, instead of driving on, she took the disappearing building as a call to action. Interrupting a trip to decorate for a Junior League charity ball, she called the owner and asked if she could rent the building from him.

"He said, 'But, Sissy, you don't understand, it's falling apart,'" she says. After assuring him that she knew the building's condition, she persuaded him to rent the cabin for $50 a month.

For more information:
Sissy's Log Cabin
2319 Camden Road
Pine Bluff, Arkansas 71603
1-888-879-3940

(Left to right) Murphy Jones, Ginger Jones Motes, Sissy Jones, Bill Jones.

A single hanging bulb lit the cement-floored interior, and her husband Murphy thought she had gone crazy, but "it looked good to us," Jones says. Borrowing $1,500 from her uncle, she emptied her attic, brought in a space heater, cleaned up the cabin and opened an antique store.

"We had to hang black and white checked cloth on the ceiling," she says, "because whenever an 18-wheeler came by it would shake the dust off."

"The $1,500 didn't last long," she says, but the customers started coming in. Some of them brought shoeboxes full of jewelry to trade or sell on commission.

"Jewelry, I didn't know anything about jewelry," she says. "What was jewelry? I decided it was time to get a little education. I bought two pairs of pliers, a pair of cutting pliers, some o-rings, and I am a jeweler."

Jones is recognized as the creator of the watch slide bracelet. She took antique watch slides and mounted them on two 14-kt. gold rope chains, then added a clasp. "I said, 'What a pretty bracelet'," she says. "We'll just make bracelets. And we were really big time." Once she perfected the bracelets, she advertised in newspapers to acquire all the slides she could. Now she designs her own slides, and holds patents and copyright on the slide product.

When she decided to make the jump from antiques to jewelry, Jones threw herself into her adopted craft with enthusiasm. She has studied at the Gemological Institute of America in California, McCarthey Jewelry Design School in Mena, Trenton Jewelry/Goldsmith School in Memphis and the University of Arkansas at Monticello. She is a licensed appraiser of antique jewelry.

Sissy Jones serves as CEO of the company. Her husband, Murphy, is secretary/treasurer. Their son Bill now serves as president, and has been recognized by Arkansas Business as one of the top 40 Arkansas business people under 40 years of age.

Bill Jones originally planned a career as a chemical engineer, attending the University of Arkansas, Fayetteville and the University of Arkansas at Little Rock. While at UALR, he would drive down and help out in the store stringing bracelets. "He fast learned what we did inside," Sissy Jones says. In 1984, he left college to join the family business full-time.

Daughter Ginger Motes worked for three years as a registered nurse, joining the Sissy's staff in 1985 when Bill Jones left for jewelry training. "And I never left," she says. She now serves as executive vice president.

Sissy's staff, called her "working family," includes eight full-time goldsmiths, a lapidarist, a master watchmaker, professional sales and service team and an in-house ad agency. The master watchmaker, Bob Hawkins, has 52 years experience in watch repair and service, including quartz analog, and is trained to service Swiss timepieces, including Rolex, Baume & Mercier, Raymond Weil, TAG Heuer, Seiko, Gucci and Cartier.

Everywhere she goes, Sissy Jones wears her products. Each piece has the price marked, and it's not uncommon for her to make a sale on the spot when someone admires her jewelry. "This guardian angel means more to me than any piece of jewelry," she says, pointing to a piece in the shape of an angel with two children on a bridge. "Those are my children," she says.

Jones credits her success to hard work, honest living, good friends, customers and family, "and the help of a few angels." Angel designs are everywhere at Sissy's Log Cabin; the theme is a Jones' favorite.

Sissy's finally outgrew the log cabin with the coming of the 90s. The business closed in the old log cabin the day before Thanksgiving, 1991, and moving from one building into three began.

"I thought, 'How am I ever going to fill all that?'" she says. "I couldn't believe all the people who showed up to help us move," Sissy Jones says. After a holiday spent hauling merchandise, the new, three-building Sissy's Log Cabin, which still includes the original structure, opened on Friday, "mostly selling out of boxes," she says.

Sissy Jones has become a regular speaker at industry events, charming and motivating her audience with her inspirational story. She gives the audience a formula for success based on four "Cs":

• Create an image with everyday fair prices. Develop a memorable slogan. Take advantage of your location, such as Sissy's inclusion on the Arkansas Parks and Tourism Historic Site list, and hire a superb staff.

• Care for your customers, your employees and your vendors. "Your friends and customers do something for you by shopping in your store," she says. "What do you do for them?" The Sissy's staff meets weekly for business and devotional purposes. And instead of treating vendors as an adversary to be mistrusted, those delivering and selling to Sissy's are treated as friends. The treatment is reciprocated.

• Communicate often. Daily five-minute morning meetings, a well-used suggestion box and birthday cakes for employees all help in this effort. When a person is named sales associate of the month, they receive a gold name tag. Each succeeding time the person wins the honor, a small diamond is added to the tag.

• Commit to your staff and customers. Sissy's invests in training programs for all, encouraging staff members to take whatever courses they are interested in, whether the subject relates directly to their job or not. The company shares goals and tracks progress. Every customer gets an angel pin and a verse card. "They only cost about a dollar but they let people know I appreciate them," Jones says.

Sissy's Log Cabin also goes through a lot of coffee and

Sissy's Log Cabin, Arkansas' leading independent jeweler.

Cokes. At the drop of a hat, the family will spring for drinks and snacks for customers and employees. "It might cost you $25 or $30," Sissy Jones says, "but those special little things you do make your life go around."

Jones has earned numerous awards in the last 29 years, among them:

• 1990 Jeweler of the Year, Arkansas Jewelers Association;

• Nine C.A.R.A.T. awards from AJA;

• 1993 Best of Show, from Jewelers of America;

• 1996 Boss of the Year, by Credit Professionals International;

• 1996 Arkansas Business of the Year, from Arkansas Business Publishing Group;

• JCK •Jewelers' Circular Keystone) Advisory Board;

• 1997 Ella Hunn Payne Award from the Junior League of Pine Bluff;

• Keynote speaker at the 1999 JCK Jewelry Show in Orlando, Fla., RJO Jewelry Show in Des Moines Iowa and the MIDA Jewelry Show in Dallas, Tex.

•1999 Small Business Person of the Year, by the Greater Pine Bluff Chamber of Commerce.

•1999 Best of Show 1st place Jewelry Store by the Arkansas Democrat-Gazette

In addition, Jones has been named one of Arkansas' "Top 100 Women" every year since 1995 by Arkansas Business.

Professional organizations that boast Jones as a member include:

• Jewelers of America;

• Gemological Institute of America, New England Appraisers Association;

• Retail Jewelers Organization;

• Jewelry Information Center and

• Arkansas Antique Dealers Association.

• New England Appraisers Association

Sissy's offers a large selection of loose diamonds, and is one of six suppliers chosen to carry the Millennium Diamond. Rolex, Cartier, Lagos, Baume and Mercier are all available at Sissy's Log Cabin, along with a huge selection of original designs featuring interchangeable earrings, enhancers, bails, rings, bracelets and links.

The store features Sissy's Collection, signed, numbered jewelry created by Sissy's own designers, who sketch designs while customers wait, then give a estimate on the spot. To ensure proper security, Sissy's takes internal photographs of precious gemstones. In addition, the customer can watch while the jeweler sets their precious stones.

The store features gift-wrapping, a bridal registry and delivery service. You can be assured of complete satisfaction with every purchase. If any item, for any reason does not measure up to your satisfaction, you may return it for a prompt refund, exchange or credit within 30 days of purchase with original invoice.

"Life's too short not to envision your dreams and realize your vision" could be an alternate slogan for Sissy's Log Cabin and its founder. Whether designing jewelry, selling antiques or assembling a staff, Sissy Jones has always surpassed expectations.

And she's kept it all in the family.

St. Vincent Health System

A Vow To Serve...The Strength To Grow...A Will To Succeed

Vow To Serve

Some hospitals begin with a dream. St. Vincent began with a vow. It was the late 1870's and yellow fever was sweeping the South. The epidemic had already reached Memphis — it seemed only a question of time before it would strike Little Rock. Without adequate medical care and professionals to combat or contain the disease, the town was at risk of being wiped out by disease. That is when a prominent local couple, Mr. and Mrs. Alexander Hagar, made a vow that proved a significant one. They vowed to God that if Little Rock was spared from the ravages of yellow fever, they would dedicate their estate to the development of the city's first hospital.

Little Rock was spared and the Hagars were true to their word. In July 1888, a "charity" hospital opened its doors to the community. Located in a residence on Second Street, the facility was operated by the Sisters of Charity of Nazareth, a religious congregation from Nazareth, Kentucky who were widely known as caregivers. A group of pioneering Sisters had made their way to Little Rock to assist in the effort to combat the spreading fever. Community support for the dedicated Sisters and the new hospital was significant.

Contributions in the form of money and prayer allowed the facility to expand rapidly. Within a year, the hospital had moved to a larger building on Center Street. It quickly outgrew that location and moved on to a new building at 10th and High. Then, in 1954, the hospital moved to a brand new facility which it occupies today at

the corner of Markham and University. The Sisters of Charity of Nazareth continue active involvement in St. Vincent's operation.

Strength To Grow

Since its founding over a century ago, St. Vincent has grown into something much more than a hospital at the corner of Markham and University. It has evolved from a small, charity hospital founded in 1888 into a sophisticated and respected health system dedicated to providing compassionate, community-oriented care encompassing a spectrum of services—from preventive care to general acute care to highly sophisticated specialty care. Today, St. Vincent extends its deeply rooted tradition of caring to every facet of medical service.

But today, it takes more than a caring spirit to assure success. The new realities of health care demand a commitment to sustained growth. Recognizing this, St. Vincent has aligned itself with Catholic Health Initiatives, one of the nation's largest Catholic health systems. Committed to leading change within the industry through new models of health care emphasizing active partnerships with community groups and other health care organizations, Catholic Health Initiatives has brought new strength to St. Vincent's community leadership.

Sharply focused on transforming traditional health care delivery through integrated delivery networks and creating new ministries to promote healthy communities, Catholic Health Initiatives, St. Vincent's parent organization, brings a level of strength to the local community unmatched by any other provider. This national connection provides St. Vincent access to the resources necessary to meet the physical, emotional and spiritual needs of Arkansans and effectively delivers the economies of a large organization.

For more information:
St. Vincent Health System
2 St. Vincent Circle
Little Rock, Arkansas 72205
501-660-3000

The founding Sisters of Charity of Nazareth.

In an effort to make quality health care available across central Arkansas, St. Vincent has taken significant strides north of the Arkansas River. St. Vincent Medical Center/Sherwood expanded early in October with the opening of a 93,000 square-foot inpatient acute care center on its medical campus in Sherwood, at the corner of Highway 67/167 and Wildwood Avenue. "Our Sherwood facility is focused on serving a significant population who have typically felt it necessary to go to Little Rock for quality acute care," says Dr. Jack Cobb, the organization's medical director. "I think from now on, you'll see that dramatically reverse as people become more aware of the quality of the services available through our new Sherwood facility."

Comprised of the St. Vincent Rehabilitation Hospital (co-owned by St. Vincent Health System and HealthSouth), an ambulatory care center, North River Surgery Center and now an 86-bed inpatient facility, St. Vincent Medical Center/Sherwood has emerged as a comprehensive medical center dedicated to serving the medical needs of residents of North Pulaski County and surrounding areas. North Little Rock Mayor Patrick Hays recently observed that, "with the evolution of medical care moving toward more outpatient procedures and shorter hospital stays, facilities like this...will match the type of care needed with the right type of facility...and will create a much better marriage in terms of technology and the delivery of health care."

Acquired in February 1998, St. Vincent Doctors Hospital is a welcomed addition to the St. Vincent Health System. To the pleasure and pride of the physicians and staff of St. Vincent Doctors Hospital, not to mention a lot of proud parents, the new St. Vincent Center for Women & Children opened in May. Merging the obstetrical staff and services of both St. Vincent Infirmary Medical Center and St. Vincent Doctors Hospital, coupled with a $4.8 million investment in the construction of a new women's unit at Doctors Hospital, has yielded a specialty center which is second to none in central Arkansas. As the leading women's center in Arkansas, with a projected 3,000 births each year, this newly renovated facility affords St. Vincent the opportunity to provide services for women and children at a single, more productive and convenient location. In addition to two neonatal intensive care units, the Center features 17 labor/delivery/recovery suites and postpartum rooms with warm colors and soft lighting to provide an at-home atmosphere. "I can't imagine that there's anything nicer or more comfortable in the area," commented Mary Jackson, administrator for the St. Vincent Center for Women & Children.

St. Vincent's sponsorship of St. Anthony's Healthcare Center (formerly Conway County Hospital), in Morrilton, provides further evidence of the organization's commitment to extend quality health services to communities throughout the state. This 84-bed community hospital offers a wide range of health care services to residents of Conway Country and surrounding areas.

St. Vincent's deep roots in compassion and caring, coupled with its commitment to building healthier communities, has led to the development of several outreach programs that significantly benefit Arkansans. An example is Project Guardian Angel, a childhood immunization program serving children who would otherwise have trouble meeting recommended childhood immunization schedules.

Supported through St. Vincent Health Clinic/East and working in partnership with the Department of Human Services, Project Guardian Angel helps keep children healthy by ensuring they get the necessary vaccines. Arkansas Department of Health Immunization Nursing Coordinator, Jerry Cox, RN, considers the program innovative, unique—and extremely valuable. "Nurses from St. Vincent Health Clinic/East go to these children, where they live and spend their time. The parent and the family do not have to take off from work, load up and travel to a medical office," Cox commented. "We have people from all over the United States requesting information on how this marvelous program operates. I can't say enough about the creativity, professionalism, and dedication of the Project Guardian Angel staff."

St. Vincent's founding spirit of charity and caring is

St. Vincent Infirmary Medical Center.

also clearly reflected in the support extended to victims of the devastating tornado which ripped through central Arkansas on January 21, 1999. Two St. Vincent hospitals treated 22 tornado victims immediately following the storm. Additionally, St. Vincent's Doctors Hospital opened its doors to more than 20 displaced residents of the Quapaw Quarter Nursing Home that sustained significant damage from the storm. Community support continued with the delivery of meals and medical services to residents of significantly damaged areas.

Scott Mosley, St. Vincent's Vice President for Corporate Development, considers community outreach vital and an essential element in the building of a strong health care network. "The demands of health care today are much different than they were a decade ago. Sophisticated medicine is no longer exclusively delivered through large medical care centers. Major medical centers have to wrap themselves with a strong network of physician clinics, home care providers, community hospitals, and other community-oriented care centers. Delivering quality care starts with the prevention of illness and addressing individual health care needs by working with individuals where they live and work."

Another important facet of St. Vincent Health System is its extensive network of affiliated primary care clinics. Maintaining affiliations with more than 80 primary care physicians working in more than 20 clinics in 7 central Arkansas communities, St. Vincent uniquely respects the value of collaboration with physicians. "St. Vincent views its physicians as partners," says A. David Hall, M.D., Senior Vice President for Medical Affairs. "Physicians are part of our leadership structure, serving on our board and administrative team, and helping oversee key parts of our operation. The resulting relationship is one that's built around mutual commitment to the organization's success and the work it does every day. We work to eliminate barriers between the organization and its medical staff and are always looking for the win-win solution. That is the only way patient care can be optimized."

Will To Succeed

St. Vincent is succeeding in its goal to provide high-quality, cost-effective health care which is responsive to the diverse medical needs of Arkansans-which makes everyone a winner. Not only does St. Vincent suport the largest primary care network in central Arkansas, but it is also the state's fourteenth largest employer.

It seems fitting that St. Vincent was founded on a vow. Especially since its vow to support community health with compassionate, quality, cost-effective care provides the foundation for St. Vincent's continued growth. St. Vincent began with a vow and a pioneering commitment on the part of six Sisters in 1888. That spirit continues to fuel a driving commitment to success. As Senior Vice President for Mission, Sr. Carole Kaucic, SCN explains, "the pioneering spirit of St. Vincent's founding congregation is very much alive today. The many Sisters who have dedicated themselves to St. Vincent over the years have successfully implanted a sense of caring and commitment within the heart of the organization which will always be there, shining clear and strong, as a beacon for all to follow."

The Courier

Your Information Source For The Arkansas River Valley For 125 Years

In Jan. 28, 1875, "Your Information Source for the Arkansas River Valley" was born. The newspaper that is known today as *The Courier* began with B.F. Jobe and James E. Battenfield serving as the paper's inaugural business manager and editor, respectively.

The Courier-Democrat was formed after the consolidation of *The Courier* and the competing weekly *Russellville Democrat* in 1898. The newspaper went daily in 1924, publishing Monday through Friday.

The newspaper was continued in operation by family members, through a lease arrangement until 1951 when the paper was bought in a joint venture by U.S. Sen. J. William Fulbright and the chain established by the late C.E. Palmer of Hot Springs. The paper was sold in 1955, to a corporation controlled by the late John Guion of Paris (Ark.) and Robert Breeden.

Five linotype machines and "hot metal" presses, in use since 1911, were phased out with the addition of an offset press, a 16-page, 4-unit Harris-Cottrell model, in 1969.

Harte-Hanks Communications of San Antonio, Texas, purchased the Courier-Democrat in 1976. W.H. "Bill" Martin became the publisher and oversaw the first Sunday edition of the *Courier-Democrat* in December 1976 with the debut of a new 32-page, 8-unit Goss Community press. *The Weekly Courier-Democrat* was phased out not long afterward and was replaced with a free circulation weekly, the *Advertiser*, which became

Courier *press foreman Eric Gray checks the color registration on one of the many commercial printing jobs that* The Courier *prints each week at their Russellville, Arkansas facility.* The Courier *currently prints dozens of newspapers and periodicals on an 8 unit Goss Urbanite press, including their Tuesday through Sunday daily newspaper.*

the *Tri-County Record* in 1997.

Harte-Hank Communications sold the newspaper to Worrell Communications on in 1987, and Paxton Media Group purchased the paper in August 1991. The third and fourth generations of the Paxton family are now involved in operation and management of the Kentucky-based company whose motto is "First, be a great newspaper." Plans were drawn and construction began for a $3 million building expansion on the east side of the existing building in 1993, which housed a new 64-page Goss Urbanite press that doubled the printing capacity of the operation and its more than 20 additional publications that are printed.

In 1994 the newspaper went through a complete

For more information:
The Courier
201 East Second
Russellville, Arkansas 72801
501-968-5252   1-800-369-5252
E-mail: dmosessa@couriernews.com
www.couriernews.com

A neon Courier *logo can be seen through the newly renovated newspaper offices of* The Courier.

redesign and the 119-year-old publication changed its name from the *Courier-Democrat* to *The Courier* on Feb. 15. Color highlights and photographs on the front page and sports sections illustrated the news.

The paper's mission was outlined in the middle of page one: "A courier is a messenger carrying important or urgent messages. *The Courier* is a messenger for the Arkansas River Valley carrying important information from around the world as well as local communities. Our 'look' is different. Our mission is unchanged."

The newspaper was converted to a 6-day morning publication in 1995, dropping the Monday edition in favor of a Saturday edition. Martin retired in late 1994, ending a successful career in the publishing industry. David Mosesso, who had previously served as publisher of the Paxton Media Group newspapers in Paragould and Searcy, became publisher of *The Courier* in 1997.

Commercial printing plays a vital role in *The Courier* operation. Word got out quickly about the quality of printing that was being done in Russellville after the installation of the Goss Urbanite press. Page and color capabilities were expanded, meeting the needs of many

current and future printing customers. Printing for customers all over the state via electronic digital file transmission, *The Courier's* printing volume has more than doubled over the past few years. *The Courier* is one of the most respected and sought after commercial printing operations in Arkansas.

Today, *The Courier* prints several weekly community newspapers, journals, grocery inserts, statewide and nationwide publications, including the *Arkansas Times*. *The Courier* also performs inserting, mailing, and distribution services for many of its customers.

Work began in 1997 on a $1.5 million total renovation of building where *The Courier* is produced. Boastfully one of the nicest newspaper offices in the state, *The Courier* office was designed for the next century. The construction project doubled the size of the original newspaper office and was completed in March of 1999.

The Courier, "Your Messenger for the Arkansas River Valley" is a vibrant newspaper serving a prospering community. Its roots run deep throughout the River Valley.

The Ranch

Idyllic Setting, Virtually In The Shadow Of Pinnacle Mountain

When talking to Bob Shults about one of his favorite subjects, The Ranch, certain buzzwords and catchphrases keep entering the conversation: quality; foresight; "doing it right".

An unassuming man in a Hermes tie, Shults, along with business partner Ed Willis, has been making The Ranch his life's work since they purchased the property from the Johnson family in 1984. A prime, 610-acre development bordered by Highway 10, Pinnacle Mountain State Park and the Little Maumelle River, it was the largest undeveloped tract of land along Highway 10 at that time. What is now known as The Ranch was left 'as is' until 1990 when street and utility work began. Until that point, Shults and Willis had traveled the South and Southwest looking at better developments and finding out what made them click with homeowners and consumers.

With Ed Willis, there was a history of developing former cattle ranches. In the 1970s, Willis purchased the property where Financial Centres I, II & III now sit at the intersection of I-630 and Shackleford Road. Look out the window of Bob Shults' office in Three Financial Centre and there is a panoramic view of West Little Rock, much of which Shults and Willis had a hand in developing. Properties such as the Holiday Inn Select, Regas Grill, Marriott Courtyard, and others have a shared history of Shults and Willis involvement.

Initially planned by a national planning firm, The Ranch was envisioned from the beginning as a community with offices, retail space, single and multi-family homes, and plenty of green space. The enormous Leisure Arts, Inc. headquarters was completed in 1991, and residential street construction began. Mindful of public scrapes involving neighborhood associations and commercial development in West Little Rock in the late 1980s, the first residential lots were laid out and homes built—virtually next door to Leisure Arts, Inc.

"The best thing we ever did," Shults allows, "was developing the residential lots next to Leisure Arts first. Those are choice lots. If you do it right, there's no stigma attached to living near an office building."

Shults also explains that The Ranch was the genesis of Little Rock's first and only "scenic corridor", the Highway 10 Overlay Zoning District. Adopted by the Little Rock City Board in 1990, this ordinance concerning the area along Highway 10 contains higher development standards and specifications than any other area of the city. Hundred-foot setbacks, 50 feet of greenbelt, thoughtful lighting, and limited building and signage heights are all part of the mix along this stretch of Highway 10.

"Later, the city added on to what we had done," Shults continues, "but we had already made our own scenic mile."

When approaching The Ranch from the main entrance at Highway 10 and Ranch Boulevard, after passing the brick gates with their lush landscaping, the first thing that catches the eye is Saddle Creek Center. A mix of retail and office space, Saddle Creek is the retail hub of The Ranch. Saddle Creek is very distinctive; its white buildings and green mansard roofs are embellished with cupolas. Its identity was forged after a trip Shults took to the Kentucky horse country, where he photographed countless buildings, barns and sheds. Upon his return to Arkansas, he showed his architect about 200 photos and said, "Something like this is what I want for Saddle Creek."

For more information:
The Ranch
Highway 10 and Ranch Boulevard
Little Rock, Arkansas 72212
501-224-9600

The view from one of the homes on Ranch Ridge Road with Pinnacle Mountain in the distance.

"I wanted that retail center to be an amenity," Shults explains, "of course I didn't want it to detract from the overall look and feel of what we have." Saddle Creek is currently home to a dry cleaner, a day care, The Productivity Institute, and a satellite office of Baptist Health.

What distinguishes The Ranch from other developments in West Little Rock and other cities? First of all, it is a mixed-use development that includes office and commercial space, along with homes and planned apartments. It is headquarters for Leisure Arts, Inc., a major publisher of craft books and materials, and a regional office for State Farm Insurance. Arkansas Baptist School System is located here, as well as various businesses located in the Saddle Creek Center.

The Ranch is also remarkable because of its distinctive look and feel. Development and construction standards are designed to maintain the pleasant, relaxed feel of the property. The average homeowner, in the market for a new home, may not be consumed with the minutiae of what constitutes a 'good' or 'bad' development, but they know what appeals to them. They may not notice immediately that there are no front-loading garages in

The Ranch, but they do notice that the overall visual effect is a pleasing one.

Shults explains the design and construction standards at The Ranch. "Early on, because there was nothing built out there, there was a lot of resistance to making homes and offices compatible with the overall design. Every year that dwindles because people see how pleasant the overall scheme is. And people have gained confidence that we're really going to do this. They can see how much thought and care has been put into the whole project."

"Basically, the gas station is required to have the same zoysia and brick as the homeowner."

The existing homes in The Ranch line sit on lots, many with mature trees, that sweep over rolling hills. Children playing and adults working on their lawns and gardens contribute to the feel of a traditional, established neighborhood. The single-family home phase currently under development surrounds Cypress Point Lake. These lots and homes, virtually in the shadow of Pinnacle Mountain, curve around the lake.

It is here that The Ranch features an amenity that

Saddle Creek Center offers retail and professional office space.

makes it unique among developments in Central Arkansas: via the Little Maumelle River, boats launched into Cypress Point can reach the Arkansas River in minutes. It is here that one realizes that the possibilities of The Ranch are almost endless, whether for active or relaxed lifestyles. With I-430, Pinnacle Mountain State Park, and the Arkansas River within easy reach, The Ranch is perfect for those whose passions are as diverse as fishing, biking, hiking, and shopping.

"This (development) has been a dream of mine and Ed's. We've had an agreement from the beginning to do this the right way. It hasn't always been easy. We've had to turn things down when they looked awfully tempting; when either loans were due or things were moving slowly. We've turned down several deals to build projects that we weren't ready for or that we didn't think would fit."

Another subtle sign of quality is the care with which the natural environment is considered. With an absolute minimum of mature trees removed during the early development, the focus now is on preserving the re-

maining trees and planting additional trees native to Arkansas. Witness the cypress planted at the Highway 10 entrance. Fast-growing, short-lived, lollipop-shaped Bradford pears are nowhere to be found. Young willow oaks line the sidewalks on the northern end of Ranch Boulevard. Nature trails and bike paths are another aspect that make The Ranch so special.

Driving through The Ranch gives one a sense of the enormous potential of the entire development. The Ranch potentially is one of the most desirable neighborhoods in Arkansas, not just now, but 50 years from now.

Future plans for The Ranch include more office and commercial space, luxury garden apartments, and more single family homes. There is also a marina in the works on the Little Maumelle River.

The Ranch offers a way of life that is unsurpassed in Arkansas. Straining against the prospect of appearing immodest, Bob Shults nevertheless lets it slip that, "Sometimes builders and other developers bring out-of-town prospects through our development." After all, what's wrong with pride in a job well done?

U. S. Pizza

It's An Unbroken Success Story With No End In Sight

Judy Waller opened her first U.S. Pizza restaurant 27 years ago in North Little Rock, and success was almost immediate. Now up to eight and counting, she has a community institution on her hands, and it all started with some college kids' desire for good pizza.

Starting in a stone building on Pike Avenue in Levy that seated 35 diners, Judy, working full-time in a chemistry laboratory at the University of Arkansas for Medical Sciences, had two secret weapons. While attending the University of Arkansas in Fayetteville, she and her husband at the time, Whit Waller, had arrived at their own recipe for excellent pizza. Along with the pizza, they made a mean buttermilk ranch dressing.

When they moved to Little Rock, Judy looked around and didn't find a good pizza restaurant.

U.S. Pizza was born.

Everything but the food was designed to keep overhead low. The Pike Avenue location rented for $100 a month, an old freezer was converted to a prep table, and, thanks to Twin City Bank and a $2,400 loan, they were in business. U.S. Pizza and TCB remained business partners throughout the life of the bank.

The food spoke for itself, and, within a month, people lined up outside for a chance to dine in the informal new pizza place. Judy soon had to quit her day job at UAMS to keep up with the demand.

Soon, one U.S. Pizza wasn't enough, and the Sherwood location opened on Highway 107 in 1976.

Reacting to pleas from the south side of the river, Judy investigated real estate and found that abandoned service stations offered good, neighborhood sites and were cheaper to remodel than building from scratch. In 1981, the first Little Rock U.S. Pizza opened on Kavanaugh Blvd. in Hillcrest. The restaurant was housed in a service station, as was the one added in 1987, also on Kavanaugh, in the Heights.

The original Levy location in North Little Rock, famous for its colorful Old Glory mural across one side of the building, finally burst at the seams with business in 1988, and the restaurant moved up Pike Avenue a couple of blocks, where it stands today. With four times the seating capacity and much more parking, it should last awhile.

Meanwhile, in 1990, the company opened its first West Little Rock location, on Rodney Parham Road. In 1993, U.S. Pizza took a major leap, carving a niche on Dickson Street in Fayetteville. Rekindling her college-days affinity with the town, Judy bought three buildings on the famous street, turning one into the only U.S. Pizza outside of central Arkansas. The location in Fayetteville features an outdoor deck and a pizza cellar served by a dumbwaiter, innovations spurred by Judy's U of A

For more information:

U. S. Pizza Co.

- *3324 Pike Avenue, North Little Rock, Arkansas 72118   501-758-5997*
- *4001 McCain Park Drive, North Little Rock, Arkansas 72116   501-753-2900*
- *8403 Highway 107, Sherwood, Arkansas 72120   501-835-5673*
- *650 Edgewood Drive, Maumelle, Arkansas 72113   501-851-0880*
- *2814 Kavanaugh Boulevard, Little Rock, Arkansas 72205   501-663-2198*
- *5524 Kavanaugh Boulevard, Little Rock, Arkansas 72207   591-664-7071*
- *9300 North Rodney Parham Road, Little Rock, Arkansas 72207   501-224-6300*

Judy and Trey Waller are the two generations behind the U.S. Pizza every Arkansan has come to know and love.

memories.

Along with the restaurant, she is renovating a 100 year-old house on Dickson Street.

Judy opened her seventh pizzeria, at 650 Edgewood in Maumelle, in 1995. In a fraction of the time it took the original, the Maumelle location has gotten too popular for its surroundings.

"It has just totally outgrown the location," Corporate Manager Lana Powers says. This time Judy has sprung for a new building, on which construction will start soon. Judy's son Trey Waller, who has become an integral part of the U.S. Pizza Corporation, has designed the initial layout and will be working with the architects through completion.

"It will be a showpiece for me, and I hope for it to be the prototype for all of our future locations," Judy says. The lakeside structure will feature a dining patio and a full bar. The full bar was first tried, with great success,

at the company's latest location, on Warden Road in North Little Rock, near McCain Mall. The company's business plan has usually called for a new restaurant about every three years, though sometimes pent-up demand has shortened the interval.

"We get calls all the time, people wanting us to put one somewhere," Lana says. The next restaurant is likely to land somewhere in West Little Rock.

"The capacity of the Rodney Parham store is at its max," Judy says. "I would love to find a location out in West Little Rock somewhere." She's looking in the Chenal or Highway 10 area, she adds.

Once established, a restaurant becomes the community's own. The only location not in its original building moved in the same neighborhood to more spacious quarters.

It seems that U.S. Pizza has always struck a chord with the community, and the affection is mutual. The company sponsors a myriad of community activities.

U.S. Pizza sends a Boy Scout troop to camp each year and sponsors an American Legion baseball team, along with another baseball team in Lakewood and youth football at Sylvan Hills. Judy also contributes to Meals on Wheels and the Red Cross.

The Rollin' Razorbacks wheelchair basketball team is a prime beneficiary of the company's community outreach. U.S. Pizza sponsors a golf tournament and in-store fund-raisers for the team.

In addition, U.S. Pizza, with its "Uncle Sam Wants You" logo, is a regular advertiser in high school yearbooks and event programs.

"She tries to do a little bit for everybody," Lana says.

U.S. Pizza bakes in "old-fashioned stone hearth ovens," which require a minimum cooking time of 25 minutes. Customers can either call orders in ahead of time, or relax in the laid-back atmosphere of the restaurants. Some customers become such fans that they have menu items shipped to them if they move away.

Aside from pizza, the key to the company's success on the dining table has been their Salad Supreme, on the menu for 27 years, and enlivened with the famous house dressing, Lana says. The restaurants do almost as much business in salads as in the stores' namesake, frequently requiring two people doing nothing but making salads during lunch. The Supreme is a combination of meat, mushrooms, black olives, onions, green peppers, mozzarella and bacon bits. Customers frequently ask for the dressing recipe, which consists simply of buttermilk, mayonnaise, and a store-bought mix, but it rarely tastes the same at home.

But Judy Waller and her restaurants aren't standing still. She scouts around for menu items, particularly when on a trip.

"When she's off somewhere, she eats Italian and brings back ideas," Lana says. Then the fine-tuning begins. Taste tests are staged, then Judy consults with the U.S. Pizza managers.

"Then when it's what she wants... we put it on the menu," Lana says.

"Heart-Smart" pizzas made with olive oil are among the more popular new items, according to Lana. The restaurants offer a whole page full of specialty pizzas, including the Victory Garden Pizza, with olive oil, onions, yellow squash, zucchini, Anaheim peppers, cauliflower, broccoli, three cheeses and spicy tomatoes. Trey Waller's own innovation, the Chloroplast Blast Pizza, explodes with three types of peppers, along with crushed red pepper, pepper jack and mozzarella cheese and chili powder. Oh, and zucchini.

The company still uses only the finest ingredients, chopping fresh vegetables and preparing the crust each morning.

Sandwiches make up a large part of the U.S. Pizza menu. All are made warm with lettuce and house dressing and served with chips and a dill spear on a Hoagie bun. Plenty of other bread choices are available, though; sandwiches also come on a wheat bun, sliced rye, sliced sourdough or Pita Fold.

And U.S. Pizza now offers desserts. Peanut butter silk pie and cheesecake swirl pie are on the menu, if you have room.

It's all available at very reasonable prices, since the money goes toward maintaining excellent cuisine and staff. Judy buys the U.S. Pizza buildings outright now, and still owns the original stone building in the shadow of the Levy I-40 bridge, now successful as a bar and grill. With an eye for fixer-uppers, she frequently snags good deals and passes the savings on to the customer.

Several U.S. Pizza alumni have taken Judy's cue and opened their own pizza restaurants. Though she hates to lose the talent, U.S. Pizza has always been up to the challenge, so Judy takes the imitators as a compliment.

As with most successful entrepreneurs, Judy keeps her ears open, listening to the customers who care enough to keep her apprised of the food quality and service level in the restaurants. Her favorite part of the business is interacting with customers, and she enjoys working in different stores, getting back to the basics the company was founded upon.

In 1999, Judy was recognized by Arkansas Business as one of the top 100 business women in the state.

"That was a real big honor for Judy," Lana says. The walls of the company's office on Rixey Road in Sherwood are dotted with awards and certificates of appreciation presented to Judy, her employees and the company.

U.S. Pizza doesn't do much advertising, relying on word-of-mouth. Every customer is a potential advertisement. In fact, customers pay to wear one of the company's t-shirts, which have become a fashion statement themselves, particularly among teenagers.

And to what does Judy Waller attribute this unbridled success? Aside from her customers, she points to two people, her lawyer, Sam Hilburn, and her "walking buddy," Earl Hill, who, at 75, is her sounding board for business strategy.

"Those two friends are probably the keys to my success," she says.